D1180976

GOOD FOOD FROM FARTHINGHOE

Nicola and Simon Cox run Farthinghoe Fine Wine and Food Ltd, a flourishing and now very well known Cookery School and retail Wine Merchant business, from their Victorian rectory near Banbury. A self-taught cook with an enquiring and experimental approach, Nicola is a former Sunday Times Cook of Britain (runner-up in the subsequent European Competition) and mother of four children. She holds cookery demonstrations at Farthinghoe and demonstrates country-wide and abroad. A leading exponent of Food Processor and Game cookery, she has demonstrated at the annual Game Fair for nine years.

Nicola, who was recently Cookery Editor of *Brides*, now writes regular columns for *Good Housekeeping* and *Decanter* and freelances widely. Her other books include *Country Cooking from Farthinghoe* (1984), *Entertaining with Magimix* (1984) and *Good Housekeeping Creative Food Processor Cookery* (1986).

Also by Nicola Cox
available in hardcover from Victor Gollancz Ltd
COUNTRY COOKING FROM FARTHINGHOE

Nicola Cox

GOOD FOOD FROM FARTHINGHOE

with line illustrations by
David Green
and photographs by Fiona Pragoff

London
Victor Gollancz Ltd
in association with Peter Crawley
1986

First published in Great Britain July 1981
by Victor Gollancz Ltd
14 Henrietta Street, London WC2E 8QJ
Second impression July 1983

This edition first published in hardback 1986

First published in Gollancz Paperbacks 1986

British Library Cataloguing in Publication Data
Cox, Nicola
   Good food from Farthinghoe.—2nd ed.
   1. Cookery
   I. Title
   641.5   TX717

   ISBN 0-575-03904-3
   ISBN 0-575-03843-8 Pbk

Printed by Clark Constable Ltd, Edinburgh

CONTENTS

ACKNOWLEDGEMENTS

On entering the *Sunday Times* Cook of Britain competition I named my dish Veal St Simon, rather as a joke, since I had never considered my husband particularly saintlike, though he did correct the recipe and get it typed for me. Now, eight years later, he has truly earned that title. He has tasted and tried dishes until he is sick of them, but has always been objective in his criticism; he has corrected recipes and checked proofs, advised, prodded, cajoled, and always given me the encouragement and support needed to produce my first book. So, to Simon the Saint, my love and thanks.

It was Margaret Costa, whose imaginative recipes I started to read and collect at the age of fifteen, who helped to fire my enthusiasm for cooking. It was exciting, therefore, to meet her when she judged the competition, and encouraging that she thought I might make a cook. Since then she has been my culinary godmother, and I am deeply grateful for all she has done to help me.

I would also like to thank our secretary, Mrs James, who waded through all my drafts and came out smiling, Sheila Bush, my editor, without whose objective scrutiny and sheer expertise this book would have lacked the professional finish and style I hope it now has, and Stephen Bray and his demonstrably expert Production staff.

May I also thank Peter Crawley, my publisher, who asked for it in the first place and has waited patiently for three years while I wrote it!

Nicola Cox

FOREWORD

When I was the cookery writer on the *Sunday Times* Magazine we launched, with the co-operation of the leading women's magazines in other countries, a prestigious competition with really handsome prizes to find the Best Amateur Cook in Europe. The response, both from men and women, was enormous; deciding which entrants merited inclusion in the British semi-final was difficult, and the final a near-run thing. But in the end the exquisite simplicity, fastidious presentation and delicious taste of Nicola Cox's Escalope de Veau St Simon won the day, hands down, against stiff opposition from the other finalists.

This success helped to settle the question of what Nicola and her husband would do when he came out of the Army. Simon Cox has a wide-ranging knowledge of wine, and their family home in a big early Victorian rectory in Northamptonshire is now the headquarters of his flourishing wine business and her cookery school. Not only is she a very good teacher and a relaxed and charming demonstrator—her services are much in demand, especially for fund-raising occasions for all kinds of good causes—but she also takes pupils in her home and sells locally, and at her demonstrations, a small range of her delicious home-frozen foods.

How she finds time to do all this with a young family to look after baffles people like me who are less well organised. I hope I have not made her sound too intimidatingly efficient—she is still the modest charming winner of our Best Cook finals long ago, and I was delighted to be asked to introduce her book. I know it will be well used in my own kitchen.

Lacy's   Margaret Costa
London 1980

INTRODUCTION

Nowadays we all have to live many different lives, and this is reflected in our cooking: one moment we are the cool career woman with food appearing as if by magic, next the harried housewife trying to get a meal in no time flat. We may live in the city one day and the country the next: we may be lavish entertainers at the beginning of the month but feel poor and in need of something inexpensive by the end. We may be keen gardeners and grow our own vegetables; we may have hordes to feed in the holidays but be single at other times. Cooking and experimenting may be our relaxation, or health and a whole-some diet our preoccupation. We probably fall into and out of these categories day by day or year by year, but one thing is certain—we all have to eat, so why not enjoy our cooking? As plants will grow for the green-fingered who love and talk to them, so food seems to respond to the enjoyment and pleasure you get from cooking it.

I have fitted into all these situations and have therefore chosen recipes with this diversity in mind. I have based this book on the five years of cookery demonstrations that we have run here at Farthinghoe; everyone who has been here has told me what they have found most useful and interesting and which recipes they liked best. They also say that they like the tips, hints, and detailed explanations, and so I have included as many of these as possible. As a virtually self-taught cook I have made every mistake that can be made, and so perhaps can tell you how not to make them.

I have divided the book into chapters for different types of entertaining but, as many of the dishes will fit numerous occasions, the index has been carefully compiled and I hope you will find it helpful.

Before Simon and I started our own wine and food business we spent twelve years travelling with the army, and in that time we had more than a dozen houses, large and small. Abroad I was lucky enough to have unusual ingredients to cook with, but sometimes essentials were almost unobtainable. Now, settled at last with four growing children and a wine and food business which I help to run, I feel I have built up some experience of cooking and entertaining. Nearly all my cooking is for what I myself am, and what I'm sure most of you are—the cook-hostess; so the minimum of last-minute dashes to the kitchen, whilst still producing good food, is our criterion.

Entertaining is my theme, for eating is a pleasure, and sharing good food with friends is even more of a pleasure. In these informal days we have so many ways of entertaining to choose from that we should never need to deny ourselves its pleasure or get bogged down in its preparation. The whole concept of entertaining has changed. Gone (well, nearly) are the large parties and formal dinners of a former age, which hung on into the hurried servantless years with the hostess valiantly trying to keep up standards and appearances. Now a much more relaxed approach can be advocated. A hostess who is warm and at her ease can make everyone feel happy, but if she is harried and flustered it can have quite the opposite effect. So rule one in entertaining must be never to set yourself more than you can do, or you won't be relaxed or enjoy yourself, always the acid test of a good party.

Our own normal form of entertaining takes place in the kitchen with simple suppers where the friendly atmosphere makes up for the informality and I can try a far wider and perhaps more interesting range of dishes. Even those special occasions for one or two friends, when only the best in food and wine will do, tend to take place in our kitchen. Only then can I make dishes which need last-minute attention or which would be impractical for more than a few. In the holidays we see numerous friends and their children, so we sit down with vast numbers of varying ages and I never count heads until just before the meal. A relaxed and easy form of entertaining with the minimum of fuss and bother is essential, and so is economy when it comes to teenage appetites! Barbeques and outdoor eating whenever the weather allows are getting even more popular, and as country dwellers and sun-worshippers we eat every possible (and sometimes totally impracticable) meal outside, so I have included some suitable recipes for these. As a party-lover and impulsive entertainer I have often jumped in with both feet and invited everyone to an impromptu party, causing immediate commissariat problems, so I have included a chapter on spontaneous entertaining. Buffet parties, even though you may not enjoy balancing a plate, are an extremely useful way of entertaining a crowd, and I've included quite a lot of dishes suitable for large numbers.

Having said that the whole concept of entertaining has changed, I must qualify that by saying that of course there is still nothing quite like the now occasional formal dinner party. A beautifully laid table with gleaming glass and silver and the quiet lapping of luxury transports us from everyday life, brings out the best in us and allows us to live on a higher plane for a brief moment.

The cost of entertaining is of enormous importance as the price of food climbs higher, but with a clever choice of dishes it is still possible to eat reasonably cheaply, and I have some extremely inexpensive dishes that I am not ashamed to set before anyone. It's the careful choice and not the cost of ingredients that counts. Time need not daunt you either, because there are many quick and easy dishes to choose from.

Having obeyed rule one and not overfaced yourself, you are relaxed enough to re-member rule two, which is to think of your guests. The art of entertaining is to give people what they would like; to put yourself in their shoes and cast around for whatever will give them most pleasure. A pinch of imagination can often save pounds of expense.

Guests from abroad will appreciate the best of British specialities like smoked salmon, asparagus, beef or game. They may well not often get them! But they will be well content with our smoked haddock and mackerel, our beautiful North Sea fish (don't forget that the Mediterranean is virtually fished out and the best fish comes from the cold northern waters), all our meats, pies and dairy products, because as a green and verdant island we have some of the best grazing in the world. Our Stilton and hard cheeses are second to none. Use our best British recipes like Lancashire Hot Pot and Lemon Meringue Pie, or some of our old English puddings like Lemon Posset, Syrup Tart or Trinity Burnt Cream. How many times have I entertained foreigners who were amazed that English food could be so good.

Your friends from the town will love the idea of simple country food. Summer Pudding tastes so much sweeter in the country, and if you can give them fresh-grown vegetables as a separate course or an Elderflower Sorbet from the hedgerows they will enjoy themselves the more. Country cousins will enjoy an unusual dish using ingredients only available in the big city—freshly-made pasta and good Parmesan, perhaps, or unusual imported fruit and vegetables. Your sophisticated friends will appreciate unusual dishes gathered from abroad using authentic ingredients. Children love simple, savoury things, preferably eaten with their fingers. Give people what they like and half the battle is won. Your reputation gains more by producing the right dish at the right moment than by sheer cookery skill.

The next thing to think about is seasons. I love the seasons, and it's sad to think how they get lost in the freezer, friend though I find it. It used to be smart and clever to serve things out of season; now the skill is to serve them in season. How many people fill their freezer with vegetables, and then have madly to eat up last year's broad beans before this year's young ones come along, thereby taking the edge off their anticipation and apprecia-tion? I find more and more that in winter I prefer to eat fresh winter vegetables like carrots, celeriac, leeks and sprouts, because they go better with winter food than frozen summer vegetables. So for me no more bending double over the bean rows or blanching over a steaming pot on the hottest days of summer. I shall freeze a few, but try to use them early or when they really suit what I'm cooking.

Menu planning is a matter of balance, achieved with colour, texture and contrast. An extra few minutes spent in planning will pay off in compliments and will help you to avoid that disconcerting last-minute discovery that you are starting with Vol-au-Vents and finishing with Tarte aux Fraises. My worst experience was a spring demonstration several years back when I was so carried away with the idea of the freshness of spring that every dish turned out green—even the pudding which was Gooseberry Fool! A rich dish on its own is good, but a rich meal becomes unbalanced, and this can easily happen when you are trying especially hard. Anyway these days we eat simply most of the time and our stomachs cannot appreciate a sudden very rich meal. The Chinese are masters at produc-ing balanced, interesting meals. Crisp clean course follows soft rich course, sharp courses

15

complement bland, with meat, fish and vegetables carefully juxtaposed. The Chinese can also teach us about slow, leisurely meals; there should be no hurry but plenty of time to savour the dishes over which you have taken so much trouble.

Once you have chosen your menu, do have a quick feasibility study. Have you the knives, forks and plates necessary? I've often had to change the menu because I could not do two rounds of little forks. Will you need the oven at two different temperatures at once? Have you too many hot courses and can you heat the plates? Don't choose something that needs an hour in the kitchen before dinner if you have three children to put to bed and yourself to produce from social hibernation. If great friends from far away have one day to spend with you don't, in your enthusiasm to do them proud, spend all day in the kitchen. These are all silly mistakes, I know, but I've made them all, and perhaps I can help you not to.

HOW TO READ THE RECIPES

The Work Involved. This is very subjective and what is easy for one may be less so for another, but I have used a simple star system to guide you.

✱ Easy   ✱✱ Straightforward   ✱✱✱ More complicated

Pre-Preparation and Planning. I used often to be caught out by starting a recipe, only to find halfway through that I should have soaked the beans overnight or whatever. Or I might find myself trying to wrap a hot leg of lamb in pastry because I had not realised it took so long to cool. So where any fundamental pre-preparation is necessary, or where there is any long or critical time-lag during cooking, I have marked the recipe with a $\mathcal{P}$. This signifies Preparation or Planning and warns you to read the recipe carefully before launching into it.

Measurements and Sizes. All these recipes are gathered from my demonstrations at Far-thinghoe over the last five years. They were conceived and originally written in imperial measurements but are now also shown converted to the metric equivalent, which you will appreciate cannot always be exact to the nearest gram. It is vital to stick to one or the other and not chop and change within a recipe. All container measurements, such as a table-spoon, use British Standards Institution sizes and are measured level unless otherwise stated. Although accurate measurements are given, your taste and the character of the individual ingredient will obviously vary; for instance, the bacon can be extra salty, the lemon extra large or the Cheddar less strong than you would like, so cook with your wits about you, taste as you go and do not follow the recipe blindly if your reason dictates otherwise.

Eggs, Flour, Sugar and Cream. Eggs are size No. 3, flour is plain, sugar is granulated and cream whipping unless otherwise stated.

Dishes which freeze well. A freezer, even if only a little one above the fridge, is almost standard in kitchens these days, and most of us rely on it heavily. We all have our own ideas about how to use it and what will freeze successfully: the criterion I try to follow is that things should come out as good as they went in, if not better. There are many freezer guides with full instructions on packaging, labelling, freezing, thawing and re-heating. This book does not set out to be a comprehensive freezer guide, so all I have done is to mark with an F the dishes which I myself find freeze successfully, and to give a few hints on points I have particularly noticed. I have also mentioned, in the case of one or two that look as if they should freeze, that they turn out disappointingly or disastrously. I'm sure you will find more that can be frozen, and of course it's one thing to cook and freeze a dish ahead for a party and another to know that leftovers can be frozen and will come out 'all right' for eating up.

It is important to remember that ingredients like egg yolks and cream in soup are much safer added upon re-heating, for if the soup should boil they will curdle. And ingredients such as frozen prawns, mussels and scampi should always be added upon re-heating.

I know that once the freezer's rapacious maw has swallowed up a dish one rarely remembers to look up the recipe again on thawing to see what other ingredients are needed for finishing it; and so those almonds and sesame seeds on top or that sprinkle of parsley and lemon rind tend to get forgotten. Waterproof Pentel pens are invaluable for freezer marking anyway, as they will write on plastic bags or containers, but I find them particularly helpful for adding any finishing instructions. You can then see at a glance, when removing a dish from the freezer, what will be needed to complete it. Masking tape is also useful as it can be stuck on container lids with details and instructions written on it, then ripped off when the dish is used, leaving the container lids clear for next time.

I think most dishes taste better when thawed before re-heating, so whenever possible take out in the morning for the evening or one day for the next. 'Quick Freeze, Slow Thaw' is the cry, particularly with meat. Try taking Sunday's joint out on Wednesday or Thursday and leave it in the bottom of the fridge so that the ice crystals will thaw slowly and have time to be reabsorbed into the meat tissue. Chicken must be fully thawed before cooking or the central meat will remain frozen and will not cook properly, and there will be a danger of salmonella poisoning.

Pâtés benefit from being slowly and thoroughly thawed, and the rich creamy sort taste much better when served at room temperature, soft and smooth and with their flavour fully developed. Rough pâtés tend to acquire a wet texture in the freezer and I have not recommended them for freezing; don't forget, though, that you can always prepare your pâté mixture ahead and freeze it uncooked for a week or so, which may ease the pressure at party time. Mousses and creamy puddings also need a long thaw as otherwise their texture can remain almost lumpy and separated.

Some dishes, of course, can be re-heated straight from the freezer, but normally they require additional cooking time.

Garlic. Make sure you always use fresh plump garlic. Many books will tell you that garlic develops an off-flavour in the freezer, but if it is fresh when you use it this is not so, and the dish may be kept frozen for months.

Dried herbs. If they are old, any mustiness will be accentuated in the freezer, giving the dish a bitter and musty taste. But good quality 'fresh' dried herbs can be used successfully.

Sauces. If sauces thin out on being re-heated from the freezer, it is probably due to the flour being insufficiently cooked in the first place; so try simmering your sauces for longer.

Equipment, Ingredients and Basic Recipes

EQUIPMENT

Knives

I might just as well get on to my favourite hobby horse now. Sharp knives, sharp knives, sharp knives, and the greatest of these is sharp knives! Suddenly a task becomes easy; time is saved, so is temper and so are fingers. Do get yourself the best knives you can afford and treat them with love and respect; put the fear of God into the family (who for two pins will prize open tins with their points, chop on formica and other terrible sins), and you will have good friends and faithful servants for twenty or thirty years. A knife should lie balanced in your hand, feeling as if it belonged there. It should have a steel shaft running the length of the handle—for stainless steel is so improved that most professionals now use it—and a rivetted handle for strength and durability; although some of the composite handles, moulded to fit your hand and completely enclosing the shaft, are extremely comfortable and hygienic and, of course, can be put in the washing-up machine.

A *Boning Knife* (**1**), with its firm inflexible blade and curved end, is indispensable when boning out shoulders or legs of lamb, jointing or boning a chicken, duck or any other bird, and for many similar tasks. The blade is on the curve, and this eases the meat off the carcass much more easily than a straight-bladed knife.

For all general slicing and chopping a straight-bladed *Kitchen Knife* (**2**) is essential, one whose blade will lie flat along the chopping board. I don't favour one quite as large or

19

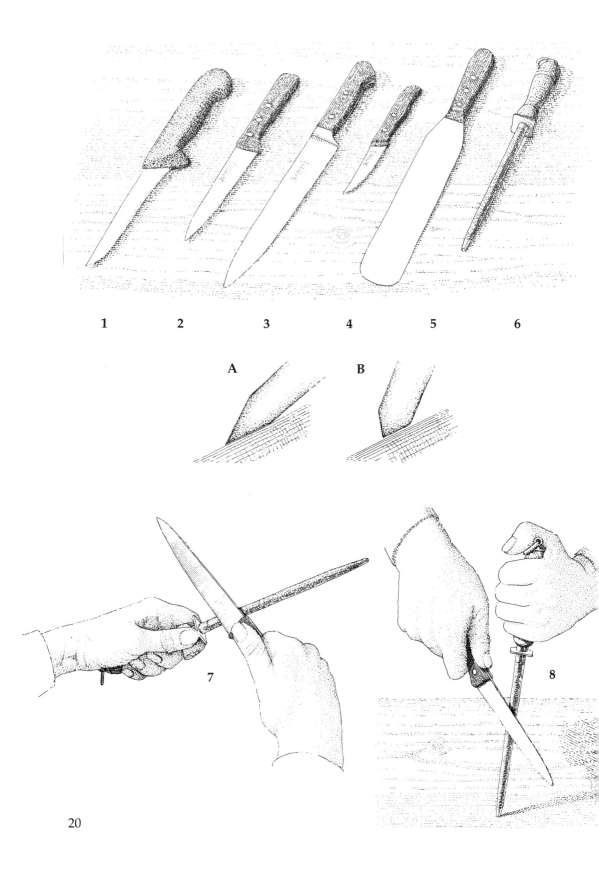

1 2 3 4 5 6

A B

7 8

20

heavy as most chefs seem to use, but it needs enough weight for the knife to do much of the work for you.

A large *Cook's* or *Butcher's Knife* (**3**) can save time if you have a considerable quantity of meat to slice or cube. It is also necessary for carving and slicing, and I personally use mine for this instead of the traditional specialist Carving Knife.

It's useful to have a *Flexible-Bladed Knife* if you find yourself doing much fish-skinning or filleting. I nearly always skin the fish fillets before cooking them, because it's so much easier to whip the skin off then than after the cooking, when the fish is hot and the skin falls to pieces under your burnt fingers.

A sharp little *Vegetable Knife* (**4**) is useful for scraping carrots, peeling onions and a thousand and two general jobs.

Then there's our old friend the *Palette Knife* (**5**), so useful for flick turning and scraping. I wouldn't want to be without him.

Finally, but very important, a *Steel* (**6**) with a finger guard to protect you. Do remember that for stainless steel knives you need a steel made for stainless steel. For years I used a steel from granny's old carving set and although it did a reasonable job, it was not hard enough to get a really fine edge. Stainless steel, as I said earlier, is greatly improved and is very hard, so do keep your knives sharp. If you allow them to get blunt it takes a long time to work an edge on to them again.

To Sharpen a Knife

The aim is to have a good long shoulder of blade on the knife; a cut-through section would look like this (A), not like this (B). A pull-through or electric sharpener massacres the knife; it may sharpen the edge but does not give much shoulder, so when you have worn off the edge it's blunt again very quickly. With a long shoulder the edge wears away much less quickly. Lay the blade against the steel at the hilt, keep it absolutely parallel with the steel, then with a slight twist of your wrist put pressure on the blade side of the knife (**7**). Draw the length of the blade along the length of the steel, just keeping pressure on the blade side, but don't tip the knife to make too great an angle. Place the other side of the blade under the steel and draw it similarly along the length of the steel. Repeat this but don't hurry; there's no magic about zipping it along so fast that no one can see! The secret is little and often.

For a stubbornly blunt knife you can get a bit more pressure by standing your steel upright, its point on a board, and drawing the blade up each side of it (**8**). But even with all this wonderful care and attention, I find that about once a year my knives need more drastic treatment. Make friends with your butcher and he will work up the edges for you on an oil stone, probably by appointment on a Monday morning when he's not too busy. But don't ever let your precious knives have their edges run down on a coarse wheel, because this spoils them and wears away too much steel.

These beautiful sharp knives now need a home, somewhere where their tips are protected and where you won't cut yourself. I like a *Magnetic Knife Rack* placed somewhere safe, behind the stove or at the back of a worktop where the knives can't drop on the children's heads.

Chopping Boards

To use knives one needs a cutting surface that is not too hard. It's ruination to chop or cut on marble or metal or on a formica board or work-top. A nice big *Wooden Chopping Board*, say 12" × 18" (30cm × 45cm) with 1" (2cm-3cm) depth, makes a very good central cooking point in the kitchen. You chop and cook on it, and because you always work in the same place you know exactly where everything else in the kitchen is in relation to you. A good-quality board is essential or it will start to warp and rock after only a little use.

Six or eight years ago, while living in Germany, I acquired from a butcher friend a new *Plastic Chopping Board* called Solidur or Rowplas, which proved so good and popular that eventually we had to track down a supplier in this country. The advantages of this excellent board are that it is a robust white plastic, with enough 'give' in it to chop on without blunting your knives but very hygienic and easily cleaned. You can chop onions on it, wash it, and immediately roll pastry without ending up with onion-flavoured apple-pie. It's also naturally cool and so makes a lovely pastry-board; pop it into your freezer or fridge for half-an-hour and it outdoes granny's marble slab any time. I'm told that it will shortly be mandatory for butchers, fishmongers, schools and hospitals instead of the old-fashioned wood. Sad in a way, but it really is a step forward.

Food Processors

A machine at the top of the market is one of those marvellous modern *Food Processors*. I have been the proud possessor of a Magimix for years, and find it absolutely invaluable. The number of working hours it saves justifies its cost many times over if you are a busy person, and the jobs it does in the twinkling of an eye—mincing, chopping, mixing, grating, slicing and liquidising! Though not essential it's a joy to use, and its neatness, versatility, and ease of operation and cleaning are remarkable.

Some Help when Making Pastry and Pasta

Although it may sound obvious, a good *Rolling Pin* is vital. I have a big long one, much easier to use than a little one, and helpful if you make your own pasta. A rolling pin should never be washed but should be rubbed with oil when you buy it, then cleaned with a dry plastic pot-scratcher when it gets bits on it. If you have to wash it, dry it out well in a warm place, re-oil and try not to wash it again. Then it will acquire the satiny, non-stick surface of a Solidur or Rowplas pin which I find the best.

A *Pastry Brush* with a good head of real bristle is most useful. Actually you need two, one clearly marked 'Garlic' and kept well segregated for making Garlic Bread and that sort of thing.

Another useful but cheap little tool is a nice old-fashioned *Pastry Wheel*. Usually made in China from bamboo cane, it is a help in cutting your pastry or pasta.

For flans, tarts and quiches I use metal *Removable Base Flan Tins*. I find them better than the china dishes in which I can never get the underneath pastry cooked properly.

We eat a lot of pasta; in fact, it's something of a tradition for Saturday lunch, and I can easily justify a *Pasta Machine*. These are marvellously easy to use, are very well made and robust and are not particularly expensive for what you get. I use mine to roll pasta for lasagne, etc., to make wide and narrow noodles, and for spaghetti. Home-made pasta is as different from even the 'fresh' bought variety as chalk is from cheese, much softer and more toothsome—but beware when cooking it because it takes much less time.

Pots and Pans

Quality pans will save on fuel bills. A heavy pan with the right base for the heat source makes all the difference. Agas and electric cookers need absolutely flat, ground bases that can't wobble so that you get a perfect contact. But too smooth a base on gas allows the flames to lick over it without really heating it, so dimple-based pans are best. Copper pans are lovely to work with (especially if you don't do the washing up—I have virtually given them up). As long as it's thick enough, a copper base on a pan gives you the heat-diffusing qualities you're looking for but without the cleaning problems.

If you use aluminium pans—and heavy aluminium is a very good work-horse—do remember that several things should never be cooked or made in them; the acid in spinach and sorrel conflicts with aluminium and produces a nasty flavour, whilst egg or wine in sauces, custards or mousses will make them discolour and go greyish if cooked in aluminium.

Don't heat your non-stick pan till it smokes or you will breathe in noxious gases. Enamelled cast iron is excellent for cooking in. It's so easy to use on the stove, in the oven or on the table. I use these casseroles all the time, but they can be too heavy for some people and then earthenware is a good solution.

Earthenware

Everything cooked in earthenware seems to taste better, and I love cooking in it. Fry, boil, simmer or stew—you can do it all if only you remember never to heat the pot empty and always heat it gradually to start with, never direct from the cold larder or fridge. I generally start mine on a heat diffuser and then put it directly on my Aga, electric or gas stove. When new, some earthenware pots need to be soaked in cold water for an hour. I use a deep *Marmita* (**9**) for soups, an open *Casserole* (**10**) for frying or sometimes with a lid for braising, and a sort of pot for stewing (**11**) which the Italians call an *Umidiera*. But they're all fairly interchangeable.

Some Useful Miscellaneous Equipment

Without a food processor, slicing a potato evenly and finely can be difficult, but it is necessary for dishes like Pommes de Terre Dauphinoise or Pommes de Terre Savoyard. A *Mandolin* is the answer, a flat metal or wooden board with a blade set in it (the best have adjustable blades, but do check that they are well made and the blade does not loosen and slip while you are using it). Potato, carrot and cucumber, etc., are sliced rapidly up and down over the blade, but watch your nails and knuckles and don't try to get the last little bit through!

For peeling potatoes, carrots and some fruits I use a razor-sharp little *Potato Peeler* (**12**), and I reckon to beat most people at a potato-peeling race. It fits right- or left-handed people. Peel away from you in long strokes; it really is magic, you waste no potato and you'll get the knack quite quickly.

Another piece of equipment I would hate to be without is a *Wire Whisk* (**13**). Invaluable for sauces (I defy anyone to make lumpy sauce using a whisk!), but do buy one with a wooden handle, so as not to get blisters, and one that's the right size for your bowls and saucepans. I recommend a 10" (25cm) whisk for normal domestic cooking, and one whose loops of wire are different lengths and unattached to each other at the whisking end so that it really does whisk. For whisking cream and egg whites I favour a *Rotary Whisk*—get the best you can. It is quicker and better than an electric beater, and you can judge the state of your cream or egg-whites more accurately. But it does take elbow power, and if you haven't too much of that I recommend the light, hand-held electric kind. You can move it round the bowl to keep everything moving, and if you can also use it over hot water it is invaluable for soufflés and mousses.

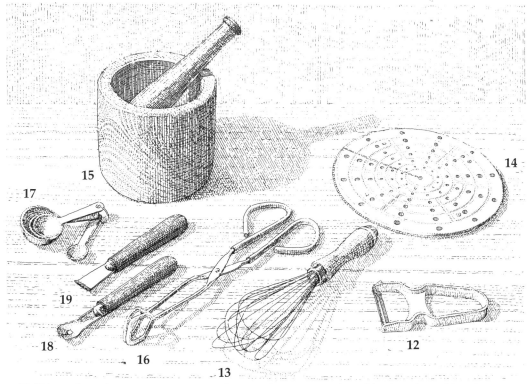

Talking about hot water, a *Heat Diffuser* (**14**) can save a lot of fuel and trouble. If you are on North Sea gas it is almost essential, because I'm sure you find simmering wellnigh impossible. With the gas set low a diffuser (two *in extremis*) will persuade anything to simmer gently. Instead of using the oven for slow cooking you can cook gently on the top.

For spiced and aromatic dishes, do try to use whole spices whenever possible. Once ground, the volatile oils are released and the spices begin to deteriorate. Unless you use spices very rapidly—and how many of us do in this country—keep them whole till you need them and preserve their flavour. A *Pestle and Mortar* (**15**) are good for grinding small quantities of spices, and I use a small wooden one, decorative but inexpensive. For larger quantities and for making Curry Powder or Garam Masala, both so different from the bought varieties, I use our small electric coffee grinder—but wipe it out carefully before and after use.

Scissor Tongs (**16**) are another useful tool for turning things over in the pan. I'd hate to be without this very cheap aid which saves me splashing fat everywhere.

A long-handled *Slotted Spoon* for removing chopped vegetables from the frying-pan is essential, and I also like to use it for folding in whipped cream and egg-whites.

A set of *British Standard Measuring Spoons* (**17**) from ¼ teaspoon to 1 tablespoon helps to keep my measurements accurate—and I always use level spoonfuls. They are only made in plastic and do break rather easily, but they are the quickest and easiest to use.

A ½ pt (300ml) *Pyrex Measuring Jug* with the fluid ounces clearly marked seems also to be in constant use in our kitchen, with a 2 pt (1.2l) plastic one for larger quantities.

Two little tools which everyone goes for in a big way are a *Decorator* or *Cannelling Knife*

(**18**) for orange and lemon julienne strips or for decorating cucumbers, courgettes etc., and a *Zester* (**19**) for taking off tiny curls of orange or lemon zest. It is much quicker to use than a grater for just a little grated lemon rind.

Finally, a really good pair of *Kitchen Scissors* will always be in use. Those with a notched place in them for cutting bones are best.

Of course everyone has their own ideas about kitchen equipment and knows what they find useful, and I haven't even mentioned *Wooden Spoons, Rubber Spatulas*, a *Fish Slice* or lots of other things I'd hate to be without. But these that I have talked about are in constant use in my kitchen at Farthinghoe, and I recommend them wholeheartedly.

INGREDIENTS

We are lucky enough to be able to use a great variety of ingredients in our daily diet, and I think it is important that what we eat should not only keep us going but should also be the source of positive pleasure. As a nation less prosperous than we should like to be, economy is pressed upon us and food is advertised and sold on the basis that it is cheaper than its competitor. But let us be quite certain that, within the limits of our purse, we choose the ingredients to make wholesome and delicious meals.

I'm not necessarily advocating expensive ingredients, just good, fresh ones. This is often a matter not of price but of choice. A French housewife will choose her oil with great care, her radishes individually and her fish with an experienced critical eye. She is feeding her family, and only the best is good enough. The care and attention with which one tomato is chosen and another rejected should certainly be a lesson to us all, and something we should actively practise with our suppliers if we are going to shame and encourage them to improve their standards. On the other hand, one must sometimes be prepared to pay for the correct ingredients to achieve the right flavour. They certainly do on the continent, so why should we be loath to do so? Our French farmer neighbours make their own Pâté de Foie Gras. When I said, 'But surely truffles are so expensive?', the answer came back, '*Oui, mais il faut!*' It is necessary! And of course Monique is right, one must have truffles to get the authentic taste. Therefore she gets them. But she has never had a holiday, and has only slept away from the farm for one night in about thirty years of married life. *Chacun à son goût.* And they think nothing of getting up with the lark to look for cèpes, the big fat mushrooms of the Dordogne, because they know that if they don't someone else will.

I like to use unusual ingredients, not just for their own sake, but because I think it is my job to encourage people to try things and give them fresh ideas, rather than just to try to teach them to cook, since most people are good cooks anyway, these days. If your greengrocer has a new vegetable, try it and use it; if no one buys it he will soon give up stocking it and we are back again to sprouts and carrots. Fight for your fresh firm garlic, never buy dried-up shrivelled heads, because they will taste stale. I'm sure this is why so many people in this country still don't like garlic, because it is horrid when it's stale.

But, thank goodness, there is now a wider interest in food in this country, born largely, I imagine, from the experience of holidays abroad, and also a better approach to the health aspect of food. But don't look for way-out, extremist views on diet in this book, only my ideas of a sane approach to food.

The Store Cupboard

I have always liked a well-stocked cupboard. If you have a good store of unperishables you can probably pick up a recipe and cook it at once without having to set off on a shopping spree. You can experiment more easily with tastes and flavours, or rescue disasters (always a sign of a competent cook) with a pinch of this or a drop of that. Build up your store-cupboard gradually and try to have a really comprehensive range of ingredients to call upon. At the same time, do be brave about your dried herbs. If they have been on the shelf for as long as you can remember, chuck them out and start again.

Some of the ingredients for the store-cupboard are fairly obvious; others come from specialist sources, Chinese stores, Soho, distant delicatessen (I buy all my cooking chocolate in Edinburgh) or abroad, and you must buy them when you can and enough to last till you go back again. I've included some in Section 7, *Spontaneous Entertaining*, but here are a few more ideas of some basic ingredients I'd hate to be without.

Oil. For everyday cooking and dressing I like a groundnut oil (Arachide in France). It's light in flavour and texture, although sunflower or safflower is lighter, better from the cholesterol point of view, but expensive. I find corn oil heavy and don't much like the taste.

Olive Oil. This is an absolute must for some dishes to give them their authentic flavour, and it is, of course, delicious in many others. I favour a medium-grade oil with quite a full flavour because you can always mix it with some groundnut or sunflower oil if you want to save on costs or lighten the taste. Some of the Spanish Andalusian ones are good, and I often buy one called Carbonella which is excellent value. It's nice to have a bottle or two of thick, green virgin oil from Tuscany, Greece, Provence or Spain. They all have their distinctive characters and can be hideously expensive, but how good their flavours and how much they add to the dish. But I'm very mean with them, almost keeping them under lock and key, and they last a long time.

Walnut Oil. This is very distinctive. I find a little goes a long way, but it's lovely and unusual in salads to make a change. The one I have comes straight from a French farmer, and one teaspoon of it to several tablespoons of groundnut oil is quite enough.

Vinegar. Wine vinegar is a must, because I find malt vinegar has only one use and that's for chutneys and pickles. Red or white wine, tarragon and sherry vinegar are all good and all have their moments. Try making your own. Put about ½ pt (300ml) wine vinegar in an open jar in a warm place with muslin to keep the flies out, add any wine dregs—never more than 1 pt (600ml) at a time—whenever you have them, and behold! you should end up with wine vinegar. It's strong, and if used discreetly for salads with good olive oil it sets the memory bells ringing for Mediterranean lands.

Parmesan. Another expensive ingredient but essential for some dishes. Buy it in the piece, never be fobbed off with the ready-grated packets or tins, which are disgusting. Bought in Soho in one of those marvellous Italian grocers like Parmigiani or Camisa it can be thirty per cent cheaper than if bought in the provinces. It keeps for ages (if you can resist using it) wrapped in greaseproof paper in the bottom of the fridge. As a substitute, take a good piece of mature strong Cheddar, wrap it lightly in absorbent paper and keep it in a dry cupboard for several months. It's nothing like as good as Parmesan, but it is useful and better than the ready-grated stuff.

Dried Mushrooms. Boletus Edulis, the cèpe mushroom of France, is sold dried in little packets; expensive, I know, but a little goes a long way and gives a great lift to a dish, adding a rich flavour to soups, stocks and sauces. I should use them more if I had to rely on stock-cubes instead of real stock as I think they help to compensate for the lack of depth of flavour.

Tinned Consommé. I like Campbell's but you have to look carefully for the one which will set to jelly; it says on the tin 'serve cold jellied'. Sainsbury's is also good. It is a necessity for making certain dishes and is a boon used in conjunction with stock-cubes to give a bit of texture and depth to instant stocks.

Stock-Cubes. I have not done a comparative stock-cube tasting, but I tend to go for Knorr as being a safe bet.

Vanilla Sugar. This is easy to make and so much finer in taste than the essence (which is usually not essence anyway but an artificial and rather nasty vanilla flavouring). Fill a 2 lb jam jar with castor sugar and tuck in several split vanilla pods. These should be shiny black and pliable, and if they are very fresh they have tiny white hairs on them. The longer they are the more expensive, and it's no wonder they are quite dear when you think that each pod has to be fertilised by hand. This is due to the fact that vanilla is not indigenous to the country in which it is now grown and there are none of the right moths and insects to do the work, and also because the curing process is rather lengthy. But the pods do last for years. If you use them to flavour custards and syrups rinse them, dry them out and pop them back in the jar.

Flour. I find that all flours need to be stored before use. This is because nowadays the flour is processed and sent from the mill to the shop so quickly that it has little time to dry out

29

and mature. This means that when you make a sauce, however carefully you do it, a rather sticky, gluey mixture can result. So now we buy flour in quite large quantities, store it in a warm dry cupboard and try to keep it for about a month before using it in rotation. We use plain flour for nearly everything, including all pastries except for one or two. I think self-raising flour in pastry gives a dry crumbly texture with a yellowish tinge and a shop-cake taste. It's the same in sauces—and who wants to taste bicarbonate of soda or cream of tartar in everything they cook? Even in cake-making it is much better to add baking powder to plain flour in the correct strength.

Strong Flour. This is sometimes called bread flour, and is made from hard wheat as grown in Canada, the States and Central Europe. It has a high gluten content, and this renders it more elastic and allows it to rise and stretch further, making it better for breads, savarins, choux pastry, puff pastry and pasta.

Wholemeal Flour. This retains up to one hundred per cent of the wheat, and we use it in great quantities for all our bread-making. Different mills and brands sell flours of a rather different coarseness and texture, and I usually mix wholemeal with some strong white flour. In fact, if you have a supply of wholemeal and strong white flour you can change the proportions and vary your bread accordingly. If you keep a few extras like nibbed wheat, bran, wheat germ and malt you can ring the changes still further and make many other different breads.

Store Cupboard Ingredients you can Freeze

I find a freezer absolutely invaluable as an aid to good cooking, and I use it to have certain important ingredients immediately available. Here are some of the things I find particularly useful.

Stock. I make this whenever a chicken carcass is available, or in great quantities from time to time, and freeze it for soups and sauces. I also like to keep any trimmings of celery or leek and parsley stalks in the freezer, for sometimes they are ingredients one does not have available, and they can easily be tossed into the stock pot from the freezer. I never blanch them for this purpose.

Breadcrumbs. This may not sound necessary, but it's always a bit of a hassle to make a few breadcrumbs. I keep a box of them in the freezer to add at will.

Cheese. Similarly, I keep a box of ready-grated Cheddar. I also keep my cooking Gruyère in the freezer as I find it's the only way to protect it from the phantom Gruyère eater who can always find it in the fridge. It grates easily from the freezer, and a tablespoonful or so on top of a dish can raise it from the ordinary to the special.

Fresh Root Ginger. The root of the fresh ginger is becoming increasingly available; pop it in a plastic bag just as it is and freeze it. When you want some, scrape off the skin while still frozen and grate it straight into your dish.

Tomato Purée. If you have to open a little tin, it's either all used up, probably making the sauce too tomatoey, or a bit is left in the fridge and this invariably has to be thrown away later. Tubes are useful but expensive. The large tins are much cheaper, and when opened can be turned into a plastic box and frozen. The purée never freezes really hard and can be cut readily into cubes, and one soon gets used to a cube rather than a tablespoonful.

Frozen Herbs. These are useful if frozen when freshly available in the summer, chopped and pressed lightly into tiny containers from which the point of a knife will winkle them out to scatter on to your dish.

Ingredients that are difficult to find. Three things I always have a struggle to find when I need them are Ricotta Cheese for one of my favourite Lasagnes, Filo Paste for Baklava or Beureks and Pitta Bread for Kebabs. All keep well in the freezer.

Butter and Cream

Butter. I use a firm New Zealand butter like Anchor for cooking. It's not made in the continental way with ripened cream, holding a lot of milky residue which will burn if you use it for frying, and which also makes a softer pastry that is difficult to roll. Soft margarines have the same problem, and one needs to fry and cook fairly gently with them. People often ask why I don't use margarine in my cooking, and I tell them that my role is to show dishes properly cooked using the correct ingredients. Others may interpret and substitute as they will, but if I start to substitute, and they substitute still further, a travesty of a dish will appear. Some dishes need a lightly salted or an unsalted butter.

Cream. We use quite a lot of cream in our dishes when entertaining, for Britain is a dairy country with some of the best cream in the world. But often we use whipping cream, which is thirty-eight per cent butterfat, as opposed to double cream which is forty-eight per cent. Whipping cream will whip to a light airy mass, good for mousses and soufflés where lightness is what one is after. For pouring, in sauces and to enrich a dish, double cream is better as it has the necessary weight and flavour. I sometimes long for the Jersey cream of my childhood in which the spoon not only stood up but got stuck! But it was difficult to use, going buttery when heated and impossible to whip without some thinning down.

Herbs

At last, after years of travelling, I am settled and beginning to build up my herb garden. I have a path edged in parsley, and I revel in the abundance. The perennials are my favourites, from the cultivation point of view; plant them once, and year after year there they are. Many are attractive and find their place in the border, preferably as close to the kitchen door as possible. It takes a while to discover what position and soil each plant likes, but the flavour from sun-baked basil, marjoram, fennel or tarragon is much better than from its shaded counterpart, whereas chervil will bolt and seed at once if planted in a sunny position. I prefer most herbs fresh rather than dried, but I do believe the Mediterranean ones are better dried—but only if you buy the best and the freshest you can find, and ruthlessly turn them out before they decline into tired old age. I have never really succeeded in growing herbs on window sills inside a room. There is not enough room, and plants grow leggy and seem rather tasteless. I'm sure outdoor windowbox culture, especially with a south or west aspect, is well worth doing, but I've never had the chance to try.

Perennial Herbs

Bay. Use it fresh or dried and grow it in a favoured place; it hates the cold March wind.

Chives. For cheese, salads and general flavouring. One never seems to have enough of this most useful member of the onion family.

Curry Plant. The somewhat tender, curry-scented Artemisia that I use in a rather interesting soup.

Fennel. Green or bronze, very pretty in a border, and the leaves, stems and seeds can all be used on fish or in salads. Plant it in a good sunny position, but beware it doesn't take over.

Lemon Thyme. Not as hardy as thyme, but I use it a lot because it's got such a lovely flavour.

Lovage. Strong in flavour and rather like celery. Use it discreetly in stocks, soups and salads. Another that will take you over given half a chance.

Marjoram. Golden marjoram is an attractive garden plant, though the flavour is not so good as the annual marjoram.

Mints. There are many of these with different uses in sauces and salads and for general flavouring. They like damp ground but can be very invasive. I grow the essential common mint, *Mentha spicata*, as well as a beautiful white variegated mint that suits our grey and white border, Eau-de-Cologne which I use for sorbets, and pennyroyal which has a strong peppermint flavour.

Rosemary. Use with discretion in roasts, sauces and soups. We grow it in a big bush outside the front door, an old Scots habit, I believe.

Sage. Not a herb I use much because of its coarse, earthy taste, but the variegated and bronze sages are pretty, if a little tender.

Sorrel. For salads, soups and sauces. A well-behaved and model plant that I sowed when we got here. Four years later, with nothing but picking and an annual chop-back, there it is, last to leave in winter and first to return in spring.

Tarragon. This is one of the best herbs for soups, sauces and salads, and indeed many other dishes. True French Tarragon is difficult to find and keep, and so often one is not sold the true *Artemisia dracunculus* in the first place but the Russian tarragon, which is not so flavoursome. It is also rather tender and does not do well without lots of sun. When I have no fresh tarragon I use the best dried, which I often buy in France and it tastes very good, often much better than the freshly grown in this country.

Thymes. Where should we be without thyme? It's in every bouquet garni. Dried thyme goes off quickly and tastes stale, but it's a hardy perennial and, thank goodness, is with us all the year. And some of the variegated ones are also very pretty.

Winter Savory. I use this in soups, stews and sauces. Rather strong and coarse-flavoured, but at least it's there all the time.

Annual and Biennial Herbs

Basil. Delicious on tomatoes, over salads and in sauces or soups. A perennial in India but a touchy annual here, happiest really in a greenhouse. If you grow it outside don't plant till the soil is warm in May. I love this herb, and never seem to have nearly enough of it.

Chervil. Rather like parsley, but with a delicate aniseed flavour that goes well in soups and sauces. It is the correct herb to use with tarragon in a Béarnaise Sauce. It seems to do best in spring and autumn if left to self-seed in a sunny spot where it keeps popping up, but in summer it likes a moist shady place. I had no real success with it until I bought the seeds in France.

Dill. Used extensively in Germany and Scandinavia for fish, cucumber, sauces and soups. It grows easily from seed which you can also use as it is.

Parsley. The essential herb, which should be sown every year. It is slow to germinate, but a kettleful of boiling water poured down the drill after planting helps it to get going.

Summer Savory. Known also as Bohnenkraut or bean herb, it grows easily in summer and is said to go especially well with beans, peas and lentils.

Sweet or Knotted Marjoram. I use this in soups, sauces and stews, find it a better flavour than the perennial marjoram and grow it easily from seed.

BASIC RECIPES

There are some recipes which come up again and again, either on their own or in conjunction with other ingredients to make so many dishes that it is well worth being completely conversant with them, to know all their quirks and the tips for making them. I am only including a very few basic recipes which I find myself demonstrating again and again, for I hate cookbooks which are always saying 'see page so-and-so' just as you have got halfway through the recipes. So though I may risk being repetitive when we come to the main chapters, I have set out most recipes in full.

Stock

Let's start with stock, such a vital part of good cooking. I know it's easy for us at Farthinghoe; we are cooking a lot of food and therefore the ingredients for stock are at hand and we have the time to give to making it. It seems to me that there are two main ways of making stock. One is a skirmish with the odd carcass, which is popped into a pot with a few vegetables and herbs and put to simmer. The other is an occasional major attack upon the stockpot as we endeavour to make a large quantity of really well-made stock to have available in the freezer for the next few months. There is also the variation of making a rich stock by browning chicken (or any kind of bones) in a frying pan or in the oven and boiling a glass of wine away, thus intensifying the flavour quite remarkably. Whichever of these you choose, with an Aga it is easy to pop a pan in the low oven all night or let it simmer away quietly on top. It is not so economical, of course, if you cook on electricity or gas.

Stock-cubes, useful though they are—and they do very adequately for some soups and dishes—are no substitute for the real thing. While you may get quite a lot of rather salty

34

tastiness from a cube, you can never achieve the texture and richness that come from the gelatine, or the depth and fullness of flavour found in a well-balanced stock.

When I checked the classic stock recipes I was staggered at the quantities of meat they recommended to make quite a modest amount of stock. Three pounds of lean veal, four pounds of giblets, four pounds of chicken bones and trimmings and four pounds of veal bones, all to make about ten pints of stock. It shows how rich and tasty their stocks must have been. Nowadays, luckily, the taste is for lighter, more delicately flavoured dishes. But remember that you can't make a silk purse out of a sow's ear; a cooked chicken carcass, picked of every scrap of flesh, is not going to render masses of tasty stock. On the other hand a raw carcass, from which you have taken the joints and portions of chicken with your boning and joining knife, is going to do a far better job and at no greater expense. Follow also the Chinese principle of chopping up the bones to release the flavour from the marrow, and get into the habit of adding half a teaspoonful of lemon juice or vinegar to help release the calcium in the bones which is good for us. Long cooking draws out the gelatine and slow cooking makes a clear stock; but fast boiling makes it cloudy as the particles get broken up and amalgamate with the liquid instead of settling on the bottom or rising to the top to be skimmed off. Your proportions of vegetables are important to get a balanced flavour, but potatoes should not be added as they also make a cloudy stock.

With a freezer, all your stock can be frozen in ½-litre or 1-litre containers. Strain it straight into plastic boxes, chill it, freeze it and turn it out of the boxes into plastic bags if you need the boxes for something else. It is then instantly available for soups and sauces, but cannot 'go off' as it will in the fridge. To use from frozen, turn into a saucepan with a little water in the bottom to stop it from burning, heat it, and it will be ready in moments.

F *   ## White Chicken Stock

Ingredients
2–3 pts (1.2–1.7l)

1 chicken carcass (preferably raw, or if cooked still with some meat on it)
giblets and wing tips if available
1 peeled onion stuck with a clove
1–2 carrots
½ stick celery (or frozen trimmings)
1 leek (or frozen trimmings)
1 bay leaf
3–4 parsley stalks
1 sprig fresh thyme
½ teasp lemon juice

1 clove garlic (optional)
4–6 black peppercorns
3–4 pts (1.7–2.25l) water or to cover
1 teasp salt

Optional extras
mushroom stalks
a few bacon rinds
¼ teasp tarragon
a little white wine

Break the bones if possible to release the flavour from the marrow and place in a pan with all the other ingredients. Cook in a very slow oven (225°F/110°C/Gas ½) overnight or for 4–6 hours, or simmer very gently on the top of the stove for 3–4 hours. Strain, chill and de-grease.

F * ## Rich Brown Chicken Stock

Ingredients
approx 2½ pts (1.5l)

1 raw chicken carcass with wing tips, giblets, trimmings and feet if you can get them
1 lb (450g) veal knuckle or bones
2 oz (50g) chicken fat, bacon fat, lard or oil
1 slice bacon or ham
2 carrots
1 unpeeled onion stuck with a clove
1 small leek (or frozen trimmings)

1 stick celery (or frozen trimmings)
6 peppercorns
½ teasp lemon juice
4–6 parsley stalks
1 sprig fresh thyme
½ bay leaf
4 fl oz (100ml) dry white wine
2–3 pts (1.2–1.7l) water (approx)
¼ teasp salt

Break the bones and carcass to release the flavour from the marrow. Brown in the fat in a large saucepan with the roughly chopped vegetables. Add the wine and reduce completely until everything is frying again. Repeat this process with water (or even better with more wine) for a strong flavour. Add water to cover and the remaining ingredients, bring to the simmer and skim, then cook in a very slow oven (225°F/110°C/Gas ½) for 4–6 hours or overnight, or simmer very gently for 3–4 hours on top of the stove. Strain through muslin and cool. For really concentrated stock, remove the fat when cold and reboil fast to reduce quantity, then season. Cool and chill.

Fumets

If you need Fish Fumet (or stock) and are going to have to chat up the fishmonger for fish bones and skins, why not make quite a batch and freeze it? It's useful to have in the freezer and, as with many things which take a little time, thought or effort, it can be made for practically nothing. Steel yourself to buy a few prawns in their shells and you can make tasty Prawn Butter and also incomparably improve your Fish Fumet to a Prawn Fumet. Do remember that fish stocks are never simmered for longer than 30–40 minutes at the most or a bitter taste of fish bones develops.

F * ## Prawn Butter

Ingredients

3–4 oz (75–100g) butter
the shells from 8 oz (225g) prawns

Heat the butter in a frying pan, add the prawn shells and toss over high heat until hot through. Turn into a food processor or liquidiser and process until finely chopped. Scrape into a square of muslin and twist and squeeze the mixture to separate the prawn butter from the shells. This sounds a sticky process, but in fact is quite easy and well worth doing. Use in sauces or add to enrich fish dishes.

F ∗   ## Fish Fumet

Ingredients
approx 2 pts (1.2l)

2 lb (900g) white fish skins and bones (turbot or sole are best)	1 tiny sprig thyme
1 small sliced onion	4–6 peppercorns
6–8 parsley stalks	¼ pt (150ml) dry white wine
1 thin slice lemon	a few mushroom stalks (optional)
½ bay leaf	about 2½ pts (1.5l) cold water to cover
	¼ teasp salt

Place the washed fish bones, with the gills removed, in a pan on top of all the other ingredients (if you put the other ingredients on top they all float up and get skimmed off). Bring to the boil, skim well and simmer for 30–40 minutes (never longer). Strain through muslin and reduce further if necessary for flavour.

F ∗   ## Prawn Fumet

Having made the Prawn Butter, add the chopped prawn shells to the Fish Fumet recipe to make it into Prawn Fumet.

Basic Sauces

Sauces seem to me to be another area where one is constantly following the same basic principle with varying quantities, proportions and ingredients to achieve specific results. How many times have you made a sauce thickened with a cooked fat and flour roux, yet do you know the quick method? And do you know instinctively how much flour per ½ pt (300ml) of liquid to allow for a thin sauce, a coating sauce or a thick sauce? I still have to think carefully, but it should be a formula we learn by heart until we do it by instinct. Though, of course, different flours have slightly different thickening capacities and one must be prepared to adjust.

$\mathcal{F}$ *   **Basic Method**

Thin Sauce	Coating Sauce	Thick Sauce
½ oz (12g) butter	¾ oz (20g) butter	1 oz (25g) butter
½ oz (12g) flour	¾ oz (20g) flour	1 oz (25g) flour
½ pt (300ml) milk	½ pt (300ml) milk	½ pt (300ml) milk
salt and pepper	salt and pepper	salt and pepper

Chop up your butter so that it will all melt quickly and evenly and put it in a saucepan over moderate heat. When melted, add the flour, stir together with a wooden spoon and cook for 2–3 minutes. If the flour is not adequately cooked at this stage, the sauce will have a floury flavour; this will only go after a further 10–15 minutes' simmering once the milk is in, and you will have to watch so that it does not catch in the pan. On the other hand, if the heat is too high the flour will go sandy and grainy, and these grains will remain in the finished sauce, leaving it not quite smooth.

Having cooked the flour, draw the pan off the stove and wait for the sizzling to stop; when it has, add the cold liquid all in one go. Replace over medium or high heat and beat with a wire whisk while it comes to the boil; then simmer for 1–2 minutes, and season. You can also add hot liquid instead of cold, but in this case make sure that your butter and flour really have stopped sizzling. If very hot liquid hits a very hot roux it can thicken before you can grab the whisk. Made in this way you will never have a lumpy sauce, and it will be just as smooth and shiny as a conventionally made sauce where the liquid is added gradually, but will take far less time. Of course, if you use non-stick pans, or copper ones lined with tin, you will have to stay with the conventional method in order not to remove the lining, or use a little birch-broom stick.

This basic sauce can be changed in a thousand ways. Made with flavoured milk it becomes Béchamel, a sauce most undeservedly despised; it can be flavoured with parsley, egg, anchovy or cheese, and then it takes the name of whatever is added. It can be made with a proportion of single or whipping cream instead of milk and instantly becomes rather more special, as it does if a little butter is beaten in at the end. Made with white stock instead of milk it becomes a Velouté sauce and can again be used in endless different ways. Made with a base of Prawn Butter and Fish Fumet a realm of fish sauces opens up.

The classic brown sauces, Espagnole, Demi-Glace and their endless derivatives, don't seem to me to have much place in a busy housewife's repertoire, and certainly I hardly ever use them; this is partly due to the time they take to make, but also because these weighty brown sauces no longer appeal; and this is epitomised in the philosophy of 'La Nouvelle Cuisine', which has only followed people's tastes. So with very little hesitation—for this is not meant to be a classic cookery book—I am leaving out most of the brown sauces.

The flour for sauces. As I said in *Ingredients*, flour should be bought ahead and kept in a warm top cupboard.

The fat for sauces. Butter makes the finest sauces and gives the best flavour. Margarine has a high water content, and so the margarine and flour need to be cooked fairly gently or there can be a danger of the sauce becoming rather grainy and lumpy. Dripping and various fats—pork, duck or chicken—give dishes their own individual flavour and are most often used where flour must be browned for gravies; these fats heat to a higher temperature without burning and also have no water content.

Keeping sauces warm. I often find my best sauces are made the day before or well ahead when I have a lot to do. So why not turn this fact to good account and make your own life easier by making special sauces for parties in advance, leaving them sitting in a pan of hot water to keep warm and mature? I have often had people ask what that delicious sauce was when all it was was our old friend, Monsieur Béchamel, made properly and kept warm!

Once the sauce is made, set it aside in a *bain marie,* a pan of hot water at about 140°F/60°C, or as hot as your finger can bear for two or three seconds, to come halfway up the sides of the saucepan or bowl. Cover with wet greaseproof paper, or wet cling film pressed down on to the sauce itself, and it will keep happily for hours in this way.

To reheat a cold sauce. Return the sauce to a saucepan and heat gently, stirring from time to time. If it is a rich cream sauce or one containing egg yolks, set it in its bowl over a pan of water to reheat, again stirring from time to time, but do not let it get so hot that the yolks could scramble.

Beurre Manié. A last-minute way of adjusting the thickness of a sauce. Soft butter and flour, usually in equal quantities or with a little more butter to flour, are creamed or kneaded together, then added in very small pieces to a sauce to thicken it at the end of its cooking time. The sauce is stirred, or just shaken and swirled if there are bits that could break up in it (like fish fillets), until it comes to the boil and thickens; the flour is so lightly cooked that it does not have time to develop a floury taste. If you freeze a sauce that has been thickened with *beurre manié,* it may well thin out when re-heated from the freezer because the flour has not been well cooked.

Cornflour, Potato Flour and Arrowroot. These can all be added to soups, sauces, stews or puddings to thicken them. Cornflour is used frequently in Chinese cooking. I find potato flour a very useful thickener, especially for freezer dishes. Arrowroot is the most delicate and digestible of starch thickeners and is used for fine sauces and sweet dishes. Mixed with a little cold liquid, these flours are then stirred into the hot but not quite boiling liquid, which is then boiled and stirred for a minute or so until thickened and smooth.

Emulsion Sauces

*   Mayonnaise by Hand

For special occasions or extra special dishes nothing is better than hand-made mayonnaise; it does not take long and is not difficult, and is most rewarding. It certainly is not the ogre it's sometimes made out to be, and any problems are usually not real but only in the mind of the maker. Once you know how to solve any that may arise, you relax and then they don't usually happen! I'm sorry to go on about this, but I'm so amazed at the number of good cooks who come to the Farthinghoe demonstrations and quake and say, 'Mayonnaise! Oh, I can't do that.' So I feel that it must need saying.

Ingredients
approx ½ pt (300ml)

2 egg yolks
½ teasp Dijon mustard
½ pt (300ml) oil (olive oil and sunflower
    oil mixed is good)

½ lemon or a little wine vinegar
plenty of salt
pepper

Have everything at room temperature; don't take your eggs from the fridge or the oil from a cold larder. If they are a bit cold, warm the bowl before you start because this aids emulsification and inhibits curdling. Place the yolks in a roomy warm bowl standing on a folded wet cloth to stop it from sliding about. Add the salt, pepper, mustard and a few drops of lemon juice or vinegar and whisk with a wire whisk for about a minute until it thickens slightly (this means it will absorb the oil more easily). Drop by drop add the oil (this is most easily done from a jug), whisking all the time. When 2–3 tablespoons are incorporated and you have a stiff mixture, add a few more drops of lemon or vinegar to thin a little and then add more oil. You can add it a little faster now, in a thin trickle. Make sure it is all absorbed before you add more, but don't dwell on it, taking too long or beating too hard, or it will get very stiff and white and you will have to keep adding lemon to thin it; then it will end up too acidic and will look and taste machine-made. When all the oil is added, correct the seasoning and lemon or vinegar; it should be thick enough to hold on your whisk, translucent and shiny. A tablespoon or so of boiling water added at the end helps mayonnaise to keep well and lightens it, but I'm not altogether in favour of this as I think it detracts a little from its texture; it may be a good idea if you are using a very heavy olive oil. Two yolks to ½ pint of oil is about right; more yolks make a lovely rich yellow mayonnaise or you can get away with adding a little more oil, if you are feeling mean, without jeopardising the mayonnaise.

Keeping Mayonnaise. Keep the mayonnaise covered or it will quickly form a discoloured layer. It will keep for 7–10 days in the fridge, but remove it and let it come to room temperature before using or stirring it. It may curdle if stirred straight from the fridge.

Curdled Mayonnaise. The mayonnaise suddenly breaks up as you are beating and the oil starts to separate, or it simply will not thicken, however much you beat it. There are several reasons why the mayonnaise may curdle; if the ingredients were too cold; if the oil was added too fast; or if the weather is very sultry and thundery. Very rarely, certain heavy olive oils will curdle. If it persistently does so, take the oil back and the shop should change it; of course, if you brought it back from your holiday in Spain this may not be easy! In that case try mixing it with another, lighter oil. If your mayonnaise curdles do not despair because there are several things you can do. Take another egg yolk in a warm bowl, beat it well, then very gradually add your curdled mixture teaspoon by teaspoon, beating it stiff and smooth until you have it all back together. Or you can warm a bowl (rinse it in hot water, then dry it), add a teaspoon of Dijon mustard, and very gradually beat your recalcitrant mixture into that; it saves a yolk and takes no time at all.

To Freeze Mayonnaise. If you freeze mayonnaise it will curdle when it thaws, but with a teaspoon of Dijon mustard and a warm bowl you can have it back together again in much less time than it takes to make the sauce from scratch. So don't hesitate to freeze surplus mayonnaise if you want to. I only discovered this when we catered for a wedding for two hundred or so. I made enough mayonnaise, to go with the salmon, for two hundred people as greedy as I, and we were left with about eight pints! So into the freezer it went and I blessed it every time I took it out and reamalgamated it.

*   **Mayonnaise by Machine** *(Liquidiser or Food Processor).*

One usually takes whole eggs instead of just yolks (though yolks alone can be used in the food processor), which gives a lighter, paler mayonnaise, very good for coleslaws, salads and mousses. It's incredibly quick to make but, useful though it is, to my mind a machine-made mayonnaise is never quite as good as a hand-made one for those extra special occasions.

Ingredients
approx ½ pt (300ml)

1 whole egg
½ lemon or a little wine vinegar
½ teasp Dijon mustard
½ pt (300ml) oil
salt and pepper

Place the egg, salt, pepper, mustard and a little lemon juice or vinegar in the processor bowl or liquidiser goblet and process for 10 seconds; then gradually, drip by drip to start with, pour in the oil; when about a third has gone in the mayonnaise should have 'taken'. You will hear a change of note and the mixture will go slurp, slurp, slurp; now add the rest of the oil as quickly as you dare to avoid too tight an emulsion (the more you dwell on it, the thicker and whiter your mayonnaise will become). Add lemon or vinegar to taste and correct the seasoning.

41

*   # Hollandaise Sauce

This is not a difficult sauce to make. It does not take endless whisking, it can be made several hours ahead and it does not need any last-minute attention. Make in a heavy non-aluminium pan (to avoid discolouration) over extremely low direct heat if you are very confident about it; otherwise use a bowl resting over a pan of hot water, which is usually what I do.

The egg yolks thicken as they cook, but at about 155°F/68°C they will coagulate and 'scramble'; by having a cube of cold butter or an ice cube at your elbow, ready to throw in to lower the temperature if the sauce looks like curdling, you can make it without trepidation. If you have to 'hold' the sauce for many hours I should use no more than 2 oz (50g) butter per yolk; you can also add a pinch of potato flour or arrowroot, but it's not really necessary.

Ingredients
approx ½ pt (300ml)

3 egg yolks
6–8 oz (175–225g) best unsalted or lightly
    salted butter (though salted butter can
    be used)

1 lemon
1 tbs cold water
salt and pepper

Keep two ½-oz (12g) pieces of butter on one side, chop up the rest and set to melt gently, but don't let it get too hot. Place the egg yolks in a bowl which will fit over a pan of hot, but not quite boiling, water with the water not quite touching the bowl. Before placing the bowl over the pan whisk the yolks for about ½ minute with a wire whisk, because well-beaten yolks thicken better. Stir in 1 tbs cold water and 1 tbs lemon juice, add one piece of your reserved butter and stand the bowl over the pan of hot water; now stir until the butter melts and the yolks thicken (this is the part that cannot be hurried). When the yolks are thick enough (so that you can just see the bottom of the bowl for a moment when you draw the whisk across), remove the bowl from the saucepan quickly before they cook further and curdle, and toss in the remaining piece of cold butter to arrest the cooking and lower the temperature. If the bowl is still very hot or the mixture begins to look curdly round the edges, quickly add another bit of cold butter or an ice cube. Whisk until the butter melts, then, still off the heat, gradually drip in your melted butter, whisking the while (if you have used salted butter leave out some of the white salty residue). The sauce should be thick and creamy; season lightly and add more lemon if necessary, but re-member it is a delicate sauce and it is the flavour of the butter that counts.

To Keep Hollandaise Warm. Stand your bowl in a pan of tepid water and keep it at the back of the stove or near the pilot light, but nowhere too hot; it will hold for 4–5 hours like this and should be eaten just warm. I have little success if I try to rewarm it, but left-over Hollandaise is very useful in sauces, soups or scrambled eggs, added to enrich them when they come off the stove.

✱✱   Béarnaise Sauce

The prince of sauces, fuller flavoured than Hollandaise, which needs fresh, frozen or the best dried chervil and good tarragon to taste really right.

Ingredients
approx ⅓ pt (200ml)

2–3 tbs white wine vinegar
3 tbs dry white wine
1 tbs finely chopped shallots
2 teasp fresh chopped or 1 teasp dried
    tarragon
1 teasp fresh or ½ teasp dried chervil
4–6 peppercorns

5 oz (125g) best unsalted or lightly salted
    butter
2 egg yolks
salt and pepper

To Finish
1 tbs very finely chopped fresh tarragon
    and chervil

Place the wine, vinegar, shallots, peppercorns and herbs in a small saucepan and boil down until the shallots are cooked and only 2 tbs liquid remains. Strain and cool. In a small saucepan just melt 4 oz (100g) butter, keeping 1 oz (25g) chilled. Beat the yolks in a bowl really well with a wire whisk, then beat in the wine and vinegar liquid. Place the bowl over a pan of hot, not boiling water so that the bowl does not touch the water. Add half the cold butter and stir until the yolks thicken. Remove the bowl quickly from the heat and stir in the remaining cold butter to check cooking and stop the yolks from curdling. Gradually whisk in the melted butter, as if making mayonnaise, season, and stir in the very finely chopped tarragon and chervil.

Sauce Béarnaise will keep warm (and it should be only warm) for three to four hours standing in a saucepan of lukewarm water in a warm place. Use only 2 oz (50g) butter per yolk if you have to hold the sauce for long. ½ teasp potato flour beaten into the yolks makes it more stable but less good. If the finished sauce starts to curdle or separate beat in 1 tbs cold water or an ice cube.

Left-over Béarnaise can be kept in the fridge or freezer and is delicious added to soups, sauces or scrambled eggs just before serving.

Pastry

I think people are frightened of pastry these days. Perfectly good cooks say their quiches never go right; they buy mince pies from us saying that they can never make them; and if one mentions the words flaky, puff or choux pastry a glazed, hunted look comes into their eyes. In the old days cooks were in the kitchen all the time, probably making pastry nearly every day, and they got to know the feel and exactly how to make it. Now we may go for quite long periods without making pastry, and when we do may have forgotten which recipes we prefer and exactly how stiff we usually mix it. I am not a great lover of the typical English shortcrust, which I find can become dry and powdery in the mouth, but I do include two basic pastry recipes which I think are really worth getting to know well. An hour or two's rest improves the pastry, but if you are in a hurry ½-hour will do.

F *   All-purpose Pastry

An easy-to-make, easy-to-use pastry which is crisp and especially good for quiches. The method of mixing in the liquid as you rub in the butter, followed by the *fraisage* of smearing the pastry down the board to combine butter and flour, gives it its character. In a food processor it's the quickest thing ever.

       Ingredients
       For a 9" (24 cm) tart tin

1 egg yolk and about 2 tbs of cold water	**a good pinch of salt**
or **3–4 tbs cold water**	
6 oz (175g) plain flour	
3 oz (75g) firm butter	

If you are using a yolk mix it with the cold water. Sift the flour and salt into a wide mixing bowl and add the firm butter cut into hazelnut-sized pieces. Rub in the butter, sprinkling over the yolk and water mixed, or just water, as you work and pinching the whole lot into a dough. When formed into a rough dough turn out on to a board and with the heel of your hand smear the pastry down the board in egg-sized lumps finally to amalgamate it. Knead briefly into a flat disc. Rest in a plastic bag in the fridge for 1–2 hours or overnight.

In the Food Processor. Sift the flour and salt into the bowl of the food processor with the metal blade in place, add the firm butter cut into hazelnut-sized pieces and have your yolk and cold water, or just cold water, ready. Switch on and add the yolk and water at once; process until the mixture just draws together into a lump. Turn out on to a board and smear down the board in egg-sized lumps (though I hardly feel it needs this *fraisage* when made in the food processor). Knead briefly into a flat disc. Rest in a plastic bag in the fridge for 1–2 hours or overnight.

F *   Sweet Pastry

A medium rich sweet pastry with sugar and egg yolk is also a good friend, rolling out without fuss. I think one of the most important tips is to use butter firm from the fridge, for if you use kitchen-soft butter your pastry can be crumbly and difficult to roll. I also find sweet pastries much easier to work when made with icing rather than castor sugar; of course, the French fine sugar is finer than our castor sugar, and I think it is probably this which causes a lot of recipes (probably translated from the French) to be so difficult to work.

       Ingredients
       for a 9" (24cm) tart tin

6 oz (175g) plain flour	**1 egg yolk**
4 oz (100g) firm butter	**1–2 tbs iced water**
2 tbs icing sugar	**a pinch of salt**

Sift the flour, salt and icing sugar into a wide mixing bowl, add the butter cut up into hazelnut-sized lumps and rub in to breadcrumb consistency. Lift the flour high and let it trickle through your fingers; don't press and force the butter into the flour, which will make a tough pastry, but let it work in gradually. Mix the yolk with a tablespoon of water; sprinkle this over the flour mixture and work up to a dough using another tablespoon of water if necessary. Knead and work the pastry as little as possible but form into an even flat disc. Chill in a plastic bag in the fridge for ½–2 hours or overnight.

In a Food Processor. Sift the flour, salt and icing sugar into the bowl of the food processor with the metal blade in place, add the butter cut into hazelnut-sized pieces and process to the breadcrumb stage. With the engine still running, add the yolk mixed with 1 tbs cold water and switch off as the mixture combines into one lump (only use more water if necessary) and comes away cleanly from the bowl. Knead briefly into a flat disc. Chill in a plastic bag in the fridge for ½–2 hours or overnight.

SECTION 2

Buffet Parties

Buffet parties can be most useful and enjoyable, and indeed are usually necessary when you have large numbers to entertain: Here at Farthinghoe we get quite a lot of practice when we run our regular cookery demonstrations, having a different three-course lunch for thirty to cook every time. It all has to be cooked the day before and has to re-heat without attention or deterioration.

While the look of food on a buffet is important and it's lovely to feast your eyes on different coloured, shaped and textured dishes, how often is it only your eyes that have feasted? Food that looks good must also taste good because one is expecting so much more from it. A buffet with too many dishes always tempts me to try a little of everything, with the result that I end up with a plate piled high and cannot appreciate the flavour of anything. So keep it simple: it will be easier for you in your planning, shopping and cooking, and your guests won't have to make too many awful decisions.

For up to ten or even twenty we can usually visualise the quantities needed, but over that it's very easy to go quite berserk, panic madly and end up with enough for a hundred. Remember that as numbers increase so the quantity per head goes down, heaven knows why. You will also find when doubling up dishes that not all the ingredients automatically double. For instance, Coq au Vin for sixteen does not need four times the wine for four; two-and-a-half to three times will do. This is generally the case for all sauces and thank goodness it is, for this saves a bit on costs. Garlic, herbs and seasoning likewise do not need to be indiscriminately doubled or quadrupled; add and taste again.

When cooking in quantity it does help to have a few large pans. A huge saucepan makes rice cooking easy and a big colander helps for straining. Several large casseroles that will

46

fit into your oven are invaluable (do check that they fit your oven if you borrow from a friend), and so are some large bowls. I have several plastic washing-up bowls which I keep for food and they are very useful for holding salads, cooked rice, chopped up chicken and so on.

Hot food for large numbers is a problem, and I find one hot course is usually enough. Soup can be the easiest, and even just a hot potato dish or hot garlic bread will give the touch of warmth that is needed.

If time is not on your side—and it so rarely is—divide your menu up and see what can be prepared ahead; soups and puddings can often be made and popped in the freezer for a week or so. Other preparations may be spaced over two or three evenings after work.

For demonstrations or catering, for large parties or for weekends, I always sit down and plan the menu, and this is the stage at which I check the balance, availability, colour, contrast and feasibility of my initial idea. Then I get out the recipes and write down the quantities I shall use when I have doubled or quadrupled everything (as an absolute non-mathematician I find it very easy in the frenzy of cooking to double one ingredient while I quadruple another). With paper in five columns I put all my ingredients into various categories. From this I can check the store cupboard and make the shopping list. Lists do save cudgelling one's brains to think of what might be forgotten or having sleepless nights trying to remember whether or not the cream was ordered. It's funny how once you break things down into comprehensible parts the whole ceases to frighten you. I try to remember to check those all-so-easily forgotten items like candles, napkins, olives and coffee sugar. This is also the stage at which to check the plates, knives and forks to see if the choice fits the available cutlery and dishes. Change your menu if need be before you are all organised, or borrow from a friend.

Next plan your room. Here catering has taught us to look carefully at access, flow and exit. Don't get your buffet tucked right away in a corner where guests will pile up in the approach and where everyone with full plates will have to fight their jostled way back through the hungry mob. Likewise don't block a passageway with the table so that once people are crowded round it no one can get through. Arrange it so that you can get to and from the kitchen without a hundred 'excuse me's' and, with a central table, put the first course on the far side to get people into the room and have the near side ready to stagger to with dishes of the main course. A tray placed strategically in a passage-way with a couple of plates already on it will gather up empties as a honey-pot gathers wasps. Do remember that humans, when being entertained, tend to behave a bit like sheep. They crowd into one room leaving another empty; or a chair may effectively block off a part of the room and no one will venture beyond it. Trying to get someone to start eating can also be difficult, and persuading the men to help themselves with the ladies rather than all hanging back until the end, so that the sexes become neatly divided, takes a practised hostess but ensures a better party. How deep in us must be these herd instincts that they immediately re-appear when we relax and stop thinking! The entertained guests like to be led along, spoon-fed, most decisions made, all their attention left for socialising.

Having got all that worked out there is only a cooking time-plan to make. It is so much easier if you can discipline yourself to operate from a plan, and I always work backwards from the time at which we want to eat. Do be realistic about this; I tend to think, 'That won't take long' or, 'I'll allow ten minutes for that', failing to remember that one pair of hands cooking for large numbers will take much longer. And don't let yourself be tempted into making extra dishes at the last moment.

In drawing up your time-plan remember that large quantities put into an oven take far longer to heat up than the usual amount we cook. For instance, to re-heat rice and a casserole for thirty, allow 1½–2 hours in a moderately hot oven instead of the normal 30–40 minutes. Also, be realistic about the time at which you will eat. I always think we shall eat at the time I have planned, but we seldom do; it's usually a quarter to half-an-hour later at a buffet party, but at least I'm beginning to allow for this and try to choose dishes that will wait.

Lastly, don't panic; disasters can be turned into triumphs. Things do go wrong in the kitchen, and good cooking is far more often trying to sort something out than being so clever that you never get it wrong. But don't let on. Keep your cool, stay relaxed, and it's surprising what you will get away with.

Stand-up buffets can be for a variety of occasions from twenty visiting gastronomes to sixty rowdy children, so even in this one branch of entertaining you need many different dishes to choose from. I have tried to include some that are suitable for children and teenagers, some that are relatively cheap or easy, something a bit unusual, and dishes to cover the various seasons.

First Courses

F *   Rich Mushroom Soup

This soup has a real home-made taste and a rich flavour of mushrooms. It also freezes extremely well.

Ingredients

4–6 people	*25 people*
½ lb (225g) fresh mushrooms	2½ lb (1.15kg) fresh mushrooms
1 oz (25g) butter	6 oz (175g) butter
1½ pts (900ml) good stock	7½ pts (4.3l) good stock
1 tbs potato flour	4–5 tbs potato flour
½ pt (300ml) milk	2½ pts (1.5l) milk
salt and pepper	salt and pepper

To Finish	*To Finish*
a few drops of lemon juice	1–2 lemons
1 oz (25g) butter	2 oz (25g) butter
2–4 tbs cream	¼–½ pt (150–300ml) cream
some finely chopped chervil or parsley	3–4 tbs finely chopped chervil or parsley

Melt the butter in a saucepan, add the finely sliced mushrooms and cook very gently with the lid on for 5–10 minutes. Add the stock, season and simmer for ½ hour or so. Mix the potato flour and milk until smooth and add to the soup. Simmer for 10 minutes more and then liquidise (you get a more velvety smooth soup using a liquidiser for this recipe rather than a food processor).

Return to the pan and heat up, add lemon juice to taste and the cream. Check the seasoning and finish with the butter (whisked in off the stove in small flakes) and serve with chopped chervil or parsley stirred in.

F * # Cucumber and Sorrel Soup

I've never come across this combination anywhere else, but it is delicate and a little unusual. Do try to grow a small clump of sorrel somewhere; it's easy and useful. Serve this soup hot or cold, but from the freezer I prefer it hot.

Ingredients

4–6 people	25 people
1 large peeled and diced cucumber	4 large peeled and diced cucumbers
1 small finely chopped onion	4 small finely chopped onions
8 oz (225g) peeled and cubed potatoes (less for a cold soup)	2 lb (900g) peeled and cubed potatoes (less for a cold soup)
1 teasp fresh or ½ teasp dried tarragon or dill	3 teasp fresh or 1½ teasp dried tarragon or dill
1½ pts (900ml) light chicken stock	7 pts (4l) light chicken stock
1 teasp white wine vinegar	1 tbs white wine vinegar
¼ pt (150ml) cream	½–¾ pt (300–450ml) whipping cream
a good handful of sorrel, finely shredded with any tough midribs removed	several handfuls of sorrel, finely shredded with any tough midribs removed
a little cream	¼ pt (150ml) cream
salt and pepper	salt and pepper

Place the cucumber (retaining some for garnish), onion and potatoes in a pan with the tarragon, stock and vinegar, season lightly and simmer for 20–30 minutes until the potato is cooked. Purée until very smooth in the liquidiser or food processor and sieve. Put the cream and shredded sorrel in a non-aluminium saucepan (sorrel reacts with aluminium) and simmer for a few minutes until the sorrel is wilted and tender but still in strips. Stir the sorrel and cream into the soup, correct the seasoning and serve hot or chill to serve cold with a splosh of cream and a sprinkle of tiny cucumber dice.

PF **   Soupe au Pistou *(Winter Version)*

A spoon-and-fork soup stiff with vegetables and perfumed with basil; wonderful and cheap in summer but not to be scorned in mid-winter from the freezer. Makes a nice simple lunch with a cheese board and fruit to follow.

Ingredients

4–6 people	*25 people*
1¾ pts (1l) light stock or water	7 pts (4l) light stock or water
2 oz (50g) each diced onion, carrot, leek, celery and potato	8 oz (225g) each diced onion, carrot, leek, celery and potato
14 oz (400g) tin peeled tomatoes	4 × 14 oz (400g) tins peeled tomatoes
4 oz (100g) French beans (fresh or frozen)	1 lb (450g) French beans (fresh or frozen)
4 oz (100g) white haricot beans (soaked and cooked) or a small tin	1 lb (450g) white haricot beans (soaked and cooked) or use tinned
1 oz (25g) broken up spaghetti/pasta	4 oz (100g) broken up spaghetti/pasta
salt and pepper	salt and pepper

Pistou Sauce	*Pistou Sauce*
1–2 cloves garlic	3–4 cloves garlic
2 tbs tomato purée	8 tbs tomato purée
8–10 leaves fresh basil or 1½ teasp dried	handful of fresh basil or 3–4 teasp dried
½ oz (12g) freshly grated Parmesan cheese	1½ oz (35g) freshly grated Parmesan cheese
2–3 tbs good olive oil	6–10 tbs good olive oil

Garnish (optional)	*Garnish (optional)*
4–6 slices of stale French bread	25 slices of stale French bread
1 clove garlic	2–3 cloves garlic
some olive oil	¼ pt (150ml) olive oil

Place the onion, carrot, leek, celery and potato in a pan with the roughly chopped tomatoes and stock or water; season and simmer briskly for 30–40 minutes. Add the broken French beans, the haricots and spaghetti and simmer for 15 minutes.

Pistou Sauce. Place the chopped garlic, tomato purée, basil and Parmesan in the food processor or liquidiser. Process and drip in the oil until a smooth, mayonnaise-like sauce forms. If with a small quantity it doesn't liquidise, add a little of the soup. Pour some soup into the pistou sauce, stir round and return to the pan.

Serve very hot with slices of French bread rubbed with garlic, brushed with olive oil and baked hard in a low oven.

F **   Soupe de Poisson

This is something special, a bit different and definitely the best fish soup I've succeeded in making in this country. Also nice for supper parties, and freezes well, though of course any frozen fish would go in afterwards.

Ingredients

4–6 people

½ lb (225g) smoked cod or haddock
½ lb (225g) halibut, huss, coley or cod
about 4 oz (100g) shelled prawns
several well-washed scallops, with black
 thread removed, and cut up
1 lb (450g) well-scrubbed mussels in their
 shells or about 4 oz (100g) frozen shell-
 less mussels
3 fl oz (75ml) olive oil
2 medium onions
1 leek
1 stick celery
3 cloves garlic
1½–2 lb (675–900g) skinned and chopped
 tomatoes
parsley, thyme and fennel
1 bay leaf
strip orange or lemon peel
¼ pt (150ml) dry white wine
1 pkt or a good pinch saffron soaked in
 hot water 15–30 mins
1¾ pts (1l) water
salt, pepper and mace

To Finish
finely chopped parsley
grated lemon rind

25 people

1½–2 lb (675–900g) smoked cod or
 haddock
1½–2 lb (675–900g) halibut, huss, coley or
 cod
¾–1 lb (350–450g) shelled prawns
several well-washed scallops, with black
 thread removed, and cut up
2 lb (900g) well-scrubbed mussels or
 ¾–1 lb (350–450g frozen shell-less
 mussels
8–10 fl oz (225–300ml) olive oil
6–8 medium onions
3–4 leeks
3–4 sticks celery
6–8 cloves garlic
6 lb (2.7kg) skinned and chopped
 tomatoes
2 tbs each chopped fresh parsley and
 fennel
1 tbs chopped fresh thyme
2 bay leaves
3 strips orange or lemon peel
¾ pt (450ml) dry white wine
2–3 pkts saffron soaked in hot water for
 15–30 mins
7 pts (4l) water
salt and pepper
¼ teasp mace

To Finish
4–5 tbs finely chopped parsley
grated lemon rind

some or all of these

Cover the bottom of a large pan with good olive oil and heat gently. Add the finely sliced onions, leek and diced celery and fry gently until beginning to brown, taking 15–20 minutes. Add the chopped garlic, tomatoes and a little thyme, parsley, fresh fennel (or fennel seeds), the bay leaf and lemon peel. Cook for 4–5 minutes before adding the wine, a very little salt and pepper, the soaked saffron, a pinch of mace and the water. Simmer briskly for 20–30 minutes.

Skin and bone the fish and cut into large cubes. Add first the smoked fish and fresh mussels (if used); four minutes later the fresh white fish; and finally, three minutes later, the prawns, scallops and frozen mussels, which only need 3–5 minutes. Sprinkle with chopped parsley and grated lemon rind before serving with hot French bread.

✳✳   Pâté en Croûte

This pâté en croûte does not use a mould, just a sympathetic pastry that's easy to handle and a piece of paper cut into a rectangle as a pattern. It looks very good on a buffet.

Ingredients

6–8 people

Pâté
¾ lb (350g) lean pork
½ lb (225g) back pork fat
½ lb (225g) chicken livers
¼ lb (100g) pork sausage-meat
1 egg
1 small finely chopped onion
2 tbs brandy
1 clove garlic
¼ teasp ground mace
¼ teasp quatre épices or a good pinch of cloves, nutmeg, cinnamon and ginger
1 teasp salt (approx)
pepper

Pastry
1 lb (450g) plain flour
5 oz (125g) firm butter
3 oz (75g) lard
2 eggs
2–3 tbs cold water
½ teasp salt

25 people

Pâté
2¼ lb (1kg) lean pork
1½ lb (675g) back pork fat
1½ lb (675g) chicken livers
¾ lb (350g) pork sausage-meat
3 eggs
2 finely chopped onions
5 tbs brandy
2 cloves garlic
¾ teasp ground mace
¾ teasp quatre épices or several pinches of cloves, nutmeg, cinnamon and ginger
1–1½ tbs salt
1 teasp pepper

Pastry
3 lb (1.35kg) flour
15 oz (425g) firm butter
9 oz (250g) lard
6 eggs
6–8 tbs cold water
1½ teasp salt

Pastry. Sieve the flour and salt into a bowl and add the butter and lard cut into hazelnut-sized pieces. Mix the eggs with a little water, rub in the fats, adding the egg and water as you do so to make a flexible pastry; then roll and turn three times. Or make it in a food processor half at a time and combine to roll. Set aside to rest for 2 hours.

Pâté. Keep 2–3 chicken livers whole and steep in the brandy. Mince or process in the food processor (which gives a moister pâté) the pork, pork fat, the remaining livers, the onion and crushed garlic, and beat in the sausage-meat, seasoning and egg (keep a little back as egg wash for the pastry). If possible leave in a cool place for 2–3 hours or overnight for the flavours to blend before cooking.

Cut off one-third of the pastry for a lid. Roll the remainder into a rectangle 10″ × 14″ (25cm × 36cm) laid on tinfoil on a baking sheet. Trim all the edges. Beat the brandy from the chicken livers into the pâté and spread a layer down the centre of the pastry leaving a 2″ (5cm) margin all round. Place the chicken livers down the centre, well bedded in, and cover with the remaining pâté. Turn up the pastry all round, mitre the corners, moisten with cold water and press together. Roll out the remaining pastry for a lid, moisten the edges and fix in place. Decorate with pastry leaves, brush with egg wash and insert a meat thermometer if you use one. Bake in a hot oven (400°F/200°C/Gas 6) for 15 minutes or so to set the pastry, then turn down to very moderate (325°F/170°C/Gas 3) and bake for a further 1 hour 10 minutes or until cooked (170°F/75°C on the meat thermometer). Cover the top if it gets too brown. Serve hot or cold.

Variation for 25 people. Make three standard pâtés en croûte or two larger ones—10″ × 21″ (25cm × 52cm)—if your oven is big enough. You will find the cooking time will be longer with more in the oven.

** Terrine de Campagne

The trouble involved in making terrines and pâtés seems well worth it for large numbers. It's getting the ingredients together which takes time. This one is not powerful and redolent with garlic but moist, succulent and of fine flavour.

Ingredients

8–10 people	*25 people*
1 lb (450g) lean belly of pork	2½ lb (1.1kg) lean belly of pork
¾ lb (350g) pigs' liver	1¾ lb (800g) pigs' liver
½ lb (225g) lean veal, pork or best pork sausage-meat	1¼ lb (550g) lean veal, pork or best pork sausage-meat
¼ lb (100g) back pork fat (failing that use streaky bacon)	10 oz (275g) back pork fat (failing that use streaky bacon)
6–8 juniper berries	12–14 juniper berries
1 clove garlic	2 cloves garlic
¼ teasp ground mace	½ teasp ground mace
¼ teasp allspice	½ teasp allspice
4 fl oz (100ml) dry white wine	6–8 fl oz (175–225ml) dry white wine
2 tbs brandy	4 tbs brandy
2 eggs	4 eggs
about 1½ teasp salt	1 tbs salt
pepper	pepper

Mince or process in the food processor (which always gives a more succulent result because it chops rather than squeezes) the belly pork, the liver and the veal, pork or sausage-meat. Add the back pork fat (or streaky bacon) cut into little dice and the crushed juniper berries and garlic. Blend in the spices, salt and plenty of pepper, and beat in the wine, brandy and eggs; a good beating lightens the texture of any pâté. Fry a little bit, taste to check the seasoning, then if possible leave to marinate for the flavours to blend for an hour or two or overnight in a cool place. Turn into a 2 pt (1.2l) terrine or several smaller ones. Place the terrine in a roasting tin with boiling water to come at least halfway up. Cook uncovered in a slow oven (300°F/150°C/Gas 2) for 1¼–2 hours. The pâté is cooked when it comes away from the sides of the dish and when a skewer stuck in it produces no pink juice.

Remove the terrine and leave to cool, then press with 3–4 lb or 1½–2 kg weight. Keep for a day or two in a cool larder or fridge before serving with fresh bread or hot toast, butter if you like, and gherkins.

$\mathcal{F}$ * Rillettes

A speciality from the Touraine region of France which is easy and inexpensive to make. It is unusual, but seems to be enjoyed by everyone I've tried it on. It freezes very well or will keep in the fridge for some time.

Ingredients

6–8 people	*25 people*
1 lb (450g) meaty belly of pork	3 lb (1.35kg) meaty belly of pork
½ lb (225g) pork fat (back fat or flair)	1½ lb (675g) pork fat (back fat or flair)
1 oz (25g) lard or pork dripping	1 oz (25g) lard or pork dripping
½ clove garlic	2 cloves garlic
2 tbs water	2 tbs water
sprig of thyme	2 sprigs of thyme
¼ teasp quatre épices or pinch of cloves, nutmeg, cinnamon and ginger	1 teasp quatre épices or ¼ teasp each of cloves, nutmeg, cinnamon and ginger
salt and pepper	1 tbs salt (approx)
	plenty of pepper

Cut the meat and fat into ½" × 1½" (1cm × 4cm) strips. Melt the lard in a heavy pan, add the meat, pork fat, the water, the crushed clove of garlic and the thyme and seasoning. Cover and cook in a slow oven (300°F/150°C/Gas 2) for about 4 hours (or it can be cooked *very* gently on the top of the stove). When very soft, tender and well cooked, pour the mixture into a sieve over a bowl to separate the fat. Then pound the meat in a mortar or process briefly in a food processor with a plastic blade to form a thready pâté. Check the seasoning and pack into terrines. Covered with the strained fat (but *no* meaty juices) to a depth of ½" (1.5cm), your rillettes should keep for 6 months to one year in a cool dry larder, though I feel happier freezing them. Serve at room temperature with fresh bread.

$\mathcal{F}$ * Smoked Mackerel Pâté

A smooth light pâté, quick to whip up and appreciated at any time of the year.

Ingredients

4–6 people	*25 people*
2 smoked mackerel fillets, together weighing about 12 oz (350g)	3 lb (1.35kg) smoked mackerel fillets
4 oz (100g) butter	1 lb (450g) butter
¼ pt (150ml) cream	1 pt (600ml) cream
1 lemon	3–4 lemons
salt, pepper and mace	salt, pepper and mace

Gently melt the butter. Skin the mackerel, place the flesh in a food processor or liquidiser and process, adding the butter, lemon juice and seasoning. Turn into a bowl and when cold fold in the softly whipped cream and any additional lemon juice to taste. Pack into containers. Serve at room temperature for full flavour and creaminess.

** Oeufs au Printemps

The mounds of eggs under the delicate green of the mayonnaise make this a very attractive dish for a buffet, although it must not be put together until the last minute.

Ingredients

4–6 people	*25 people*
4–6 hard-boiled eggs	25 hard-boiled eggs
2 oz (50g) soft butter	6 oz (175g) soft butter
1 small pkt Philadelphia or 3 oz (75g) cream cheese	8–10 oz (225–275g) Philadelphia or cream cheese
2 teasp Dijon mustard	2 tbs Dijon mustard
a little cream	¼ pt (150ml) cream
salt and pepper	salt and pepper

Mayonnaise Verte	*Mayonnaise Verte*
1 bunch watercress	3 bunches watercress
fresh parsley, chervil, dill and tarragon	a good bunch fresh parsley, chervil, dill and tarragon
1 egg	
1–2 teasp wine vinegar	3 eggs
6 fl oz (175ml) oil	2 tbs wine vinegar
salt, pepper, Dijon mustard	1¼ pts (750ml) oil
	1 teasp salt and plenty of pepper
	1 tbs Dijon mustard

Cut the eggs in half lengthways and remove yolks. Cream the butter well, sieve in the yolks, add the mustard and cheese and beat well together, or process in the food processor. Season with salt and pepper and moisten with cream if necessary. Fill into the egg whites and reform.

Mayonnaise Verte. Pick over the watercress and herbs and blanch in boiling water for 1–2 minutes; drain and refresh under the cold tap to set the colour, and squeeze dry. Break the egg into the food processor or liquidiser, add salt, pepper, mustard and vinegar. Process and gradually drip in the oil, adding the watercress and green herbs until pale green (a liquidiser gives a smooth green mixture, a food processor a speckledy green). Correct the seasoning, and if necessary thin to coating consistency with water. Pour over the eggs and serve within half-an-hour, or the mayonnaise verte will discolour.

To prepare ahead. Prepare the filling, keeping the egg whites in cold water, as they toughen if left exposed to the air. Fill the eggs and keep tightly packed in plastic boxes to exclude as much air as possible. Make the mayonnaise ahead, blanch the watercress and green herbs and add as late as possible or the beautiful green colour goes dull. Lay out the eggs and pour over the sauce at the last minute.

P * # Herring Fillets in Lemon Cream

When fresh herring are in, this dish of raw filleted fish in a lemon cream dressing can be made a day or two ahead and is most unusual and popular.

Ingredients

4–6 people	*25 people*
2–3 fine herrings	10–12 fine herrings
⅓ pt (200ml) double cream	1⅓ pts (800ml) double cream
1 lemon	3–4 lemons
3 tbs olive oil	8 fl oz (225ml) olive oil
3–4 tbs white wine vinegar	½ pt (300ml) white wine vinegar
1 very finely sliced small onion	2 very finely sliced onions
2 peeled, cored and diced sharp apples	6–8 peeled, cored and diced sharp apples
2 bay leaves	4–6 bay leaves
salt and pepper	plenty of salt and pepper

Fillet the fish (or get the fishmonger to do so) and cut first into strips and then into bite-sized pieces. Season very well with salt and pepper. Whisk the cream lightly, adding grated lemon rind, juice, vinegar and oil. Stir in the onion, apple and whole bay leaves and season well. Fold in the herring bits and turn into a serving dish. Cover and marinate in the fridge for 24–48 hours before serving cold with brown bread and butter.

* # Coupe Juli

A fresh crunchy starter, excellent if you have a rich dish to follow. It can be done in individual dishes or glasses for easy serving.

Ingredients

4–6 people	*25 people*
some cauliflower florets	1 cauliflower
1–2 avocado pears (depending on size)	6–8 avocado pears (depending on size)
2 pears or ¼ small melon	8–10 pears or 1 good melon
4" (10cm) cucumber	1½ cucumbers
Dressing	*Dressing*
½ teasp honey	3 teasp honey
½ teasp Dijon mustard	3 teasp Dijon mustard
2 tbs lemon juice	6 tbs lemon juice
6 tbs olive oil	½ pt (300ml) olive oil
1 tbs each of fresh, finely chopped chives, parsley and mint	4 tbs each of fresh, finely chopped chives, parsley and mint
salt and pepper	salt and pepper

Toss the cauliflower florets into boiling salt water for 2 minutes to blanch, and refresh in cold water until chilled; drain well.

Dressing. Mix the salt, pepper, mustard and honey with the lemon juice, then gradually beat in the oil to make a dressing. Stir in the herbs. Peel and dice the avocado, pear (or melon) and cucumber and turn into the dressing with the cauliflower. Mix thoroughly and leave to chill for 2–4 hours, mixing once or twice.

Serve well chilled in individual glasses accompanied by Sesame Fingers (*see page 242*) or brown bread spread with anchovy butter and rolled up.

* Guacamole

This Mexican avocado pâté, hot or mild as you please, makes a good first course or cocktail party dip with crunchy vegetables or crisp toast.

Ingredients

4–6 people	*25 people*
2 ripe avocado pears	8–10 ripe avocado pears
2 spring onions	8–10 spring onions
1 clove garlic	3 cloves garlic
2 limes or 1 lemon	6–8 limes or 3–4 lemons
few drops Tabasco or Mexican green pepper sauce to taste	few drops Tabasco or Mexican green pepper sauce to taste
4–6 tbs olive oil	$\frac{1}{2}$ pt (300ml) olive oil (or more)
3–4 peeled, seeded and finely diced tomatoes	$1\frac{1}{2}$–2 lb (675–900g) peeled, seeded and finely diced tomatoes
2 tbs finely diced celery	3–4 sticks finely diced celery
2 tbs finely diced green pepper	1 finely diced green pepper
1 tbs finely chopped parsley	4 tbs finely chopped parsley
salt	1 tbs salt (approx)

Peel the avocados and crush the flesh or process in the food processor. Add the chopped onion and garlic crushed with salt. Season with Tabasco. Beat well and drip in the oil and lime or lemon juice (made in a food processor it becomes a wonderful smooth mixture). Stir in by hand the chopped tomato, celery, pepper and parsley. Turn into a bowl and press cling film or wet greaseproof paper on to the mixture to delay discolouring. Do not make this too far ahead. Serve with fresh bread or crisp toast, or with lengths of raw vegetables, celery, carrot or cauliflower.

Main Courses

***   Quenelles de Saumon, Sauce Nantua

For visiting Wine and Food Society members we have served these Salmon Quenelles in a Nantua Sauce. They taste delicious, with all the hard work done beforehand and just careful attention needed in the re-warming. Try this recipe made from any firm white fish such as haddock, cod or coley. It is essential to have fresh, unfrozen fish (the tissues of frozen fish are broken down and they will not always hold the eggs and cream successfully) and double cream.

Ingredients

4–6 people

25 people

Quenelles

10 oz (275g) fresh, raw salmon (weighed without skin or bone)
3 egg whites
about ½ teasp tomato purée, just enough for colour (optional)
⅓–½ pt (200–300ml) double cream
salt, pepper and mace

Quenelles

4 lb (1.8kg) fresh, raw salmon (weighed without skin or bone)
18 egg whites
2–3 teasp tomato purée, just enough for colour (optional)
2½ pts (1.5l) double cream
salt, pepper and mace

Sauce Nantua

2 oz (50g) prawn butter (see p. 36)
½ pt (300ml) prawn fumet (see p. 37)
1½ oz (35g) plain flour
¼ pt (150ml) milk
the prawns from 8 oz (225g) prawns in their shells
¼ pt (150ml) double cream
lemon juice
salt and pepper

Sauce Nantua

10 oz (275g) prawn butter (see p. 36)
2½ pts (1.5l) prawn fumet (see p. 37)
7½ oz (210g) plain flour
1¼ pts (750ml) milk
the prawns from 2 lb (900g) prawns in their shells
1¼ pts (750ml) double cream
lemon juice
salt and pepper

Make the prawn butter and the prawn fumet, prepare the quenelle mixture, and while this rests make the Sauce Nantua.

Quenelles. Remove all skin, bones and sinews from the fish and dice. Process the fish with the egg whites in a food processor with a metal blade, or mince twice and then liquidise until very smooth. Season with salt, pepper and mace, and add tomato purée for colour if necessary. Process, and gradually add the cream. Keep the mixture firm enough to stand up on a spoon, but do not process for more than 20–30 seconds or the cream may turn to butter. Sieve and set aside in the fridge for at least ½ hour.

Bring a large, flattish pan of salted water to the boil, then turn down heat so that it just trembles. With a dessertspoon dipped in warm water take a generous rounded spoonful of the quenelle mixture, make into a good egg-shape, if necessary with another wet spoon, and lower into the water (tap the spoon on the bottom of the pan to detach the quenelles). Continue forming quenelles and poach for 8–10 minutes, turning once carefully with a slotted spoon, until each is just firm. Remove with a slotted spoon and drain on kitchen paper. Place in a warmed, buttered gratin dish.

Sauce Nantua. Melt the prawn butter in a pan (preferably non-aluminium as wine and cream sauces can discolour), add the flour and cook gently for 3–4 minutes. Draw the pan off the stove, wait for the sizzling to cease and add the prawn fumet and milk; bring to the boil whisking hard and simmer gently for 5–10 minutes. Add the prawns, cut into 2–3 pieces, thin with cream until of coating consistency and season. Then heat through gently and finish with a squeeze of lemon juice.

To serve. Have the Sauce Nantua ready, keeping it hot in a *bain marie*. Cover well with cling-film if it has to wait for a while. Pour it over the hot quenelles and serve. Alternatively, the quenelles can be poached ahead and rewarmed in a moderate oven (350°F/ 180°C/Gas 4) for 20–30 minutes, very closely covered with tinfoil or a lid, then sauced and served. The sauce may form a skin and discolour if it is poured over the quenelles too soon and not closely covered. It should flow over the quenelles evenly, but you still want to see their shape, otherwise when people help themselves they will dig in anywhere and spoil the dish.

F ✳✳ Spiced Lamb with Almonds

One of my favourite kinds of dish, spicy with fragrant fresh spices but not peppery—neither hot nor curried. Do try to use whole spices and grind them yourself. The yoghurt and ground-almond finish to this dish gives it a smooth rich taste.

Ingredients

4–6 people	*25 people*
1½–2 lb (675–900g) boned shoulder or leg of lamb	6–8 lb (2.7–3.6kg) boned shoulder or leg of lamb
2 cloves garlic	3–4 cloves garlic
1″ (2.5cm) piece of fresh root ginger	3″ (8cm) piece of fresh root ginger
½ pt (300ml) water	1 pt (600ml) water
¼ pt (150ml) yoghurt	1 pt (600ml) yoghurt
1 teasp whole coriander seeds	3 teasp whole coriander seeds
1 teasp whole cummin seeds	3 teasp whole cummin seeds
½ teasp ground or 3–4 whole cardamoms with the shells removed	1½ teasp ground or 9–12 whole cardamoms with the shells removed
⅛ teasp ground cloves	½ teasp ground cloves
1 tbs ground turmeric	3 tbs ground turmeric
½ teasp ground cinnamon	1½ teasp ground cinnamon
1 teasp paprika	3 teasp paprika
2 oz (50g) butter	4 oz (100g) butter
2 tbs oil	4 tbs oil
2–3 finely sliced onions	8 finely sliced onions
2 oz (50g) ground almonds	8 oz (225g) ground almonds
1 teasp potato flour or cornflour	4 teasp potato flour or cornflour
½ lemon	1–1½ lemons
salt and pepper	salt and pepper

Pound the crushed garlic and peeled ginger in a mortar or process fairly briefly in a food processor or liquidiser, and add the water; steep for ½ hour. Drain the yoghurt in a muslin-lined sieve (or use a clean J cloth, double kitchen paper or coffee filter) to remove excess moisture.

Pound the whole coriander, cummin and cardamom, and mix with the ground cloves, turmeric, cinnamon and paprika.

Cut the lamb into 1″ (3cm) cubes. Gently fry the onions in the butter and oil until soft and golden; remove to a casserole. Turn up the heat, and fry the lamb in the remaining butter and oil until a golden brown. Add the spices to the pan and fry for 1 minute, then pour over the strained garlic-ginger water. Turn into the casserole and season with plenty of salt and pepper. Cook in a moderate oven (350°F/180°C/Gas 4) for 1½ hours or until very tender, or simmer very gently on the stove.

Stir the ground almonds into the yoghurt with the potato flour, gradually beat in some of the hot sauce (having removed some fat if the juice is very fatty), return this to the meat in the pan and bring to the simmer. Stir one way only, as this stabilises the yoghurt so that it will not curdle. Add a good squeeze of lemon juice and check the seasoning. Leave in a slow oven (300°F/150°C/Gas 2) for 20 minutes or so. This is best served with rice over which I like to sprinkle a few flaked browned almonds and some raisins, plumped up in hot water for a few minutes.

Variation for 25 people. The cooking takes rather more than 1½ hours.

F ** ## Hungarian Goulash

This Middle European dish can be made with half-pork and half-beef, or wholly of one or the other. The sauce should be thick, rich and spicy with paprika, carraway and marjoram. For a goulash with more bite use some strong paprika and always make sure your paprika is fresh.

Ingredients

4–6 people	*25 people*
1 lb (450g) braising or stewing beef	4 lb (1.8kg) braising or stewing beef
1 lb (450g) boned shoulder of pork	4 lb (1.8kg) boned shoulder of pork
1 lb (450g) sliced onions	4 lb (1.8kg) sliced onions
2 oz (50g) dripping, lard or oil	8 oz (225g) dripping, lard or oil
2½ tbs mild paprika (Rosenpaprika)	10 tbs mild paprika (Rosenpaprika)
½ pt (300ml) water	1¼–1¾ pts (750ml–1l) water
1 clove garlic	3 cloves garlic
1 tbs fresh or ½ teasp dried marjoram	3–4 tbs fresh or 1½ teasp dried marjoram
¼ teasp carraway seeds	1 teasp carraway seeds
2 tbs wine vinegar	6–8 tbs wine vinegar
4 oz (100g) tomato purée	1 lb (450g) tomato purée
1 green pepper	3–4 green peppers
¼ pt (150ml) sour cream	½ pt (300ml) sour cream
salt	salt

Melt the dripping in a large casserole or frying pan and gently fry the sliced onions until transparent. Add half the paprika, ¼ pt (150ml) water and the cubed meat, and cook and stir until the liquid has all but boiled away and the meat is almost frying again (this takes ages, especially with the large quantity). Add the sliced green pepper, chopped garlic, tomato purée, vinegar, salt, carraway and marjoram to the pan with the remainder of the water. Turn into a casserole if you have used a frying pan, cover and cook in a slow oven (300°F/150°C/Gas 2) or simmer gently for 1–2 hours. Add the remaining paprika and a little more liquid if necessary. Cook for a further hour or until tender; check the seasoning. Serve with buttered noodles flavoured with freshly grated nutmeg, and with the sour cream spooned over the goulash.

Variation for 25 people. Still add only ¼ pt (150ml) water with the meat, using the remainder for the simmering.

ℱ ✳✳ Lasagne con Ricotta

An unusual dish, using very little meat but plenty of cheese, which works out economically for large numbers. Freeze only uncooked, as once cooked the cheese goes rubbery.

Ingredients

4–6 people	*25 people*
5 oz (125g) green or white lasagne or ¾ batch of home-made (see p. 144)	1¼ lb (550g) green or white lasagne or 3 batches of home-made (see p. 144)
6–8 oz (175–225g) minced beef	2 lb (900g) minced beef
2 tbs olive oil	6 tbs olive oil
1 clove garlic	2–3 cloves garlic
14 oz (400g) tin tomatoes	4 × 14 oz (400g) tins tomatoes
4 oz (100g) tomato purée	12 oz (350g) tomato purée
1 tbs fresh or 1 teasp dried oregano	2 tbs fresh or 2 teasp dried oregano
1 tbs fresh or ½ teasp dried basil	3 tbs fresh or 2 teasp dried basil
¾ lb (350g) ricotta or curd cheese or substitute with cottage cheese	3 lb (1.35kg) ricotta or curd cheese or substitute with cottage cheese
1 egg	3 eggs
a little milk to make the cheese spreadable	a little milk to make the cheese spreadable
4 oz (100g) Mozzarella cheese or substitute with 6–8 oz (175–225g) Cheddar cheese	1 lb (450g) Mozzarella cheese or substitute with 1¼–1½ lb (550–675g) Cheddar cheese
1 oz (25g) freshly grated Parmesan cheese	3–4 oz (75–100g) freshly grated Parmesan cheese
salt and pepper	salt and pepper

Heat the oil in a casserole or pan and brown the meat. Add the finely chopped garlic, the roughly chopped tomatoes and the tomato purée. Season and add the herbs. Simmer for 35–45 minutes. Beat the ricotta cheese and egg together until smooth, adding a little milk if necessary.

Cook the lasagne in plenty of boiling salted water with a tablespoonful of oil added. Cook for 15–20 minutes until just *al dente* (firm to the bite) for bought pasta, or 3–5 minutes for home-made. Drain, rinse in cold water and keep in the minimum of cold water until ready to use (so much easier than spreading it all round the kitchen on cloths). Take a shallow buttered gratin dish and spread just enough meat sauce to prevent the lasagne from sticking. Layer with half the drained lasagne, cover with half the meat, and spread with half the ricotta and thin slices of Mozzarella. Sprinkle with Parmesan. Repeat with the remaining lasagne, meat and cheeses. Bake in a moderately hot oven (375°F/190°C/ Gas 5) for ½–¾ hour until brown and bubbling.

Variation for 25 people. Brown the meat in batches and simmer the meat sauce for 1–1½ hours. Finally bake for about ¾–1¼ hours if it is in two large dishes. You will probably need to cook the lasagne in two or three batches.

𝓕 **   **Koftas with Sunflower Seeds**

Another light, cheap and easy dish enjoyed by children and the young is this Middle Eastern dish of meat balls in tomato sauce. It is especially delicious when made with lamb. The toasted sunflower seeds are nearly as good as the authentic, but astronomically priced, pine-kernels, and are much cheaper.

Ingredients

4–6 people	*25 people*
1 lb (450g) lean shoulder or leg of lamb or braising beef	5 lb (2.25kg) lean shoulder or leg of lamb or braising beef
1 small finely chopped onion	4 small onions
1 egg	5 eggs
2 oz (50g) white breadcrumbs	8 oz (225g) white breadcrumbs
½ lemon	2 lemons
2 tbs finely chopped parsley	8–10 tbs finely chopped parsley
½ teasp pounded cummin	2 teasp pounded cummin
½ teasp pounded coriander seeds	2½ teasp pounded coriander seeds
3–4 tbs cold water	4–5 fl oz (100–150ml) cold water
plenty of salt and pepper	1 tbs salt (approx) and plenty of pepper
oil or fat for frying	oil or fat for frying
Sauce	*Sauce*
2½ oz (60g) tomato purée	10 oz (275g) tomato purée
¼ pt (150ml) water	1 pt (600ml) water
salt and pepper	salt and pepper
½ lemon	2 lemons
1–2 tbs sunflower seeds	4–6 tbs sunflower seeds

With a Food Processor. Remove all gristle and sinews from the meat and chop finely, using the metal blade; then add the onion, egg, grated lemon rind, lemon juice, seasoning, herbs and breadcrumbs. Process to a smooth paste, adding cold water for lightness.

Without a Food Processor. Mince the meat finely, then blend with the other ingredients as above in a liquidiser until very fine and smooth.

With wet hands form into marble-sized balls and fry gently in a little hot oil until golden; shake the balls round the pan so that they brown all over. Pour off any excessive fat and add the sauce. Stir in the brown tasty bits from round the pan. Season lightly and simmer very gently uncovered for 20–30 minutes until the sauce is rich and reduced. You can also cook the meat balls in a moderate oven (350°F/180°C/Gas 4). Brown the sunflower seeds lightly in a drop of oil in a frying pan and scatter over the top of the meat balls on serving. Serve with buttered noodles or rice.

Sauce. Mix the tomato purée with lemon juice, seasoning and water.

Variation for 25 people. Fry in batches and turn into a wide roasting tin or casserole.

P F ✱✱✱ Cassoulet de Toulouse

A winter filler to stick to the ribs which is only worth doing for a fair number of people, although it freezes well. Time, trouble and planning must be taken over this wonderful dish, and it is quite extravagant on meat. Confit d'Oie or de Canard is available in tins, though expensive. Put the casseroles together well ahead, allowing time for the flavours to blend; it produces a symphony of flavour which is hard to beat.

Ingredients

10–12 people

2–2½ lb (900g–1.15kg) piece of shoulder
   of pork or loin joint
several pieces of Confit d'Oie or Confit de
   Canard (or ½ a roast duck or the
   equivalent amount of roast goose)

The Beans
2 lb (900g) haricot beans (the best, and this
   year's)
½ lb (225g) pork skin cut into very small
   pieces
¾ lb (350g) piece of salt pork or bacon
2 roughly chopped onions
bouquet garni of 4–5 parsley stalks, 2
   sprigs of thyme and a bay leaf
3 cloves
4 cloves garlic
1 lb (450g) fresh pork boiling sausage (de
   Toulouse, de Campagne, Italian or Polish)
salt and pepper

The Braised Lamb
2–2½ lb (900g–1.15kg) boned shoulder of
   lamb
3–4 tbs good duck or pork fat
½ lb (225g) thickly sliced onions
4–5 cloves garlic
4 tbs tomato purée
1–1½ pts (600–900ml) stock
sprig of thyme and a bay leaf
salt and pepper

To Assemble
plenty of stale white breadcrumbs

25 people

Double all ingredients

Roast the pork joint. (You may like to do this a day or so ahead, using a larger piece and having a meal off it first). Cook the duck or goose—if you are not using the Confit, which *does* give this dish its characteristic flavour.

The Beans. Add the beans and pork skin to a large saucepan of boiling water, the water to cover the beans well. Boil for 2 minutes, then leave on the side of the stove for 1 hour; this saves soaking the beans overnight, which you can do if you prefer. Leaving the beans still covered in water by 1"–2" (3cm–5cm), add the piece of salt pork, the onions and the bouquet garni. Simmer very slowly or cook in a very moderate oven (325°F/170°C/Gas 3) for about 1½ hours until the beans and salt pork are just cooked. Add the whole sausage after ¾ hour and only season towards the end of cooking. Drain, reserving the liquid.

The Braised Lamb. Cut the lamb into generous pieces and brown quickly in hot goose, duck or pork fat; remove to a casserole. Fry the onions until golden and pour off the excess fat. Add them to the meat with stock barely to cover, together with the crushed cloves of garlic, the tomato purée, herbs and seasoning. Add any bones, cover closely and simmer or cook in a very moderate oven (325°F/170°C/Gas 3) for about 1–1½ hours until tender.

To Assemble. In a deep earthenware gratin dish or large casserole place a layer of drained beans. Cover with a layer of mixed meats: the roast pork cut into pieces, the salt pork cut into chunks, the cubed lamb, sausage slices and joints of confit, duck or goose. Season lightly. Continue the layers, finishing with beans. Moisten first with the sauce from the lamb and any de-fatted roasting juices and then with bean liquid, but not quite to cover the beans. Cover with a good layer of breadcrumbs and bake uncovered for 1½–2 hours or longer in a moderate oven (350°F/180°C/Gas 4) until a beautiful brown crust forms. Allow an extra half-hour or so if you are putting it into the oven cold, and leave plenty of time to get the consistency just right; the cassoulet will keep warm quite happily for ages. Add a little more liquid if it seems too dry; or if it seems too fatty or moist stir in the breadcrumbs and add another layer. This can be done several times.

Serve straight from the casserole. The beans should be soft and creamy but not mushy, and the various flavours should be beautifully blended. Follow with a sharply dressed salad.

*** Boned Stuffed Turkey

This is a bit of a cheat because you only remove the breastbone, then fill the backbone cavity with a pâté stuffing which allows you, when the turkey is reformed, cooked and cold, to carve delicious half-and-half slices (breast and pâté) for twenty or more people, with the leg meat extra.

Ingredients
10–12 people hot or 15–20 people cold

8–10 lb (3.6–4.5kg) turkey or capon
a little stock or water
a little butter and oil

Stuffing
2 oz (50g) butter
2 finely chopped onions
4 oz (100g) sliced mushrooms
the turkey liver
1 finely chopped clove garlic
1 lb (450g) lean pork
1 lb (450g) best pork sausage-meat
8 oz (225g) breadcrumbs
8 oz (225g) back pork fat
3 oz (75g) large raisins
2 oz (50g) dried apricots
4 oz (100g) toasted hazelnuts
grated rind of 1 lemon
½ teasp dried basil
¼ teasp dried oregano
2 tbs finely chopped parsley
2–3 eggs
salt and pepper

Lemon Butter
2 oz (50g) butter
grated rind and juice of ½ lemon
salt and pepper

Stuffing. Fry the onion gently in the butter until soft and golden. Turn up the heat and add the diced liver and mushrooms and toss until browned. Mince or chop the lean pork in a food processor and cut the pork fat into fingernail-sized dice. Toast the hazelnuts and rub off the skins, and roughly chop the apricots. Combine all the ingredients, beat really well together and fry a little bit of the mixture to taste if the seasoning is just right.

Lemon Butter. Cream the butter with the lemon rind, juice and seasoning.

To Prepare Turkey or Capon. Cut through the skin of the bird all along the breastbone, peel back the skin on both sides and carefully remove the breast, detaching at the wing joint. With a strong pair of kitchen scissors or poultry shears cut out the breastbone completely, cutting along the bottom of the ribcage and breastbone. Fill the cavity with stuffing, but do not overfill, and lay the breasts back on top. Spread them with the lemon butter before reforming the skin. Draw the skin together and sew up with a strong needle and button thread. Truss the bird and pass a long skewer through the thighs and body. Tie 2–3 times round with string to take the pressure off the stitching and insert a meat roasting thermometer if used.

Place in a roasting tin and rub the skin really well with oil. Spread with a little butter or fat and add a little stock or water to the roasting tin. Roast in a hot oven (400°F/200°C/ Gas 6) for 20–30 minutes until a golden brown, then cover loosely with tinfoil. Turn down to moderate (350°F/180°C/Gas 4) and continue to cook for 2–2½ hours (a meat thermometer reading of 175°F/80°C), basting from time to time. Leave 1–2 days in the cool for the flavour to develop before carving.

P ∗   Fig-Baked Ham

This is a recipe adapted from Apicius, the Roman scholar-cook, and is the best way of cooking a ham I have come across. Originally it was baked in an olive oil and flour pastry crust using a pint or so of olive oil which was then thrown away. I do not think that would be very popular these days!

Ingredients
up to 30 people

12–14 lb (5.4–6.3kg) ham
1 lb (450g) dried figs
6–8 bay leaves
½ pt (300ml) wine, cider or water

To Glaze (optional)
6 oz (175g) soft brown sugar
or
toasted breadcrumbs to roll the ham in

Enquire when you buy the ham if it needs soaking: mostly nowadays this is unnecessary, though it may need 3–4 hours in a large tub or the baby's bath! And make sure it will go in your oven.

Take a double layer of extra wide tinfoil and lay it on your largest roasting tin; make a bed of dried figs and bay leaves, lay your ham on it and add the wine. Take another double layer of tinfoil to cover the ham and seal the edges together very tightly all round, but leaving room inside for the steam to surround the ham. Bake in a slow oven (300°F/150°C/ Gas 2) for 4–6 hours. A meat thermometer plunged through the tinfoil into the interior of the ham will tell you how it's doing. Cook to a reading of 180°F/80°C.

To Glaze. You can unparcel the ham while still hot, skin it, score the fat across and across diamond fashion and baste with the sugar mixed with ¼ pt (150ml) of the cooking liquid. Then bake in a moderate oven (350°F/180°C/Gas 4) for 20–30 minutes, basting from time to time to a good brown. Otherwise you can leave the ham to cool in its parcel, then skin it and roll in toasted breadcrumbs. Sadly, I can find no use for the figs.

P ** **The Spiced Beef**

This recipe from my great-great-grandmother's manuscript cooking book means that you can tackle the hard work well ahead of the day. Marvellously easy for large numbers.

Ingredients

10–12 people	*25 people*
4–5 lb (1.8–2.25kg) piece of well-hung silverside, topside or boned unrolled brisket	8–10 lb (3.6–4.5kg) piece of beef Other ingredients as for 10–12 people
½ lb (225g) soft dark brown sugar	
1 oz (25g) saltpetre	
1 lb (450g) coarse sea salt	
1 teasp black peppercorns	
1 dozen cloves	
1 blade of mace	
2 bay leaves	

Up to 10 lb (4.5kg) of meat can be salted with each 1 lb (450g) spiced salt. Choose brisket if you like a mixture of fat and lean, or silverside or topside for all lean meat. Combine the saltpetre and sugar, rub well into the meat and place in a non-metal container; cover loosely and put in a cool airy place (or the fridge). Next day pound the bay leaf and spices, mix with the salt, spread over the meat and rub well into the now moist joint. Turn the meat daily or every second day and rub well with the spiced salt for 7–21 days according to size—or longer if it suits. A thin piece of meat will be done quite quickly, but it takes a long time for the salts to penetrate to the centre of a thick joint. The saltpetre keeps the meat pink so if, when you carve it, you find a little grey area in the middle, you know the salt did not quite reach the centre, but never mind. Keep the meat in a cool place.

To Cook. Rinse off the spices and salt and tie the meat into a good shape (thick brisket is better done in a slab rather than trying to roll it). Place the beef in a casserole with ½ pt (300ml) cold water. Cover the beef with butter papers, some suet or an inverted plate. Cover the casserole with a double layer of tinfoil pressed down in the middle so that moisture drops back into the pot. Put the lid on tightly. Cook in a slow oven (275°F/140°C/Gas 1–2) for 5 hours.

Remove from the oven to a cool place and leave sealed until cold. Remove the beef, wipe well, wrap in muslin or greaseproof paper and press between two boards with a 3–4 lb or 1½–2kg weight. Serve sliced thinly with salads, baked potatoes, spiced fruit and pickles. Once cooked it keeps very well and produces an incredible number of slices.

P ** ## Spiced Pork

There are many variations of this dish. This is based on one of Elizabeth David's recipes, and I find it invaluable and economical. We have fed twenty-five ladies off a 5½ lb (2.5kg) hand. Get your butcher to skin and bone the pork. I sometimes spice and freeze it all ready to cook when it comes out of the freezer.

Ingredients
12–20 people

4–6 lb (1.8–2.7kg) skinned and boned
   hand of pork
skin and bones from the pork
10–12 juniper berries
1 tbs sea salt
1 teasp peppercorns
½ teasp cummin seed
1 clove garlic
2 bay leaves
2 fresh or dried fennel stalks or ½ teasp
   seeds
2 slices lemon
½ pt (300ml) dry white wine or cider as
   second best

Pound together the salt, peppercorns, cummin, garlic and juniper berries in a mortar and rub well into the meat. Tie the joint in a good roll, tucking the leg bit into the hole, and lay in a tight-fitting casserole with the skin underneath and the bones around it. Tuck in the bay leaves, lemon slices and fennel stalks or seeds and leave in a cool place for 12–24 hours. Add the wine and enough water to cover the meat, cover with greaseproof paper or tinfoil and a tightly-fitting lid and cook in a slow oven (275°F/140°C/Gas 1–2) for 4–6 hours until well done and soft when prodded with a skewer. Leave to cool in the stock, then take out and dry well if you are not using for a day or two. Keep in the cool. Serve thinly sliced with baked or sauté potatoes and salads. Strain the stock, which should be very good, clear and jellied; it makes delicious soups or sauces. Any fat from the top will be tasty for frying.

P ✳✳   # Veal or Chicken in Tonnato Sauce

For a summer party try veal or chicken in a tonnato mayonnaise. This Italian sauce, based on mayonnaise with anchovies, tunny and capers added, is poured over sliced veal or poached and chopped-up chicken, and is good for a stand-up buffet.

Ingredients

4–6 people

3½ lb (1.6kg) chicken or use a 3–4 lb (1.35–1.8kg) boned shoulder, loin or leg joint of veal, which is the minimum practical size and will feed 8–10 people; other ingredients remain the same only use a little more oil in the sauce
4–6 anchovy fillets
1 onion
2 carrots
1 stick celery
1 slice lemon
3–4 parsley stalks and 1 sprig lemon thyme
2 cloves
2 bay leaves
½ pt (300ml) dry white wine
light stock or water to cover
salt and pepper

Sauce
1 whole egg or 2 yolks
pepper
mustard
lemon juice
8 fl oz (225ml) olive oil or mixed oils
4 oz (100g) tuna fish
6 anchovy fillets
2 teasp capers
2–3 fl oz (50–75ml) strong stock

25 people

Allow 4 chickens or 6–8 lb (2.7–3.6kg) joint of boned veal
double the anchovy fillets and stock ingredients and be as generous with the wine as you can!
three times the sauce quantities

Make holes with a knife in the boned, rolled and tied joint or chicken and push in bits of anchovy. If you like, marinate overnight in the wine with the vegetables and herbs. Place all in a casserole, adding any veal bones, and add stock or water barely to cover. Cover tightly with tinfoil and a lid and cook in a slow oven (300°F/150°C/Gas 2) for 1½–3 hours or until tender (chicken can be simmered very gently on the stove and may take only ½–1 hour). Leave to cool in the stock. Boil ½ pt (300ml) or more stock down to ¼ pt (150ml) for the sauce.

Tonnato Sauce. Place the whole egg or the yolks in a food processor (use the whole egg for a liquidiser), add 1 tbs lemon juice, pepper, mustard, tuna, anchovies and capers. Process, and very gradually add oil to make a mayonnaise. Correct the seasoning and lemon and thin with a little strong stock to make a coating sauce (beware, if your stock is jellied, not to thin too much; ½ hour in a hot room can melt the stock and thin the sauce). Carve the veal into thin slices, arrange on the serving dish, and pour over the sauce. Cover closely and leave for several hours or overnight. If you are using chicken, cut into bite-sized pieces, mix with the sauce in a bowl, cover, and leave for several hours or overnight, until you are ready to eat it. Then transfer to a serving dish. Decorate with very thin slices of lemon and little bunches of parsley. The surface of mayonnaise sauces will always discolour in contact with the air, so never dish up too far ahead.

✳✳ Avocado Chicken Salad

Cold cooked chicken tossed in a curried orange vinaigrette with potatoes and avocados. You can poach the chicken as in the Chicken with Tonnato Sauce (*see page 70*); it will be succulent, and will leave you with some good stock.

Ingredients

4–6 people

3½ lb (1.6kg) cold cooked chicken
1 lb (450g) new or firm waxy salad
    potatoes
½ sliced red pepper
½ sliced green pepper
½ cucumber cut into large cubes
10–12 stoned black olives
¼ lb (100g) firm button mushrooms
1 avocado
some lettuce leaves
1 lemon

Potato Dressing
1 finely chopped shallot
1–2 tbs white wine vinegar
4 tbs olive oil
a dash white wine
salt and pepper

Orange Dressing
2 oranges
1 teasp Dijon mustard
1 finely chopped shallot
6–8 tbs olive oil
½–1 teasp curry paste or powder
1 tbs finely chopped parsley and chives
salt and pepper

25 people

3 × 4–4½ lb (1.8–2kg) or 4 × 3½lb (1.6kg)
    cold cooked chicken
3–4 lb (1.3–1.8kg) new or firm waxy salad
    potatoes
2 sliced red peppers
2 sliced green peppers
2 cucumbers cut into large cubes
½ lb (225g) stoned black olives
1 lb (450g) firm button mushrooms
2–3 avocados
some lettuce leaves
1–2 lemons

Potato Dressing
1–2 finely chopped shallots
4–6 tbs white wine vinegar
10–12 tbs olive oil
some white wine
salt and pepper

Orange Dressing
4 oranges
1 tbs Dijon mustard
1–2 finely chopped shallots
12–16 tbs olive oil
2–3 teasp curry paste or powder
2–3 tbs finely chopped parsley and chives
salt and pepper

Boil the potatoes in their skins in salt water until just cooked. Skin, cut in large cubes or slices. Season and dress with potato dressing while hot. Toss well and leave to cool.

    Take julienne (matchstick) strips from one orange skin and place in a saucepan of cold water; bring to the boil and blanch for 5–10 minutes until they are no longer bitter. Drain and refresh under the cold tap to set the colour. Set aside.

Potato Dressing. Mix the salt, pepper and shallot with the vinegar, stir well and whisk in the oil and the white wine.

Orange Dressing. Grate the rind from the remaining orange into a glass jar and add 4 tbs orange juice, the shallot, salt, pepper, mustard and curry. Screw the lid on tightly and give a good shake. Add the parsley, chives and oil and shake again. Add a little lemon juice or vinegar if not sharp enough.

Cut the chicken flesh into bite-sized pieces, season, and marinate with the sliced mushrooms in the orange dressing for 2–8 hours. Add the red and green peppers to the chicken, together with the cucumber and olives, fold in the potato salad and pile on to lettuce leaves on a large plate. Sprinkle with orange julienne strips and the peeled and sliced avocado. Brush the avocado with lemon juice to delay discolouration.

Variation for 25 people. Add 8–10 tbs orange juice in the orange dressing.

Rice, Potatoes, Vegetables and Salads

*   Boiled Rice

Time and time again one has to turn to rice for a buffet, so it is essential to be able to cook large quantities perfectly.

Ingredients

4–6 people	25 people
2 oz (50g) long grain rice per head	2½–3 lb (1.15–1.35kg) long grain rice
3½ pts (2.1l) water in a 7-pt (4.2l) sauce-pan (approx)	18 pts (11l) water in a 4½ gallon (22l) saucepan (approx)
1 tbs salt	a handful of salt

We always use a large pan and plenty of water, allowing head-room for it to bubble up when the rice is in and it is boiling fast. Bring the pan of water to the boil and then salt it. Scatter in the rice, keeping the water at a fast boil, boil for 10–14 minutes and test the rice, which should be firm but cooked. Drain into a colander, rinse with hot water, shake well and turn into a serving-dish. Pop into the oven for a few minutes to dry out and turn with a fork. Cover if not serving at once.

If you want to prepare it ahead and re-heat it (very useful for large numbers) cook the rice, turn into the colander and rinse with cold water. Shake well and drain for ten minutes or so, then turn into the serving-dish.

To re-heat, cover and put in a moderately hot oven (375°F/190°C/Gas 5) for 30 minutes, turning side to middle with a fork once or twice. We consistently turn out huge dishes of fluffy rice and I am always being asked how we do it. We use untreated rice, but I always try to buy good rice with a slightly golden colour and, of course, we do use large pans; but our method is quite simple.

Variation for 25 people. You may need to cook the rice in several batches. Reheat for about 1 hour.

**   Risotto with Mushrooms and Pine-Kernels

Risottos can be made for large numbers but great care must be taken. The rice, rather than being cooked in masses of water which washes the starch off, is fried to seal the starch on so that it does not make the whole dish gluey.

Ingredients

4–6 people	*25 people*
2 oz (50g) butter	6 oz (175g) butter
1 finely chopped onion	4 finely chopped onions
4–6 oz (100–175g) diced button mushrooms	1–1½ lb (450–675g) diced button mushrooms
¾ lb (350g) long grain rice	3 lb (1.35kg) long grain rice
1 pt (600ml) hot chicken stock	3–3½ pts (1.7–2l) hot chicken stock
2–3 slices dried cèpe mushrooms	6–8 slices dried cèpe mushrooms
1 bay leaf	2 bay leaves
½ teasp finely chopped fresh thyme or lemon thyme	1 tbs finely chopped fresh thyme or lemon thyme
1 oz (25g) pine-kernels browned in butter or substitute with flaked browned almonds	3–4 oz (75–100g) pine-kernels browned in butter or substitute with flaked browned almonds
a speck of butter	½ oz (12g) butter
salt and pepper	2 teasp salt
	plenty of pepper

Soak the cèpe mushrooms for 30 minutes or more in a little of the hot stock. Melt the butter in a casserole and gently fry the onion and diced mushrooms until all the moisture has evaporated and they are frying again. Add the unwashed rice, stir over moderate heat for 2–3 minutes until the rice first glistens, then goes whitish; this seals in the starch so that the rice does not become sticky (pre-prepared rice will not go whitish as the starch has already been washed off). Add the hot stock and the chopped-up cèpe mushrooms and their liquid (watch out for sand in the bottom from the cèpes), season, and add the bay leaf and thyme. Bring to the boil and cook in a moderate oven (350°F/180°C/Gas 4) for 15–18 minutes. Test the rice, which should be *al dente*, with a little bite in it, but do not stir. All the liquid should have been absorbed. Toss the pine-kernels in a speck of butter to brown, and scatter over the risotto on serving. This risotto will keep warm quite happily.

Variation for 25 people. The initial frying time will be about 20–30 minutes as the rice will take longer to seal. Also allow a little longer cooking time.

**   Brown Rice with Almonds and Raisins

Brown rice, which is unrefined and has the husk on, is delicious, and very good for us. In fact, I use it most of the time. But do remember that it takes a long time to cook.

Ingredients

4–6 people	*25 people*
2 oz (50g) butter	6 oz (175g) butter
1 finely chopped onion	4 finely chopped onions
10–12 oz (275–350g) long grain brown rice	3 lb (1.35kg) long grain brown rice
4 oz (100g) sliced mushrooms	1 lb (450g) sliced mushrooms
3 tbs flaked almonds	3 oz (75g) flaked almonds
2 tbs raisins	3–4 oz (75–100g) raisins
¾–1 pt (450–600ml) chicken stock	3–3½ pts (1.7–2l) chicken stock
salt and pepper	2 teasp salt
	plenty of pepper

Fry the onions in the butter in a casserole until softened, add the mushrooms and fry for several minutes before adding the rice, almonds and raisins. Fry for another 2–3 minutes, cover with boiling stock, season and cook, very well covered, in a slow oven (300°F/150°C/Gas 2) for about 1½–2 hours, or simmer very gently until done.

Variation for 25 people. Allow about 20–30 minutes for the initial frying time. Bring the casserole to the boil, having added the boiling stock, and allow a rather longer cooking time.

**   Oriental Rice Salad

This bright yellow mound of rice, flecked with green and red peppers and covered with crunchy brown almonds, looks great on a buffet.

Ingredients

4–6 people	*25 people*
8–12 oz (225–350g) long grain rice	2–2½ lb (900g–1.15kg) long grain rice
1 teasp turmeric	1 tbs turmeric
½–1 teasp lime or lemon pickle (optional)	1–2 teasp lime or lemon pickle (optional)
1 tbs vinegar	2–3 tbs vinegar
2–3 tbs oil	4–6 tbs oil
½ red pepper	2 red peppers
¼ green pepper	1 green pepper
1 small tin pineapple pieces	1 large tin pineapple pieces
1 small tin drained sweetcorn	½ lb (225g) drained sweetcorn
1 oz (25g) browned flaked almonds	4 oz (100g) browned flaked almonds
salt and pepper	salt and pepper

Boil the rice in plenty of boiling salt water, with the turmeric added, for 10–14 minutes until firm but cooked. Drain into a colander and rinse with cold water, shake well and drain for 10 minutes or so. Make a little dressing with the chopped lime pickle (if used), salt, pepper, oil and vinegar. Add the rice and mix well. You will find it needs only very little dressing. Stir in the diced peppers, bits of pineapple and sweetcorn. On serving scatter generously with the browned flaked almonds.

✱✱   Gratin Dauphinois

There are many recipes for this, one school of thought saying categorically that there is *pas question de fromage*, another using Franche-Comté or Gruyère cheese. The wonderful thing about it is that it can be made quite simply with potatoes, milk and a bit of Cheddar; perhaps in that case it should only be called a Gratin de Pommes de Terre, but it accompanies Monday's cold meat admirably. This version, with that fine combination of garlic, nutmeg, cream and Gruyère which is wickedly lavish, cries out 'Eat me on my own, I'm so delicious'. It makes a feast with cold meats and salad.

Ingredients

4–6 people	*25 people*
2½ lb (1.15kg) peeled and thinly sliced potatoes (salad type are best)	8–10 lb (3.6–4.5kg) peeled and thinly sliced potatoes (salad type are best)
½ pt (300ml) milk	1½ pts (900ml) milk
1 clove garlic	2–3 cloves garlic
2 oz (50g) butter	6–8 oz (175–225g) butter
2 oz (50g) grated Gruyère cheese	6–8 oz (175–225g) grated Gruyère cheese
¼ pt (150ml) double cream	½–¾ pt (300–450ml) double cream
salt, pepper and nutmeg	salt, pepper and nutmeg

Rub a shallow gratin dish with the cut clove of garlic, then crush it, add it to the milk in a pan and heat. Generously butter the dish and put in a layer of the potatoes. Dot with butter, sprinkle with cheese and season with salt, pepper and a little freshly grated nutmeg. Continue the layers and finish with the cream and seasoning. Remove the garlic from the milk and pour carefully over, then sprinkle with the remaining cheese and dot with the last of the butter. Bake for about 40 minutes in a hot oven (400°F/200°C/Gas 6) until golden and tender.

    This dish will keep warm very happily and can be re-heated in a moderate oven (350°F/180°C/Gas 4); keep undercooked at the first cooking and do not let it dry out. You cannot prepare it and leave it aside to cook later as the potatoes will discolour.

Variation for 25 people. Do not make too deep a dishful. Add the milk as you layer the potato, which should never be awash. You should just be able to see the milk. Allow about 1 hour cooking time.

** Pommes de Terre Savoyard

This dish, using stock, is less rich, but useful when accompanying dishes with rich sauces. The main problem with all these potato dishes is slicing the potatoes. Those with a food processor will be laughing because it slices perfect, even, thin slices, but those without this miraculous machine will have to claim danger money and use a mandolin. But do watch your nails and knuckles.

Ingredients

4–6 people	*25 people*
2½ lbs (1.15kg) peeled and thinly sliced potatoes (salad type are best)	8–10 lb (3.6–4.5kg) peeled and thinly sliced potatoes (salad type are best)
1 pt (600ml) chicken stock	3–3½ pts (1.7–2l) chicken stock
1 clove garlic	2 cloves garlic
3–4 oz (75–100g) grated Gruyère cheese	8 oz (225g) grated Gruyère cheese
3 oz butter	8–10 oz (225–275g) butter
salt, pepper and nutmeg	salt, pepper and nutmeg

Rub a shallow, preferably earthenware, gratin dish with a cut clove of garlic, then put the flattened clove of garlic to heat in the stock. Butter the dish lavishly with soft butter and layer with the thinly sliced potatoes, seasoning each layer lightly with salt, pepper and nutmeg. Pour over the hot stock; you should just be able to see the stock, but the potatoes should not be awash. New potatoes will take up less stock than old.

Cover with the grated cheese and little nuts of butter and bake in a moderately hot oven (375°F/190°C/Gas 5) for 35–40 minutes until a beautiful golden crust has formed. Test with the point of a knife to see if the potatoes are cooked. This dish will keep warm very happily, or it can be made ahead and re-heated, though don't let it dry out.

Variation for 25 people. Add a little butter and cheese amongst the potato layers and do not let the potato get too deep, or it will be all potato and not enough of the lovely brown top. Add some of the stock as you layer the potatoes to prevent them from discolouring or compacting. Allow about 1 hour cooking time.

⊏ ✳✳ Epinards Gratinés à ma Façon

Good with frozen spinach if better with fresh, it goes with many dishes and will keep warm happily.

Ingredients

4–6 people

2 lb (900g) frozen or 3–3½ lb (1.35–1.6kg)
   fresh spinach
3 oz (75g) butter
2 tbs olive oil
1 finely chopped onion
2 oz (50g) finely diced ham
a little very finely chopped rosemary
salt, pepper and nutmeg

Sauce
¾ oz (20g) butter
¾ oz (20g) flour
½ pt (300ml) milk
3–4 tbs breadcrumbs
a few flakes of butter
salt and pepper

25 people

6–8 lb (2.7–3.6kg) frozen or approx. 12 lb
   (5.4kg) fresh spinach
12 oz (350g) butter
8 tbs olive oil
4 finely chopped onions
8 oz (225g) finely diced ham
1 tbs very finely chopped rosemary
salt, pepper and nutmeg

Sauce
2½ oz (60g) butter
2½ oz (60g) flour
1½ pts (900ml) milk
8–10 tbs breadcrumbs
1 oz (25g) butter
salt and pepper

Cook the fresh spinach in plenty of boiling salt water in a non-aluminium pan until just tender, then drain and refresh under the cold tap. Take handfuls, squeeze dry and roughly chop. Frozen spinach needs only to be thawed, lightly squeezed and chopped.

Gently fry the onion and ham in the butter and oil in a non-aluminium pan. When the onion is soft and golden add the roughly chopped spinach, the rosemary and the salt, pepper and nutmeg. Frozen spinach will need to cook gently at this stage with a lid on until tender. Toss over high heat until sizzling and buttery and the excess moisture has gone. Turn into a buttered gratin dish and top with the light sauce; this is only a thin layer just to stop the spinach from getting dry while it keeps warm. Scatter over the bread-crumbs and a few flakes of butter and brown under the grill. Keep warm or re-heat in a moderate oven (350°F/180°C/Gas 4) for 30–40 minutes.

Sauce. Melt the butter, add the flour and cook over a moderate heat, stirring, for 2–3 minutes. Draw off the heat, wait for the sizzling to cease, and add the milk. Bring to the boil, whisking hard, simmer 1–2 minutes, season and use.

Variation for 25 people. Large quantities of spinach are difficult to deal with and to dry out, but unless you get rid of the moisture you won't have the lovely buttery flavour. So work in reasonable sized batches, squeeze the spinach well, and use a wide shallow pan to toss it over high heat to dry out. Spinach often seems to taste even better re-heated the next day, so do prepare it ahead.

**   Broad Bean and Artichoke Casserole

Here I have adapted the Greek dish of artichoke hearts cooked with broad beans to a winter dish of Jerusalem artichokes and frozen beans. The flavours have a great affinity and an elusive quality.

Ingredients

4–6 people	*25 people*
1 lb (450g) frozen broad beans	3½ lb (1.6kg) frozen broad beans
1–1½ lb (450–675g) peeled root artichokes	4 lb (1.8kg) peeled root artichokes
1 oz (25g) butter	3 oz (75g) butter
1 oz (25g) flour	3 oz (75g) flour
1 clove garlic	2–3 cloves garlic
1 lemon	3–4 lemons
2–3 oz (50–75g) dry white breadcrumbs	8 oz (225g) dry white breadcrumbs
2–3 oz (50–75g) grated Gruyère or Cheddar cheese (optional)	8 oz (225g) grated Gruyère or Cheddar cheese (optional)
½ oz (12g) butter	1–2 oz (25–50g) butter
salt and pepper	salt and pepper

Peel the artichokes and cut any large ones in pieces. Combine in a pan with the broad beans and chopped garlic and cover with about 1 pint (600ml) boiling water. Add salt and the juice of half the lemon. Boil for about 7–10 minutes until the artichokes are just tender and the beans are cooked. Drain off the cooking liquid, retaining ¾ pt (450ml), return this liquid to the beans and artichokes. Cream the butter and flour together and add in little pieces to thicken the sauce. Stir until melted, simmer for 1–2 minutes, and correct the seasoning and lemon. Turn into a buttered gratin dish and cover with breadcrumbs, the cheese if you wish, and little dabs of butter. Brown under the grill and serve. This will keep warm, or re-heat in a moderate oven (350°F/180°C/Gas 4) for 30–40 minutes.

Variation for 25 people. Cover with about 3 pints (1.7l) boiling water. Add the juice of 3 lemons. Retain 2¼ pints (1.35l) cooking liquid to return to the beans and artichokes. Reheating time will be about 1 hour.

*   Caesar's Salad

This American salad is authentically made with Cos lettuce, and wonderfully fresh and crunchy it is. But try it also with Chinese leaves and see if you like it.

Ingredients

4–6 people	*25 people*
1 good crisp Cos lettuce (I use any really crunchy lettuce or Chinese leaves in winter)	4–6 good Cos lettuce (I use any really crunchy lettuce or Chinese leaves in winter)
1 clove garlic	1–2 cloves garlic
2 tbs freshly grated Parmesan cheese	8–10 tbs freshly grated Parmesan cheese
½–1 lemon	2–4 lemons
3 tbs olive oil	12–14 tbs olive oil
a dash Worcester Sauce	4–5 dashes Worcester Sauce
1 egg	3 eggs
3–4 anchovy fillets cut in pieces	2 small tins anchovies
3–4 rashers streaky bacon grilled until crisp or a handful of garlic croûtons	¾ lb (350g) streaky bacon grilled until crisp or 4–5 handfuls garlic croûtons
salt and pepper	salt and pepper

Rub a large salad bowl really well with the cut clove of garlic, add the crisp lettuce leaves (Chinese leaves should be cut into ½" (1–2cm) slices) and sprinkle with salt, pepper and cheese. Add the lemon juice, oil and Worcester sauce. Break an egg over the salad and toss really well until the salad glistens and no trace of egg remains. Add the chopped anchovy fillets and bacon (preferably hot) or the croûtons, and serve at once. It must be tossed only just before you eat it.

∗ Oriental Dressing

This is a favourite dressing I'm always being asked for. We use it with Chinese leaves, sliced cabbage or crisp lettuce.

Ingredients

8–10 people	*25 people*
1 finely chopped clove garlic	Double all ingredients
a little grated fresh ginger	
1 small slice finely chopped raw onion	
3 teasp sugar	
1 teasp tomato purée	
1 teasp French mustard	
1 teasp dried mint	
2 tbs wine vinegar	
¼ pt (150ml) oil	
salt and pepper	

Combine all the ingredients except the oil and stir well to dissolve the salt. Gradually beat in the oil or use a liquidiser or food processor. Serve sliced Chinese leaves or white cabbage or lettuce tossed in some of this dressing.

* # Tomatoes with Lemon Cream Dressing

The creamy dressing thickens with the addition of lemon juice. Poured over the sliced tomatoes and sprinkled with chives, it makes a very pretty dish.

Ingredients
4–6 people

1–1½ lb (450–675g) tomatoes
plenty of finely chopped chives
salt and pepper

Lemon Cream Dressing
1 teasp sugar
juice and rind of ½ lemon
3 tbs oil
2–3 fl oz (50–75ml) cream
salt and pepper

25 people

6–8 lb (2.7–3.6kg) tomatoes
4–6 tbs finely chopped chives
salt and pepper

Lemon Cream Dressing
3 teasp sugar
grated rind of 1 lemon
juice of 1½ lemons
4 fl oz (100ml) oil
8 fl oz (225ml) cream
1 teasp salt
plenty of pepper

Peel the tomatoes by pouring boiling water over them; after about 30 seconds plunge into cold water so that they don't cook and go mushy under the skin. Peel, slice thickly and arrange in a wide serving dish. Season with salt and pepper and pour the dressing over the centre of the tomatoes, leaving a border showing, and scatter heavily with chives.

Lemon Cream Dressing. Place the salt, pepper, sugar, lemon juice and rind in a bowl, whisk, add the oil and cream and whisk again until thick.

* # Spinach and Bacon Salad

Although spinach leaves don't taste all that nice when you pick and taste them in the garden, once dressed with this hot bacon dressing they become a delicious salad.

Ingredients
4–6 people

1 lb (450g) fresh leaf spinach
4–6 slices streaky bacon
1 lemon
4 tbs olive oil
salt and pepper

25 people

3–4 lb (1.35–1.8kg) fresh leaf spinach
1 lb (450g) sliced streaky bacon
3–4 lemons
8 fl oz (225ml) olive oil
salt and pepper

Wash and dry the spinach. Pick over carefully, removing the stems, break up and place in a salad bowl. Fry the bacon until crisp, crumble up and add to the spinach with its fat. Dress with pepper, salt only if necessary, oil and lemon juice, and serve while still warm.

Opposite, from top, left to right: Sesame Fingers, Soupe de Poisson, Guacamole, Coupe Juli, Smoked Mackerel Pâté, Tarte aux Fraises

Puddings

⌐ **   **My Syrup Tart**

This is not too sweet and sticky; the lemon and apple in the filling give a light fresh taste, and the rich pastry we use makes it a pudding for any occasion.

Ingredients

4–6 people

Pastry
6 oz (175g) flour
4 oz (100g) firm butter
2 oz (50g) icing sugar
2–3 drops vanilla essence
2 egg yolks

Filling
6–8 good tbs golden syrup
2 oz (50g) butter
3 tbs cream or milk
6–8 tbs fresh white breadcrumbs
grated rind and juice of 1 lemon
1–2 peeled and grated eating apples

25 people

Make four 9″ (24cm) tarts using three batches of pastry, using trimmings for the fourth tart.

Filling
2½ lb (1.15kg) golden syrup
8 oz (225g) butter
8 fl oz (225ml) cream or milk
6 oz (175g) fresh white breadcrumbs
grated rind of 3, and juice of 4, lemons
6–8 peeled and grated eating apples

Pastry. Sift the flour and sugar into a bowl or food processor with a metal blade and add the butter in hazelnut-sized pieces. Rub in or process to the breadcrumb stage, then bind with the yolks. Form into a flat disc and rest the pastry in the fridge for 2 hours. Roll and line a 9″ (24cm) removable base flan tin. Prick, line with tinfoil and gravel or dried beans, and bake blind in a hot oven (400°F/200°C/Gas 6) for 8–10 minutes until the pastry is set. Remove the foil and outer ring and cook 2–3 minutes more until just beginning to colour. Fill with filling and finish baking until golden brown in a moderately hot oven (375°F/ 190°C/Gas 5) for 20–30 minutes.

Filling. Gently melt the butter and heat, together with the syrup and cream. Remove from the heat and add the lemon juice and rind, the grated apple and enough breadcrumbs to make a soft dropping consistency.

*   # Magical Lemon Pudding

A good winter filler for teenagers or for a sportsman's lunch. Crusty sponge on top, lemon sauce miraculously underneath.

Ingredients	
4–6 people	*25 people*
Sponge	*Sponge*
4 oz (100g) butter	1 lb (450g) butter
6 oz (175g) castor sugar	1½ lb (675g) castor sugar
2 eggs	8 eggs
4 oz (100g) self-raising flour	1 lb (450g) self-raising flour
Topping	*Topping*
1 lemon	6 lemons
½ pt (300ml) cold water	2 pts (1.2l) cold water
2 oz (50g) castor sugar	8 oz (225g) castor sugar
3 teasp cornflour	3 tbs cornflour

Sponge. Cream the butter, grated lemon rind and sugar, beat in the eggs and fold in the sifted flour (or use a food processor). Turn into a buttered pie dish.

Topping. Mix the lemon juice, sugar, cornflour and water and pour over the sponge. Stand in a baking tin of boiling water to come halfway up and bake in a moderate oven (350°F/180°C/Gas 4) for about 1–1½ hours until the sponge is cooked and golden brown with the sauce now underneath.

Variation for 25 people. Use a large shallow gratin dish and bake for 2–2½ hours.

F *   # Rhubarb and Fresh Ginger Fool

Of the fruity puddings, this one fits the spring bill, but you do need nice pink sticks of rhubarb. I once used greenish sticks and the pudding ended up sludge brown-green, not very appetising, showing me how slightly wrong ingredients can completely change and often spoil a dish.

Ingredients	
4–6 people	*25 people*
1½ lbs (675g) good pink rhubarb	6 lb (2.7kg) good pink rhubarb
1" (2–3cm) fresh root ginger	4" (10cm) fresh root ginger
6–8 oz (175–225g) sugar or to taste	2 lb (900g) sugar or to taste
⅓ pt (200ml) double cream	1½ pts (900ml) double cream

Cut the rhubarb into 1" (3cm) lengths and cook with the skinned and grated ginger, the sugar and a drop of water until tender. Purée the rhubarb without its juice and cool. Whip the cream until it holds its shape, fold into the cold rhubarb purée, add a little more grated ginger or sugar if necessary and turn into a bowl or individual glasses. Serve with sponge fingers or little biscuits.

**   Tarte aux Fraises

These open French flans always look so appetizing and attractive.

Ingredients

4–6 people

Pastry
8 oz (225g) flour
2 oz (50g) icing sugar
5 oz (125g) firm butter
2 egg yolks
½ teasp vanilla essence
a pinch of salt

Filling
1 lb (450g) fresh strawberries
⅓ pt (200ml) double cream
1 egg white
vanilla sugar to taste

25 people

Make four 9" (24cm) tarts using three batches of pastry, using the trimmings for the fourth tart

Filling
4 lb (1.8kg) fresh strawberries
1⅓ pts (800ml) double cream
3 egg whites
vanilla sugar to taste

Pastry. Sift the flour, icing sugar and salt into a bowl or the food processor, add the butter cut into hazelnut-sized pieces and rub in with the fingertips or process to the breadcrumb stage. Add the vanilla and yolks and work up to a paste. Turn the pastry on to a board and smear down the board in egg-sized lumps with the heel of your hand. Knead briefly into a flat disc and chill for 2 hours. Roll the pastry and fit into a 9" (24cm) removable base flan tin, prick, line with tinfoil and gravel or dried beans and bake in a hot oven (400°F/200°C/Gas 6) for 8–10 minutes. When the pastry has set remove the tinfoil and outer ring and continue to bake in a moderate oven (350°F/180°C/Gas 4) for about 20–30 minutes until cooked through and *very* lightly browned. Cool on a rack.

Filling. Whip the cream and lightly sweeten with the vanilla sugar. Whip the egg white until just holding a peak and fold into the cream. If you are preparing the cream ahead, turn it into a muslin-lined sieve or colander so that any liquid can drip out.

Hull the strawberries and halve or quarter them if large. Sprinkle them with a tiny bit of pepper to bring out their flavour. Just before serving fold together the cream and most of the strawberries, pile into the pastry shell and decorate with the remaining berries.

ℱ ✳   Peaches in Raspberry Sauce

This is one of the best puddings in the world, and it looks fabulous on a buffet. It is not difficult to make, but for eating standing up whole peaches can be a bit tricky to manage, and you may want to halve them.

Ingredients

4–6 people

4–6 large peaches
6 oz (175g) castor sugar
¼ pt (150ml) water
8 oz (225g) fresh or frozen raspberries
juice of ½ lemon

25 people

25 large peaches
1½ lb (675g) castor sugar
1 pt (600ml) water
2 lb (900g) fresh or frozen raspberries
1–2 lemons

Dissolve the sugar in the water and boil for 2–3 minutes to form a syrup. Pour boiling water over the peaches and peel them. Poach the peaches gently in the syrup until tender, and remove to a serving dish to cool. Purée the raspberries with some of the cold syrup, sieve and sharpen with lemon juice. Pour over the peaches several hours before you want to eat them, and serve chilled.

To prepare ahead. The peaches can be poached several days ahead but keep them submerged in the syrup in a cool place. Don't put too many into one container or the bottom ones come out looking squashed. Purée the raspberries on the day and mix with only enough syrup to make a thick sauce.

✳✳   Peasant Girl in a Veil

A Danish apple dish, just right for autumn. It looks pretty in a glass dish topped with its veil of cream and grated chocolate.

Ingredients

4–6 people

4–6 oz (100–150g) brown breadcrumbs
3 oz (75g) Demerara sugar
2 oz (50g) butter
½ teasp cinnamon
2½–3 lb (1.15–1.35kg) cooking apples
1 slice lemon
sugar to taste
⅓ pt (200ml) double cream
2 oz (50g) grated chocolate

25 people

1–1½ lb (450–675g) brown breadcrumbs
12 oz (350g) Demerara sugar
8 oz (225g) butter
1½ teasp cinnamon
10–12 lb (4.5–5.4kg) cooking apples
½ lemon
sugar to taste
1⅓ pts (800ml) double cream
6 oz (175g) grated chocolate

Fry the breadcrumbs in the butter over moderate heat; as they begin to crispen, which will take some time, add the Demerara sugar and cinnamon and fry until crisp and the sugar has caramelised slightly.

Peel, core and slice the apples. Cook to a thick purée with sugar to taste, a little water and the lemon slice, removing the lemon when the apple is cooked.

Make a layer of half the apple, crumbs and chocolate in a glass bowl, then add a second layer of apple and leave until cold. Not more than 1 hour before serving sprinkle on the remaining crumbs and decorate with the whipped cream and remaining chocolate.

𝐹 ✳✳   Apricot Orange Mousse

For deep midwinter (or any other time of the year for that matter!) dried apricots give us this delicious mousse. It freezes like a dream and is pretty when decorated with chocolate rose leaves. Use curls of chocolate when there are no rose leaves about.

Ingredients

4–6 people	*25 people*
½ lb (225g) dried apricots	2 lb (900g) dried apricots
6 fl oz (175ml) can frozen orange juice concentrate	4 × 6 fl oz (175ml) cans frozen orange juice concentrate
¼ pt (150ml) cream	1 pt (600ml) cream
3 egg whites	12 egg whites
2 tbs apricot brandy or Grand Marnier (optional)	6–8 tbs apricot brandy or Grand Marnier (optional)
1 oz (25g) chocolate	3–4 oz (75–100g) chocolate
a few rose leaves (optional)	1 dozen or so rose leaves (optional)

Soak the apricots in undiluted orange juice overnight and simmer gently until soft, adding a little water if necessary. Purée, sieve and flavour with apricot brandy. The purée should just drop off a spoon and be about the consistency of whipped cream. Fold in the cream, whipped until just holding its shape, and finally the egg whites whipped until they will just hold a peak. Turn into a serving dish. Serve decorated with chocolate rose leaves.

Chocolate Rose Leaves. Melt the chocolate on a saucer over hot water. With the handle of a teaspoon spread chocolate over the wiped rose leaves and leave to harden. Peel off the rose leaves and use the chocolate leaves as decoration. Do not overheat the chocolate or it will acquire a whitish bloom when cold.

** ## Orange Flummery

This is adapted from an age-old English recipe. It can be a bit of a bore because you have got to be around to beat it as it sets, but if you're cooking for a large party you are bound to be in the kitchen anyway. It's light, fresh, inexpensive and much enjoyed by the young.

Ingredients	
4–6 people	*25 people*
A 2 lemons	A 6–7 lemons
6 fl oz (175ml) can frozen	3 × 6 fl oz (175ml) cans frozen
orange juice concentrate	orange juice concentrate
10 fl oz (300ml) water	1¾ pts (1l) water
B 1 tbs gelatine	B 3½ tbs gelatine
4 fl oz (100ml) water	12 fl oz (350ml) water
1 tbs cornflour	3½ tbs cornflour
C 7 oz (200g) sugar	C 1½ lb (675g) sugar
6 fl oz (175ml) water	1 pt (600ml) water

(A) Squeeze the lemons and mix the juice with the orange concentrate and water. Set aside.

(B) Sprinkle the gelatine on to water and soak for a few minutes, then stir in the cornflour.

(C) Dissolve the sugar and 6 fl oz (175ml) water in a saucepan and boil for 3–4 minutes. Stir the gelatine mixture into this syrup and bring to the boil slowly, stirring. Boil for *exactly* 3 minutes, remove from the heat and add the orange-lemon mixture. Whisk well and put in the fridge. Remove when cold and whisk again to a moussey consistency. Chill, but if it separates it must be beaten again. Serve chilled.

Variation for 25 people. Boil the sugar and water syrup for 6–7 minutes instead of 3–4 minutes.

** ## Caramel Soufflé

The taste of this one belies its cost. It is easy to make, looks good and is a recipe everyone should know for using up those spare egg whites. But it does not freeze successfully.

Ingredients

4–6 people	*25 people*
4 egg whites	16 egg whites
2½ teasp gelatine	3 tbs + 1 teasp gelatine
3 tbs cold water	3 fl oz (75ml) cold water
¼ pt (150ml) single or whipping cream	1 pt (600ml) single or whipping cream

Caramel Syrup	*Caramel Syrup*
8 oz (225g) granulated sugar	2 lb (900g) granulated sugar
4 tbs cold water	8 fl oz (225ml) cold water
¼ pt (150ml) boiling water	1 pt (600ml) boiling water
½ lemon	2 lemons

Caramel Syrup. Place the sugar and cold water in a heavy pan. Heat gently, stirring until every grain of sugar has completely dissolved. Turn up the heat, boil fast without stirring until it is a good dark caramel brown, and add the boiling water (watch out, it splutters like mad, but the caramel all dissolves in a moment). Cool, add the grated rind and lemon juice and pour into a measuring jug.

Sprinkle the gelatine on to the cold water in a cup and leave to soak for 3–4 minutes. Stand the cup in a pan of hot water to dissolve the gelatine and then cool a little. Whisk the egg whites until holding a peak and fold in the gelatine, followed by three-quarters of the cooled caramel syrup. Turn into an oiled 2 pt (1.2l) soufflé dish, chill and leave to set.

Turn out the soufflé by running a knife round the inside of the bowl and dipping the bowl in hot water for a few moments. Dry the bowl, cover with a serving dish and invert with a shake. If the soufflé does not come out, wrap a wrung-out hot cloth around the bowl and it should relent! Pour round the remaining caramel mixed with the cream, and serve.

F * Boodle's Orange Fool

This is a speciality of the famous London club.

Ingredients

4–6 people	*25 people*
8" (20cm) home-made sponge cake	4 × 8" (20cm) home-made sponge cakes
2 large oranges	8 large oranges
1 lemon	4–5 lemons
2–3 oz (50–75g) castor sugar	8–12 oz (225–350g) castor sugar
½ pt (300ml) cream	2¼ pts (1.35l) cream

Line a glass bowl or 2-pint (1.2l) soufflé dish with a thin layer of sponge. Whip the cream, adding sugar to taste, and the grated orange and lemon rind, and gradually drip in the orange and lemon juice. Pour into the sponge-lined bowl. Chill for at least 4 hours to allow the juice to flavour and thicken the cream and soak into the sponge.

T * # Sorbet de Menthe

Frozen puddings are my great favourites, but they are not always best for buffets as they tend to melt. Nevertheless this sorbet, with its delicate eau-de-cologne mint perfume, is so cheap and such a light, fresh end to a rich meal that I include it.

Ingredients

4–6 people	*25 people*
a good handful of eau-de-cologne mint leaves (or try any other of the scented mints)	4 good handfuls of eau-de-cologne mint leaves (or try any other of the scented mints)
1 pt (600ml) water	4 pts (2.25l) water
8 oz (225g) sugar	2 lb (900g) sugar
rind and juice of 2 lemons	rind and juice of approx. 8 lemons

Combine the sugar and water in a pan. Heat gently, stirring until the sugar dissolves, and boil hard for 5–6 minutes. Remove from the heat, throw in the mint leaves and the thinly pared lemon rind and leave to infuse for 2–3 hours. Strain the liquid and add lemon juice to taste. Turn into a shallow (preferably metal or tinfoil) dish and freeze, stirring the edges into the middle from time to time. When the whole lot is fairly firmly set turn into the food processor or liquidiser and process until smooth and light or beat really hard with a whisk. Pack into a cold container or bowl and refreeze.

These sorbets need freezing as fast as possible so that no large crystals form; before serving they need to mellow and soften in the fridge for ½ hour or so, or longer if they are in large containers. If they are kept in the freezer for months and months they may get very hard and need to be well softened, reprocessed in the food processor and allowed to firm up again before serving. Serve with Tuiles d'Amandes (*see page 243*) or little biscuits.

* # Irish Coffee

The velvet-topped glass of coffee with a powerful kick *au fond*.

Ingredients

4–6 people	*25 people*
1–1½ pts (600–900ml) strong black coffee	6 pts (3.5l) strong black coffee
sugar to taste	sugar to taste
up to ¼ pt (150ml) Irish whiskey (but Scotch will do)	1¼ pts (750ml) Irish whiskey (but Scotch will do)
up to ¼ pt (150ml) double cream	1¼ pts (750ml) double cream

Have the coffee very hot and keep the glasses, each containing a tot of whiskey, in a warm place. On serving, pour coffee into the glasses, add about 1 teasp sugar and stir briskly to dissolve. Then carefully pour cream on to the back of a teaspoon held over the glass so that it forms a thick velvety layer on top of the coffee. Serve at once.

Dinner Parties

Having said earlier that the days of formal dinner parties with their gleaming silver and glass were almost over, I must qualify that by talking of the pleasure it is to be taken briefly out of our humdrum everyday life to be set down at a well-laid table, the candles lit, the glass glistening, amongst good company and in an agreeable atmosphere. It is a very civilised pleasure, and if it is carried through to good food, fine wine and relaxed conversation it can create a marvellous evening. But to organise all this takes a lot of hard work, because everything must run smoothly while appearing to be no effort. Quite easy, of course, in the days when the hostess consulted with the cook upon the menu, with the butler about the wine and the table and with her husband about the guests; her only real tasks were to send out the invitations and do the flowers. Now the poor hostess—cook, mother or career woman—has usually to tackle most of it herself, so no wonder our dinner parties become fewer and farther between. Nevertheless, we do still give them occasionally, and so we need to know how to set about them so that we stick to rule one, a relaxed hostess who is enjoying herself.

As always, the keywords are forethought and planning; it is subtle kid-glove organisation that is needed, and teamwork between host and hostess is essential; no good the husband who insists on another round of martinis just as his wife tips him the wink that dinner is on the table. The timetable for the whole evening needs working out and must be kept to, but it should always appear a natural and unhurried progression.

Perhaps it's easiest to start with numbers. Four hardly constitutes a party; six can be very nice and friendly with general conversation, but it's a lot of hard work to entertain only four others. Eight is perhaps most usual and is a very good number; it's not too many to cook carefully for, there is time to talk to all your guests, but it's not too long-drawn-out to serve. The only disadvantage is that if your table is long rather than round host and hostess cannot both sit at an end. Ten or twelve can also make a good party if you have room and a big enough oven, and you are only entertaining once for eight or ten guests, whereas two parties of six means eight guests for virtually twice the work. If you have a lot of hospitality to repay, the time and relative expense of small dinner parties are worth avoiding if you can.

When it comes to the guests one tries to choose those who will amuse, stimulate and complement each other. We find a party goes better when our guests have somewhat different interests, for in this way one avoids getting too immersed in discussing the finer points of water-colours, golf or fishing to the exclusion of everything else. Planning who shall sit next to whom is a study in itself and can be quite Machiavellian, but in principle keep husband and wife well apart or that frightfully amusing story of one will be ruined by the other who has heard it twenty times before. And anyway husbands blossom away from their wives and vice versa.

Having settled on the guests I then probably think about the season, how much we can afford and the balance of the meal. I've already said I prefer to use ingredients in the perfection of their season, but is it to be asparagus and early strawberries or Vichyssoise and Elderflower Sorbet? Both are excellent, but the former are expensive, the latter time-consuming. One luxury is probably enough.

Dinner parties should be the occasion for fine-flavoured, elegant dishes where flavours are refined and subtle. I like to try (it isn't always possible) to build up a relatively simple start towards something of a climax, and this usually suits Simon's ideas about the wines. Sometimes, indeed, wine may take precedence over food. You may have a very special bottle or have brought back a couple of flasks from your Portuguese holiday, or you may have a wine buff coming; in this case I'm quite often asked to fit food to wine. This usually means that I go for simplicity and might, for instance, choose plain beef for a fine claret, or a fresh peach to complement those delicious, luscious dessert wines. But whichever is being matched with which, do liaise with the cellar-master in good time so that, however modest the wine, it enhances the food and is drunk at its best.

I have already mentioned season, colour, texture and contrast in planning a menu. These are all important, but an additional and vital factor to consider is the ease with which your delicious creations can be served, thus preserving the harmony of the occasion. The few dinner parties where no one has to move from the table do have an added relaxation and pleasure but that is practically impossible these days, so we must plan the simplest and most unobtrusive serving we can. If one can arrange that the first course is waiting on the table in individual dishes this can do away with one whole round of serving and get one off to a relaxed start; it is particularly useful in a small dining room.

The main course, the heart of the dinner, is the one that needs most thought, and I am always being asked for ideas which are easy, take no last-minute work and are not the hackneyed casserole. Indeed a tall order, but I have come to the conclusion that the answer often lies in some special roast or other, very often a boned and rolled joint or loin of pork or lamb. Pork chops are not particularly elegant and are fairly expensive, and a boned loin or carré of pork will stay more succulent, carve into elegant thin slices and be far more economical. Serve with some delicious sauce made much earlier and kept warm over hot water; most sauces positively improve with being kept warm and maturing, and there is so little time to get them just right at the last moment. The important thing with a joint is timing and knowing your oven. It is well worth having a meat thermometer and practising to get it right. Write down the cooking time and your preferred thermometer reading straight away, as it is surprising how easily one can forget for the next occasion.

Remember that all joints like to rest for ½ to 1 hour after cooking and before carving, as this allows the juices to spread right back through the joint, leaving it succulent and rosy throughout with the meat fibres relaxed and much easier to carve. We tend to pay lip-service to resting the joint but don't practise it conscientiously; this was brought home to me one evening when I had cooked a rack of lamb to the rose-pink perfection I had hoped for. I was just putting it to rest in the Belling hot cupboard when the telephone rang and our guests (with many apologies) said they would be an hour late. When we came to eat it, it was one of the best, most succulent joints I have ever eaten or cooked. So a joint allows one plenty of leeway so long as it does not go on cooking. A Belling hot cupboard, a warming drawer, a very low oven or a hot plate and meat cover is essential.

Back to the point of the elegant boned and rolled joints. They can be carved with your sharp knife in a few minutes into thin and attractively presented slices, and this can be done in either kitchen or dining room depending on space. In general I prefer the former, so I now beat a hasty retreat from the table to the kitchen to slice the meat rapidly and pour the sauce into a sauceboat.

Vegetables are often the hardest part of a dinner to get perfect, as so few of them like to be kept waiting. Often they should be cooked, drained and served at once, but who wants to look at their watch for four-and-a-half minutes for the broad beans in the middle of dinner and then have a cloud of steam blow through their hair? Not I, so I have concentrated on a few vegetables which prefer to be cooked ahead and then kept warm. Other main courses will not need carving but will still probably need a few minutes to dish up and finish the sauce. Anything is better than the endless casserole. In any case, course should not follow course too rapidly, and one's absence from the table for a few moments will probably go unremarked.

On to puddings. I must say I nearly always choose cold puddings, for at this stage one should be very relaxed, and the idea of messing about in the kitchen and missing the fun seems more and more abhorrent. I enjoy making puddings, and find that most people prefer them to savouries, which generally need last-minute attention to be good, though I have included a couple. If you feel that to uphold tradition you must have four courses—though I rather feel that without help with the serving three good courses are better and certainly more relaxing than coping with more plates—then serve a small entrée, cheese or a savoury.

I never feel cheese is particularly suitable for dinner, although it will certainly be offered in France, and a good cheese-board, though expensive, can be prepared in a fraction of the time it takes to make anything else. Ideas about when to serve it vary, but I normally follow the French tradition and have it before the pudding with the last of the red wine, ending up with a sweet flavour and a dessert wine.

I have strong ideas about dinner parties at this stage in the proceedings. I feel as hostess that I have gone to great trouble to gather the right guests together and have dined them well in a relaxed ambience, and by the end of dinner they have unwound and are enjoying themselves. Surely it is a waste of all one's efforts if at this juncture you drag them too hastily from the dim womb of the dining-room to a perhaps brightly-lit drawing-room? You see everyone blink and return to reality from the enchanted world to which you have transported them. So now we normally have our coffee and sit on in the candle-light, perhaps with a few people swapping places as we continue to drink our wine or a glass of port, a liqueur or an eau-de-vie. Finally, when the decanters are empty and everybody is ready, we move to the warmth and mellow lights of the drawing-room.

I have not gone into all the work of cleaning the silver, laying the table and doing the flowers. As far as the silver goes, long-term silver cloths, tissue paper and polythene bags help to keep the silver clean if it is tucked away; beware of using long-term cloths on cutlery you will put in a dishwasher, because it usually seems to bring them out in a grey bloom. Flowers? Well, if one can pick or buy them ahead, and give them a long deep drink, they are much easier to arrange and are less likely to droop as your guests walk into the room. A few favourite vases and some flower-arranging equipment make life easier, but whatever happens do avoid rushing round the garden in the rain five minutes before your guests arrive, looking desperately for presentable blooms. Bad for the flowers, worse for the hair and terrible for your cool!

So plan ahead, think it through carefully (on the bus or in the bath, a great place for thinking), and make and stick to a time-plan that is realistic. Don't be over-ambitious, and make sure you enjoy yourself!

First Courses

✶✶   Vichyssoise

A lovely soup for summer, but in England where, oh where, do you get leeks? In Germany you can buy them all the year round, and, while I am experimenting with how to grow them for summer use, I can't yet offer much help. Though you can use frozen leeks or cook the leek base in winter and freeze it for summer use, it never seems to taste quite so fresh.

Ingredients
4–6 people

1 small finely sliced onion
3–4 finely sliced medium leeks, using
   only the whites
2 oz (50g) butter
¾ lb (350g) cubed potatoes

2 pts (1.2l) good white chicken stock
⅓ pt (200ml) cream
salt and pepper

chopped chives

Melt the butter in a pan, add the onion and leek, cover and allow to cook gently or 'sweat' without browning for 10–15 minutes. Add the diced potato and stir to coat with butter. Add the stock, season well and simmer briskly for 20–30 minutes. Purée in the liquidiser or food processor, strain and chill. When you are ready to serve add the cream, correct the seasoning and scatter chopped chives on top.

* Iced Cucumber Soup

Leave half the skin on the cucumber to make a delicate jade-coloured soup with a hint of mint. Cool to look at as well as on the tongue.

Ingredients
4–6 people

1 large cucumber
1 small finely chopped onion
1½ oz (35g) butter
½ oz (12g) flour
1½ pts (900ml) good white chicken or veal
   stock
a good sprig of mint

⅓ pt (200ml) cream
salt and pepper

Garnish
chopped chives
tiny dice of cucumber

Retain 2″ (5cm) cucumber to cube for garnish, and half peel and roughly dice the remainder. Melt the butter in a saucepan, add the onion and cucumber and gently 'sweat' for 4–5 minutes without browning. Sprinkle in the flour and stir, add the stock, mint and seasoning, and simmer for 20 minutes or so. Liquidise or purée very smooth and sieve. Chill. Blend in the cream, correct the seasoning and serve sprinkled with tiny dice of peeled cucumber and finely chopped chives.

ℱ ∗∗   Prawn Bisque

This is a soup that really does freeze well, though I usually just freeze extra prawn butter and prawn fumet. If you are going to flutter your eyelashes at the fishmonger for fish bones and skins, you might as well get plenty and make a really good batch.

Ingredients
4–6 people

2 oz (50g) prawn butter (see p. 36)
1 oz (25g) flour
1½ pts (900ml) prawn fumet (see p. 37)
¼ pt (150ml) milk
½ teasp paprika
the prawns from ½ lb (225g) prawns in
    their shells
2 egg yolks
¼ pt (150ml) cream
2 tbs dry sherry
finely chopped chervil, parsley or chives
salt and pepper

Melt 1½ oz (35g) of the prawn butter in a saucepan, add the flour and cook over moderate heat for 2–3 minutes. Take off the heat, wait for the sizzling to cease, then add the prawn fumet, milk, salt, pepper and paprika; bring to the boil, whisking well, and simmer for 3–4 minutes.

Process half the prawns in a food processor until smooth and add the soup (in a liquidiser process all together). Strain, and add the remaining chopped prawns.

Whisk the egg yolks well in a bowl and add the cream; gradually whisk in drop by drop about ½ pt (300ml) of the hot soup, then return all to the pan. Re-heat gently—but *DO NOT BOIL*—until the yolks cook and the soup thickens. Keep warm in a *bain-marie*. On serving add the sherry, whisk in the remaining prawn butter and serve sprinkled with chopped herbs.

ℱ ∗   Game Pâté with Green Peppercorns

This can be made from a variety of cooked game (but don't try to get away with using just the tough and gristly scraps); it is light but creamy, and spiked with green peppercorns which prevent it from becoming cloying. This is the kind of rich smooth pâté that freezes most successfully.

Ingredients
4–6 people

6–8 oz (175–225g) cooked game meat
1 small finely chopped onion
1 bay leaf
1 clove garlic finely chopped
4 oz (100g) butter
1 teasp brandy

4 fl oz (100ml) cream
2 teasp green peppercorns
salt, pepper and mace

Gently fry the onion with the whole bay leaf in half the butter until golden, add the finely chopped garlic and brandy and cook a moment before removing the bay leaf and scraping into the food processor or liquidiser bowl. Add the diced game meat with no skin or sinews and process until very smooth. Add seasoning and the remaining unmelted but soft butter (if you add all the butter melted the mixture will curdle), and process until you have a smooth purée. Stir the whole green peppercorns into the cooled pâté. Whip the cream until it is just holding its shape, then fold in. The game purée should be cold but not setting when you fold in the cream. If it's warm the cream will thin out, but if it's set too much you won't be able to fold it in. Pack into pots and serve at room temperature with hot toast or melba toast and lemon quarters.

**   Pâté aux Herbes

A light, green, herby pâté, only really practical in summer as most of the herbs must be fresh. It's nice to make when you have some fat and lean from a ham to use up. I like to serve it with a quickly made Brioche Loaf or fresh rolls, as toast-making at the last minute usually ends in the all too familiar waft of burning and the frantic scratching of the knife.

Ingredients
6–8 people

½ lb (225g) ham fat or back pork fat
½ lb (225g) lean pork
½ lb (225g) cooked ham cut into matchstick strips
½ lb (225g) streaky bacon cut very thin
1 teasp gelatine
the grated rind and juice of 1 lemon
1 small finely chopped onion
2 cloves garlic

1 handful fresh parsley
1 handful fresh marjoram (less of strong
   annual variety)
¼ handful fresh lemon thyme or thyme
a few sprigs fresh basil or 1 teasp dried
   basil
¼ lb (100g) cooked spinach
2 eggs
salt, pepper and nutmeg

Sprinkle the gelatine on to the lemon juice in a little bowl, soak for several minutes, then melt by standing the bowl in a pan of hot water. Chop the onion, the crushed garlic and all the herbs very finely together, or use a food processor. Mince the spinach, fat and pork together or process in a food processor. Combine with the herbs, the ham strips, the melted gelatine, eggs and seasoning, and beat well to lighten the texture (use the plastic blade of the food processor). Fry a little to taste and correct the seasoning. Line a 1½-pint (1-litre) terrine with the de-rinded streaky bacon, pack in the pâté mixture and fold the bacon over the top. Place the terrine in a roasting tin with boiling water to come halfway up the terrine, and bake in a slow oven (300°F/150°C/Gas 2) for 1½–2 hours. It's cooked when no pink juice comes out when pricked with a skewer. Cool, chill and press lightly. Turn out and serve in slices.

If there is too much moisture in the spinach and herbs you will have a wet pâté. So squeeze your spinach well before using, and add a little more gelatine if the herbs seem very wet after rain.

✳✳ Egg Mousse

This is a delicious egg mousse, smooth and creamy with a thick layer of chopped chives topped with a deep brown translucent layer of jelly. Make well ahead, as the consommé takes time to set, and do make sure you get one which will set to jelly, so check the instructions on the can. When you have not got masses of chives, use the diced celery and pepper.

Ingredients
4–6 people

4 hard-boiled eggs	2 teasp gelatine
1 pt (600ml) Campbell's beef consommé	½ lemon
⅓ pt (200ml) cream	lots of chives *or* 1 stick celery and
1 teasp anchovy essence	1 slice green pepper
1 teasp Worcester sauce	salt and pepper
1 slice onion	
1 teasp tarragon vinegar	

Sprinkle the gelatine on to 2 tablespoonfuls of consommé in a little bowl, leave to soak for a few moments and stand in a pan of hot water to melt. Stir into the rest of the consommé with the tarragon vinegar and a good squeeze of lemon juice, and set half of it aside. Place the remainder, the chopped-up eggs, anchovy essence, Worcester sauce, slice of onion and seasoning in the liquidiser and process until absolutely smooth. In a food processor, process the egg until quite smooth before adding the remaining ingredients. Pour through a sieve into a large bowl and chill, stirring from time to time until it begins to thicken. Whip the cream until it is just holding its shape and fold in. Pour into a 2-pint or 1-litre soufflé dish or glass bowl and leave to set in the fridge.

Cover very thickly with chopped chives or the celery and green pepper cut into very tiny dice, then spoon over a little of the reserved consommé (warm it gently if it has already set). Leave this to set before pouring over the rest of the reserved consommé (if you don't the chives will float to the top and spoil it). This will keep in the fridge for 1–2 days and is nice served with little cress sandwiches or melba toast.

Opposite: Choux-fleurs Sauce Verte, Watercress and Orange Salad, Gigot d'Agneau Farci à la Bordelaise and Mushrooms with Garlic and Thyme

** Avocado Mousse with Spiced Prawns

This mousse is a delicate green and very smooth (beware if you have unripe or discoloured avocados; the former can make it lumpy and bitter and the latter can play havoc with the colour); the spicy prawns just held together with a little cream make a lovely contrast. Try to make it not more than 24 hours ahead and keep tightly covered for a good colour. I usually make it in one big dish, but you could easily do individual ones if you prefer.

Ingredients
4–6 people

2 avocados
1 slice onion
1 clove garlic
¼–½ teasp Worcester sauce
a drop or two Tabasco sauce
the juice of ½ lemon
¼ pt (150ml) + 3 tbs cold water
1 tbs gelatine
3 fl oz (75ml) cream
¼ pt (150ml) mayonnaise
½ teasp salt

Spiced Prawns
½ teasp whole coriander seeds
1 clove garlic
½" (1cm) fresh root ginger
the juice of ½ lemon
1 teasp sugar
¼ teasp curry powder
2–3 drops Tabasco sauce
¼ lb (100g) peeled prawns
3 fl oz (75ml) cream
ground black pepper
½ teasp salt

Sprinkle the gelatine on to 3 tbs cold water in a small bowl, soak for a few moments, then stand in a saucepan of hot water to melt. Place the chopped onion, crushed garlic and skinned, stoned and chopped avocados in a food processor or liquidiser and purée, adding the lemon, salt, Worcester sauce, Tabasco, the remainder of the water and the dissolved gelatine. When very smooth turn into a bowl and fold in the mayonnaise, followed by the cream, whipped until it is just holding its shape. Pour into a 1½-pint (1-litre) bowl, and leave to set before serving chilled and topped with the spiced prawns.

Spiced Prawns. Pound the coriander seeds, then add grated fresh ginger and the garlic, salt, pepper, sugar and curry powder. Pound well and moisten with the lemon juice, adding Tabasco to taste. Toss the peeled prawns in this mixture and marinate for several hours. Whip the cream, beating in any liquid from the prawns, fold in the prawns and spread on top of the mousse. Sesame fingers (*see p. 242*) are good with this mousse.

*   # Minted Pears

Fresh herbs give this clean first course, based on Robert Carrier's delicious Pears Vinaigrette, a fine springlike flavour, and make it one of my favourite starters when rich dishes are to follow.

Ingredients
4–6 people

4–6 ripe pears
3 tbs fresh chopped mint
2 tbs fresh chopped parsley
1 teasp fresh chopped tarragon or
    ½ teasp dried tarragon

1 teasp Dijon mustard
2 tbs lemon juice
5 tbs olive oil
salt and pepper

Place the salt, pepper and mustard in a bowl, add the lemon juice and stir well to dissolve the salt. Gradually beat in the oil to produce an emulsified vinaigrette and stir in the finely chopped herbs (if using dried tarragon, steep in a few drops of boiling water for a few minutes before using). If you are using a food processor chop all the herbs finely, then add the seasoning, mustard, lemon juice and oil. Peel, core and slice the pears into the dressing, leave for an hour or so to marinate and chill, turning once or twice, then put in individual bowls or glasses and spoon over the dressing. Serve with crisp cheese straws or Sesame Fingers (*see page 242*).

*   # Seafood en Cocotte

Very delicately curried with a hint of fennel and fresh ginger, these prawns are served in individual ramekins, bubbling hot, brown and cheesy.

Ingredients
4–6 people

½–¾ lb (225–350g) peeled prawns
1½ oz (35g) butter
1½ oz (35g) flour
8 fl oz (225ml) good chicken stock
2 fl oz (50ml) dry white wine
¼ teasp fennel seeds
a small slice fresh root ginger
1 crushed clove garlic
¼ teasp curry powder

¼ pt (150ml) double cream
½ lemon
4–6 tbs grated Gruyère cheese
4–6 tbs breadcrumbs
½ oz (12g) butter
salt and pepper

Combine the stock, wine, bruised fennel seeds, garlic and ginger in a saucepan; heat and infuse gently for 10 minutes, then strain. Melt the butter in a saucepan, add the curry powder and flour and cook for 2–3 minutes over moderate heat. Draw the pan off the stove, wait for the sizzling to cease, then pour in the strained liquid and bring to the boil, whisking hard. Simmer for 1–2 minutes and add the cream. Add the prawns, correct the seasoning, and give a squeeze of lemon juice. Spoon into buttered ramekin dishes and top with the breadcrumbs, grated cheese and flakes of butter. Brown under the grill or, if made ahead, heat through in a hot oven (400°F/200°C/Gas 6) for about 15–20 minutes until bubbling and brown.

* Smoked Haddock and Avocado au Gratin

Individual ramekins of smoked haddock in a creamy sauce covered with slices of avocado, liberally topped with cheese and browned under the grill.

Ingredients
4–6 people

½ lb (225g) smoked haddock
1 oz (25g) butter
1 oz (25g) flour
½ pt (300ml) creamy milk (use top of the
   milk or add a little cream)
pepper and mace
1 bay leaf

1–2 avocados (depending on size)
6–8 tbs grated Gruyère or mature Cheddar
   cheese

Place the skinned fish in a saucepan with the bay leaf and milk, bring gently to the simmer and draw to the side of the stove; cover and leave for 5–10 minutes (the fish will then be cooked). Melt the butter in another saucepan, add the flour and cook for 2–3 minutes over moderate heat. Draw off the stove, wait for the sizzling to cease (make sure it does, as you are adding hot liquid), and add the strained milk from the fish. Whisk with a wire whisk and bring to the boil. Simmer for 1–2 minutes, fold in the flaked fish, and season with pepper and mace, adding salt only if necessary. Spoon into individual ramekins, top with slices of peeled avocado, sprinkle heavily with cheese and grill until brown and bubbling.

⊤ **   Petits Choux aux Fruits de Mer

Choux buns filled with a rich seafood mixture.

Ingredients
4–6 people

Choux buns
¼ pt (150ml) water
2 oz (50g) butter
3 oz (75g) 'strong' flour
2 eggs
salt and pepper

Seafood
½ oz (12g) butter
4 oz (100g) peeled prawns
8 oz (225g) diced scallops or lobster or
    monkfish or a mixture
3 tbs dry vermouth
salt, pepper and mace

Sauce
1 oz (25g) butter
1 oz (25g) flour
½ pt (300ml) milk (approx)
1 oz (25g) Gruyère cheese
2 egg yolks
3 tbs cream
½ lemon
salt, pepper and mace

Choux buns. Place the water, butter, salt and pepper in a saucepan and bring to the boil to melt the butter. Draw off the stove and add all the sifted flour at once. Stir until the mixture is smooth and leaves the sides of the pan, then cook for 1–2 minutes over medium heat until a skin forms on the bottom of the pan. Cool for 5–10 minutes. Gradually beat in the eggs (or use a food processor and add the eggs all at once), beating like mad until the mixture is smooth and shiny and keeping its shape. Make 12 buns with the mixture by dropping spoonfuls, spread well apart, on to a greased baking sheet (or use a forcing bag). Bake in a hot oven (425°F/220°C/Gas 7) for 15–20 minutes or until well browned and firm. Make a slit in each bun to let the steam out and return to a slow or turned-off oven to dry out for about 10 minutes. Cool on a rack.

Seafood. Heat a frying pan and add the butter. When it is very hot toss in the prawns and diced seafood and cook fast for 1–2 minutes. Add the vermouth and seasoning and toss and cook until the liquid has gone (don't boil the seafood for long—remove or draw to one side of the pan while the liquid boils and reduces), then return and toss in the richly flavoured syrupy juices. Set aside.

Sauce. Melt the butter in a saucepan, add the flour and cook for 2–3 minutes. Draw off the heat, wait for the sizzling to cease and add nearly all the milk. Bring to the boil, whisking hard, and simmer for 1–2 minutes. Add the cheese and season with salt, pepper and mace. Beat the egg yolks and cream in a bowl and very gradually beat in the hot sauce spoonful by spoonful. Return to the pan and slowly bring to the simmer, whisking all the time; simmer for 1 minute, then fold in the seafood, adding the reserved milk if the mixture is too thick. Sharpen with a squeeze of lemon juice and turn at once into a bowl.

Cut the tops off the buns and fill with the seafood mixture. Replace the tops and heat through in a moderate oven (350°F/180°C/Gas 4) for 10 minutes or so.

**   Timbales de Foies de Volaille, Sauce Hollandaise

Delicately garlic-flavoured chicken liver creams, prepared ready to pop into the oven for a carefully timed period. Serve turned out (for large numbers or ease of serving leave in the ramekin dishes) and cover with a spoonful of Sauce Hollandaise. Don't forget that Sauce Hollandaise will keep warm for 4–5 hours and is very simply made.

Ingredients
4–6 people

½ lb (225g) chicken livers
¾ oz (20g) butter
½ oz (12g) flour
¼ pt (150ml) milk
1 whole egg and 1 yolk
½ small clove garlic
3 tbs double cream
1 tbs Marsala or brandy
salt, pepper and nutmeg

Sauce Hollandaise
3 egg yolks
4–6 oz (100–175g) unsalted butter
1 lemon
1 tbs cold water
salt and pepper

Melt the butter in a saucepan, add the flour and cook over moderate heat for 1–2 minutes. Draw off the stove, wait until the sizzling ceases, then add the milk and bring to the boil, whisking well with a wire whisk. Simmer 2–3 minutes, add the seasoning and cool. Place the carefully picked over livers (remove any green-tinged liver, as it will be bitter from the bile), the whole egg and the yolk in a food processor or liquidiser and process until absolutely smooth. Add the sauce, cream, Marsala, garlic and seasoning. Process again and strain through a sieve into buttered ramekin dishes. Place these in a roasting tin with boiling water to come halfway up the ramekins and bake in a moderate oven (350°F/180°C/Gas 4) for 25–30 minutes until the mixture is just firm. Serve turned out or in the pots with a spoonful of Sauce Hollandaise poured over.

Sauce Hollandaise. Keep 1 oz (25g) butter ice cold. Melt the rest chopped up in a small pan over low heat. Whip the egg yolks well in a bowl with a wire whisk, then beat in 1 tbs lemon juice and 1 tbs cold water. Place the bowl over a pan of hot, not boiling, water so that the bowl does not touch the water. Add half the cold butter and stir until it melts and the yolks thicken so that you can see the bottom of the bowl for a moment. Add the remaining cold butter to arrest the cooking, and remove the bowl from the heat. Whisk well, and when the butter has melted drip in the melted butter as you whisk (if you are using salted butter leave out some of the salty white residue). Season with salt and pepper and finish with a little more lemon if necessary. The sauce can now be kept warm by standing the covered bowl in a pan of *lukewarm* water in a warm, not hot, place.

Main Courses

* ### **Baked Trout and Fennel Sauce**

Make this when you've got fennel fresh from the summer garden, or try it with dill, chervil or even parsley.

Ingredients
4–6 people

4–6 trout	*Sauce*
a little butter	**6 tbs double cream**
a bunch fresh fennel	**2–3 tbs fresh chopped fennel**
salt and pepper	**6 tbs yoghurt**
	¼ teasp arrowroot or potato flour
	1–2 oz (25–50g) butter
	few drops lemon juice
	salt and pepper

Butter a shallow ovenproof dish well and lay in the prepared trout, each stuffed with some fennel. Season with salt and pepper, cover with well-buttered butter papers and tinfoil, and bake in a moderately hot oven (375°F/190°C/Gas 5) for 15 minutes or until done (the eye goes white and the flesh feels firm and will just flake).

Sauce. Heat the cream with the chopped fennel until well flavoured, combine the yoghurt and arrowroot and stir in. Bring to the simmer slowly, stirring all the time. Simmer for 1–2 minutes until thickened, draw off the stove and whisk in the butter in little pieces, season, and add a squeeze of lemon juice if necessary. Keep well covered if not serving at once.

**   Poulet Sauté à l'Orange

The chicken joints are sautéd until half-cooked, then finished slowly and served with a small quantity of delicious sauce rather than plenty of ordinary sauce. One of the main faults of English cooking is not reducing sauces to intensify their flavour.

Ingredients
4–6 people

3½–4 lb (1.6–1.8kg) good chicken	1 tbs marmalade (preferably Cooper's
2 oz (50g) butter	Oxford) chopped very fine
a few drops oil	a good pinch ground cardamom
bouquet garni of parsley stalks, sprig	6 fl oz (175ml) dry white wine
of thyme, bay leaf and 2 crushed	6–8 fl oz (175–225ml) double cream
cardamom pods	
2 tbs brandy	
salt and pepper	

Joint the chicken and season with salt and pepper. Melt the butter with a few drops of oil in a sauté pan or casserole. When hot add the chicken joints in one layer and sauté to a golden colour on all sides; this takes about 10 minutes. Pour over the brandy and flame. Add the bouquet garni and the seasoning and lay the broken carcass on top (this keeps the chicken succulent and adds some rich juices to the pan). Cover and cook very gently for about 15–20 minutes until the chicken is just tender. Remove the breasts first, then the remaining joints when they are done, and keep warm. Remove the bouquet and squeeze, take out the carcass and add the marmalade, cardamom and white wine to the pan. Reduce until only a few spoonfuls of rich syrupy juice remain. Return the joints and keep warm. When ready to serve remove the joints to a serving dish, boil up the sauce, add the cream and reduce to a thick rich sauce. Pour over and serve at once.

ℱ ∗∗   Coq au Vin

This is really only practical when you can buy small pickling onions, so authentically it is a late summer to midwinter dish. If it is to be good you must be generous with the quantity and quality of your wine. If you can get proper thick-cut lardons of bacon rather than making do with rashers which crumble into the sauce, so much the better. The idea is for the portions of chicken, the whole mushrooms, the little onions and the lardons of bacon to be combined in a smooth rich wine sauce while yet retaining their shape and individuality.

Do allow time for reducing the sauce properly, as this can take fifteen to thirty minutes, and the chicken should look purple-tinged from cooking in the wine, unlike so many restaurant versions where chicken and sauce meet only briefly as they come to the table. This dish is all the better for being made ahead and reheated carefully. It can also be frozen, though the mushroom and onions are never quite so good, and sauces thickened with *beurre manié* may thin out.

Ingredients
4–6 people

3½–4 lb (1.6–1.8kg) good chicken
2 oz (50g) butter
a few drops of oil
1 × 3 oz (75g) slice of streaky bacon
3 tbs brandy
1 pt (600ml) good red wine
1 clove garlic
bouquet garni of parsley stalks, sprig of
    thyme and a bay leaf
1 oz (25g) flour
1 oz (25g) butter
salt and pepper
heart-shaped crôutes of stale bread fried
    in butter and olive oil

Onions
12–24 little pickling onions
½ oz (12g) butter
1 tbs oil
2–3 tbs stock
1 teasp sugar

Mushrooms
8 oz (225g) button mushrooms
1 oz (25g) butter
a few drops oil

Joint and season the chicken. Heat the butter and oil in a frying pan or casserole and sauté the bacon, cut into ⅜" × 1" (1cm × 2cm) rectangles (sometimes I blanch the bacon in boiling water to remove the salt and moisture which can stick to the pan). Remove when lightly browned, sauté the chicken to a good brown all over, return the bacon and flame with the brandy. Add the wine to the casserole with the bouquet and crushed garlic and season lightly. Simmer gently on top of the stove or cook in a moderate oven (350°F/180°C/Gas 4) for 20–30 minutes until the chicken is just tender.

Remove the chicken, with the bacon, from the casserole and keep warm. Skim the excess fat from the sauce, then boil fast to reduce to about ¾ pint (450ml). Cream the butter and flour together for *beurre manié*. Thicken the sauce lightly by whisking in little bits of *beurre manié* and simmering the sauce briefly to thicken. Add the cooked mushrooms and onions to the chicken and strain the sauce over them.

This dish can be heated through and served at once; it can be kept warm; or it can be reheated. Serve surrounded by the hot heart-shaped croûtes, which take only 5–10 minutes to heat in the oven.

Onions. Sauté the onions in butter and oil in one layer in a saucepan until brown, add the stock and sugar and season lightly, cover and simmer for 15–30 minutes, shaking well until just tender. Remove the lid and boil fast to evaporate any remaining liquid, leaving the onions glazed and golden.

Mushrooms. Sauté the mushrooms fast in hot butter and oil until brown.

F **   Chicken Shalimar

This is based on a dish produced by one of the other competitors in the *Sunday Times* Cook of Britain Competition, but with the spice quantities cut down from those used by 'old India hands' to English dinner-party proportions. These freshly spiced dishes are some of my favourites, and this one, with its cream and almond sauce, is certainly up to dinner-party standard.

Ingredients
4–6 people

4–6 chicken breasts or joints of chicken	½ teasp ground cardamom
¼ teasp or 1 pkt saffron	½ teasp ground coriander seeds
¼ pt (150ml) plain yoghurt	1½" (4cm) fresh root ginger
½ teasp cornflour	juice of 1 lemon
2 oz (50g) butter	salt and pepper
a few drops oil	¼ pt (150ml) double cream
¼ pt (150ml) strong chicken stock	3 oz (75g) ground almonds
½ teasp ground cinnamon	1 oz (25g) flaked browned almonds

Prepare the chicken breasts or joint the chicken. Infuse the saffron in 2–3 tbs hot stock for 20–30 minutes. Mix the cornflour with the yoghurt. Heat the butter in a frying pan or casserole with a few drops of oil to prevent the butter from burning and gently brown the chicken pieces on both sides; sprinkle with the ground spices and fry for another minute. Remove the chicken, cool the pan a little before adding the yoghurt-cornflour mixture to the pan, then heat gently to the simmer, stirring all the time (this stabilises the yoghurt and stops it from curdling). Add the stock, the peeled and grated ginger, the saffron and the lemon juice. Season with plenty of salt and pepper. Return the chicken to the casserole. Cook in a moderately hot oven (375°F/190°C/Gas 5) for 20–25 minutes or until just done.

Mix the cream and almonds. Skim most of the excess butter off the chicken (but leave some, as it combines with the sauce and enriches it), pour the hot sauce into the almond-cream mixture and return all to the pan. Check the seasoning. Add a squeeze of lemon juice and boil up fast for a minute or two to reduce and amalgamate the sauce. Place in a low oven (300°F/150°C/Gas 2) for 10–15 minutes, or keep warm for longer. Serve the chicken on a flat dish, spoon the sauce over and sprinkle heavily with browned almonds.

Rice is the best accompaniment to this dish; toss it with any excess butter from the chicken.

F **   **Pheasant St Sulpice**

A pheasant (or for that matter chicken) dish named by me after the village in France where we gather the juniper berries from the hillside. Juniper berries take two years to ripen on the bush; the first year the prickly bushes are covered in green berries but in the second summer these blacken and go slightly squashy, and the hillside hums with heat and bees and the resinous tang of juniper tickles one's nose. The children go out picking the berries to make some pocket money, but the spiky bushes guard their seed well and they come home with red and prickled fingers. The sauce mixture of cream and yoghurt is lighter and sharper than cream on its own, and the redcurrant jelly offsets the austere juniper tang which is always so good with game.

Ingredients
3–4 people

1 plump pheasant	¼ pt (150ml) plain yoghurt
1 sliced onion	¼ pt (150ml) double cream
1 sliced carrot	1–2 teasp redcurrant jelly
1 sliced stick celery	2 teasp cornflour
2 oz (50g) butter	salt and pepper
a few drops oil	
6–8 bruised juniper berries	
1 bay leaf	
¼ pt (150ml) good pheasant or chicken	
stock	

Melt the butter with a few drops of oil in a casserole which will just hold the pheasant and brown the bird all over for about 15 minutes or so; remove and gently fry the vegetables until light brown. Return the pheasant to the pan, add the juniper berries, bay leaf, stock and seasoning, cover tightly and simmer very gently or cook in a moderate oven (350°F/ 180°C/Gas 4) for 30–45 minutes or until the pheasant is just done. Remove and keep warm.

Boil down the juices to reduce to ⅓ pt (200ml), remove the juniper berries and bay leaf and dissolve the redcurrant jelly in the sauce. Mix the yoghurt, cream and cornflour in a food processor or liquidiser, add all the sauce, process until smooth and strain back into the pan (or just mix and sieve). Bring to the boil and simmer gently for several minutes. Check the seasoning. Keep well covered if not using at once. When ready to serve, joint the pheasant, pour the sauce over it and serve.

The pheasant can be jointed and rewarmed in the sauce, but it's never quite so good and the sauce may thin a little.

P ✳✳   Roast Duck with Cherry Sauce

Roast duck is always a treat and is quite easy done in this way. It can be served with an orange salad or this cherry sauce.

Ingredients
4–6 people

4–5 lb (1.8–2.25kg) duck

Sauce
½ pt (300ml) duck stock made from the giblets
3–4 tbs red wine vinegar
3 tbs sugar

½–1 teasp arrowroot or potato flour
4 tbs port or red wine
20–40 fresh cherries or a jar of stoned morello cherries
½ oz (12g) butter
lemon juice
salt and pepper

Get the duck skin as dry as possible for a nice crisp finish. You can do what the Chinese do and place the duck in a bowl and pour a kettle of boiling water over it; take out, dry, and hang up with string in a good draughty place for 4–8 hours. Otherwise just hang it up to dry. Remove the preen glands on either side of the tail (parson's nose) because they give a musty flavour. Place the duck on a rack in a roasting pan, prick the skin along the sides with a fork to let the fat out, and roast in a hot oven (400°F/200°C/Gas 6) for 1¼–1½ hours. Do not baste, but cover lightly with tinfoil if it is getting too brown. I like to joint the duck by snipping straight down the breast bone and the backbone with a good pair of scissors, then cutting each half into two or three pieces. Use a knife for the skin and flesh and scissors for the bone. This makes a large looking portion, but there is never much meat and it's the best way for crispy skin. Duck is best fairly well cooked and served straight from the hot oven for crispness, though it will keep warm for half an hour or so, as will the sauce.

Sauce. Reduce the stock down to ¼ pint (150ml) to make it stronger. Sprinkle the sugar into a small frying pan and heat gently until it melts and turns to brown caramel. Add the vinegar and then the reduced stock (watch out—it spits like mad, but the caramel should bubble straight off). Toss the stoned cherries in ½ oz (12g) butter in a frying pan for 2–3 minutes, then pour the port over and boil up. Add to the sauce and thicken lightly with potato flour mixed with a little water. Season, simmer a few minutes, and set aside covered. Finish with a few drops of lemon juice and serve in a sauceboat with the jointed duck.

P ** # Longe de Porc au Gruyère

Boned loin of pork with a filling of Gruyère and ham which melts into the meat on cooking to give an unusual flavour.

Ingredients
4–6 people

2½–3 lb (1.15–1.35kg) boned but
   unrolled loin of pork
2 tbs brandy
2 tbs Marsala or sherry
2 tbs olive oil
3 oz (75g) cooked ham
3 oz (75g) Gruyère cheese
1 tbs chopped parsley
1 teasp lemon thyme
bouquet garni of parsley stalks, sprig of
   thyme and bay leaf

2 oz (50g) butter
1 tbs olive oil
1 finely sliced onion
2 finely sliced carrots
salt and pepper

Remove the skin from the pork, leaving only a ½" (1cm) layer of fat. Place the fat side down on the table, then make two long parallel cuts about 1"–1½" (2cm–4cm) apart down the whole length of the meat, but don't cut right through. Lay the meat cut side up on a dish and sprinkle with salt, pepper, the brandy, the Marsala and olive oil. Cover and keep in the larder or fridge for about 6 hours or overnight.

Chop the ham and mix with the grated Gruyère cheese, pepper, parsley and lemon thyme. Pack some filling down each cut in the meat, then press the meat together to reform the joint, folding the flap over, and tie with string. Gently brown the onions and carrots in the butter and oil in a frying pan and remove to a casserole to make a bed for the pork. Brown the pork all over in the hot butter for 10–15 minutes and lay it on the vegetables in the casserole, adding the bouquet garni and any marinade, pork bones or skin. Cover tightly with tinfoil and a lid and cook in a very moderate oven (325°F/170°C/ Gas 3) for 1¾–2½ hours (a meat thermometer reading of 170°F/75°C). When cooked remove the meat and keep warm, de-grease the juices and boil down to concentrate. Correct the seasoning and strain into a sauceboat, pressing the vegetables well to expel the juices. Otherwise purée and sieve them for a thicker sauce. This meat is delicious cold, possibly even better than hot.

* Jambon Braisé au Madère

When you've seen enough of your lovely cold ham, carve some generous slices for this dish.

Ingredients
4–6 people

1½–2 lb (675–900g) thick slices of cold cooked ham
1 finely diced carrot
1 finely diced onion
3½ oz (85g) butter
¼ pt (150ml) Madeira

¼ pt (150ml) good stock
1 bay leaf
1 teasp–1 tbs potato flour or arrowroot
4 oz (100g) button mushrooms
salt and pepper

Melt 1 oz (25g) butter in a casserole and gently brown the carrot and onion. Lay the slices of ham on top of the vegetables, pour over the stock and Madeira, add the bay leaf and bring to the simmer on top of the stove. Cover and place in a slow oven (300°F/150°C/ Gas 2) for 30 minutes or longer. Slice and sauté the mushrooms in 1 oz (25g) butter.

Strain the hot liquid from the ham into a small saucepan, thicken lightly with potato flour mixed with a little water and bring to the boil, stirring all the time. Add the mushrooms, correct the seasoning and simmer for 1 minute. Draw off the stove and beat in the remaining 1½ oz (35g) butter to thicken and enrich the sauce. Pour over the ham slices and serve at once.

* Porc à l'Orange

Here we come to one of the elegant boned joints I wrote of earlier, either a loin or carré, which is six to eight chops in one piece and coming from in front of the loin. You can also use pork fillets which will cook rather more quickly. The sauce can be a rich orange gravy which will freeze or can be finished with cream if this suits your menu better.

Ingredients
4–6 people

2–3 lb (900g–1.35kg) loin or carré of pork with most of the fat removed
1 lb (450g) cut up veal or pork bones
1½ oz (35g) butter
a few drops oil
½ lb (225g) carrots
2 tbs brandy

½ pt (300ml) dry white wine
a sprig of thyme
1 bay leaf
3 oranges
salt and pepper
⅓ pt (200ml) double cream (optional)
1 bunch watercress

Bone the pork and trim off all but ½" (1cm) fat, roll and tie, or get the butcher to do this. Heat the butter with a few drops of oil in a deep casserole or frying pan, brown the pork all over, browning the carrots cut in rounds and the bones at the same time. When well browned flame with brandy and add the white wine, thyme and bay leaf. Season well, cover closely and cook in a very moderate oven (325°F/170°C/Gas 3) for about 1¾–2¼ hours or until tender.

Take julienne strips from 2 oranges, blanch for 5 minutes in boiling water, then refresh under the cold tap to set the colour. Squeeze the juice of these two oranges. Cut the peel, pith and skin from the remaining orange and slice. Remove the pork from the oven, cover and keep warm. Strain the sauce (the carrots are delicious and can be picked out and served with the pork or used for soup), return to the pan and add the orange juice and julienne; boil and reduce to about ¼ pt (150ml). Serve like that, or for a richer cream sauce reduce still further to a few tablespoons, then add the cream and boil to a light coating consistency, returning any juices from the waiting pork before pouring over the sliced meat. Surround with half slices of orange, add a bunch of watercress and serve.

∗   Rack of Lamb with Mint and Tarragon Sauce

Here we take a whole trimmed and chined best end of lamb, roast it to perfection, rest it, then carve it into cutlets and serve with a butter-enriched mint and tarragon gravy. A best end is seven cutlets, and you should allow two cutlets per head.

Ingredients

1 best end of lamb with the backbone removed	2 tbs brandy
3–4 oz (75–100g) unsalted or lightly salted butter	6 tbs good strong stock (preferably jellied veal)
1 tbs fresh chopped mint	salt and pepper
1 tbs fresh chopped tarragon or 1 teasp dried tarragon	

Remove the skin and any excess fat from the lamb and expose the ends of the bones to a depth of ½"–1" (1cm–3cm). Remove the cartilaginous tip of the blade bone which you will find tucked into the meat at one end, and score the fat lightly in a criss-cross diamond pattern (or get the butcher to prepare the joint). Roast in a hot oven (400°F/200°C/Gas 6) for 25–30 minutes uncovered and with no added fat. (For two best ends set together and tied as Guards of Honour allow 40–50 minutes.) Rest and keep warm for 15–30 minutes before serving.

Melt 1 oz (25g) butter in a small saucepan and gently cook most of the mint and tarragon for 3–4 minutes. Add the brandy and bubble up, then add the stock, season very lightly and leave to simmer very gently for about half-an-hour. When ready to serve boil up the sauce, remove from the stove and whisk in the remaining mint and tarragon and the softened butter in small pieces. Do not boil again. The sauce should remain amalgamated and creamy.

113

$\mathcal{P}$ ***   Gigot d'Agneau Farci à la Bordelaise

Here the whole leg is boned out and stuffed, quick roasted to seal, cooled completely, then enveloped in a pastry and cooked. The Bordelaise filling of cèpe mushrooms, garlic and parsley is delicious, but I would not use it with English lamb when at its very best, preferring this quite simply roasted.

Ingredients
6–8 people

4 lb (1.8kg) leg of lamb with the shank-bone unbroken if possible (have this boned with the shank bone left as a handle)

Stuffing
¼–½ oz (6–12g) dried cèpe mushrooms
2–3 cloves garlic
3–4 tbs finely chopped parsley
2–4 tbs breadcrumbs
1 teasp fresh or ¼ teasp dried tarragon
a little chervil (optional)
2–3 tbs olive oil
2–3 shallots or very small onions
salt and pepper

Pastry
1 lb (450g) flour
½ lb (225g) butter
2 egg yolks
3 fl oz (75ml) cold water (approx)
½ teasp salt

Pastry. Sift the flour and salt into a bowl, rub in the butter and work up to a stiff paste with the egg yolks and water (in a food processor make half at a time). Rest for several hours or overnight.

Stuffing. Soak the dried mushrooms in tepid water just to cover for 1–2 hours, drain (keep the water for stock or soup) and dice. Cook the finely chopped shallots gently in the oil until golden; add the diced mushroom and fry gently for 3–4 minutes, then add the finely chopped garlic and seasoning. Cover and cook very gently for 5 minutes. Add the herbs and enough breadcrumbs to absorb the oil, and toss over heat for several minutes more.

Lamb. Spread the boned leg with the stuffing, form into a good long shape and sew up, using a large darning needle and button thread and leaving a long end. Tie 2–3 times with string. Roast in a hot oven (425°F/220°C/Gas 7) for 30 minutes, cool, chill and remove string.

Roll the pastry, wrap round the leg, sealing with egg-wash and leaving the bone exposed and the end of the thread out, and decorate the top. Insert a meat thermometer (if used) into the thickest part of the meat. Brush with egg wash and roast in a hot oven (425°F/220°C/Gas 7) for 20–30 minutes to set the pastry, then turn down to moderate (350°F/180°C/Gas 4) and continue to cook for ¾–1¼ hours (155°F/68°C on the meat thermometer for medium or 165°F/73°C for a little more done). Pull out the thread. Rest for 10 minutes only before carving, or the pastry may go soggy.

** Glazed Loin of Lamb with Garlic Sauce

For this dish the loin—which follows on the back from the best end and is plumper—is boned and rolled, roasted to a shiny brown and served with a delicate and creamy garlic sauce. Please don't be afraid of the garlic—it's lovely as long as you use a firm plump head.

Ingredients
4–6 people

2–3 lb (900g–1.35kg) boned loin of lamb
1 clove garlic
a sprig of lovage, lemon thyme or
    rosemary
1 tbs olive oil
1 teasp soy sauce
salt and pepper

Garlic Sauce
12 plump garlic cloves
1/2 pt (300ml) strong lamb, veal or chicken
    stock
a sprig of lovage, lemon thyme or
    rosemary
1/4 pt (150ml) double cream
2–3 teasp potato flour or arrowroot
1/2–1 oz (12–25g) butter
1 tbs finely chopped parsley
salt and pepper

Bone out the loin of lamb if not already done by the butcher, remove the skin, score the fat lightly in a diamond pattern and rub the salt and pepper well into the fat. Roll and tie in 3 or 4 places. Place the meat in a roasting tin with a flattened, unpeeled clove of garlic and a sprig of lovage beneath it. Roast in a hot oven (400°F/200°C/Gas 6) for 1–1½ hours (a reading of 150°F/65°C on a meat roasting thermometer for medium rare and 165°F/72°C for well done). Add a little water or stock to the pan if the juices look like burning, and brush the meat with mixed oil and soy sauce several times towards the end of the cooking time for a good brown finish. Rest for 15–20 minutes before carving.

Garlic Sauce. Toss the garlic cloves, separated but unpeeled, into a saucepan of cold unsalted water, bring to the boil, boil for ½ minute, then drain and peel. Bring to the boil twice more in cold unsalted water, draining each time. Gently simmer the blanched garlic with the lovage in the stock for 20–30 minutes until the garlic is absolutely tender. Liquidise or purée, then sieve and reheat with the combined cream and potato flour. Bring to the boil and simmer for several minutes to thicken, correct the seasoning, cover and keep warm. On serving beat in a little butter and the finely chopped parsley.

Vegetables and Salads

**   Creamed Garlic Potatoes

When you need creamy mashed potatoes for mopping up a good sauce, try these garlic potatoes; the delicacy of the flavour quite belies the number of garlic cloves.

Ingredients
4–6 people

	Garlic Sauce
2½ lb (1.15kg) peeled potatoes	1 head garlic (8–10 cloves)
2 oz (50g) butter	1½ oz (35g) butter
3–4 tbs cream	½ oz (12g) flour
4 tbs chopped parsley	½ pt (300ml) milk
a little milk	salt and pepper
salt and pepper	

Garlic Sauce. Drop the garlic cloves into boiling water; boil for 2 minutes, drain and peel. Melt the butter in a saucepan and cook the garlic very gently, covered, for about 20 minutes, until tender but not brown. Blend in the flour and cook for 2 minutes. Away from heat, beat in the milk and seasoning. Bring to the boil and simmer 1–2 minutes, whisking with a wire whisk. Sieve or liquidise sauce.

Boil the potatoes in salted water, and when tender drain and mash, preferably through a potato ricer or sieve. Beat in the butter, salt and pepper and a little milk. Beat in the garlic sauce, cream and parsley to make a soft purée and serve at once.

    If you want to keep them warm for a while, smooth the top of the potatoes, pour over the garlic sauce and cream, cover closely and stand over a pan of hot water until ready to serve. Then beat the sauce and parsley into the potatoes.

**   Le Véritable Gratin Dauphinois de Fernand Point

This recipe from Fernand Point, the great chef, was created, or so I believe, to take nothing away from his great sauces. It is bland, complementary, and stays firmly in the background, forming no juices to run round your plate.

Ingredients
4–6 people

2½ lb (1.15kg) potatoes (yellow-fleshed varieties for preference)	2 eggs
2 oz (50g) butter	¾ pt (450ml) milk
1 clove garlic	2 tbs double cream
	salt and pepper

Take a shallow fireproof gratin dish and rub with a cut clove of garlic. Salt lightly and butter heavily. Cover with a layer of very thinly sliced potatoes that have been peeled and wiped only. Salt and pepper lightly; continue with the layers of potato and seasoning. Boil the milk, beat the eggs and combine the milk, eggs and cream; pour over the potatoes and finish by covering with little nuts of butter. Start cooking the dish on the stove over a low heat for 5–10 minutes and finish in a slow oven (300°F/150°C/Gas 2) for 30–40 minutes. Serve from the dish still boiling, with several more nuts of butter on top. You can also cook it at a slightly higher temperature (350°F/180°C/Gas 4) without first starting the cooking on the stove. Allow 45–60 minutes.

If making in large quantities, add the egg and milk mixture as you layer the potatoes. If it's poured on top afterwards it sits on the potatoes and they compact into a firm mass underneath.

* **Lemon New Potatoes**

Quite sharp and lemony and nice when you want to do something a bit different with new potatoes.

Ingredients
4–6 people

1½–2 lb (675–900g) small new potatoes	2–3 teasp fresh dill or fennel
1 lemon	salt and pepper
1½ oz (35g) butter	

Scrape the potatoes. Place in a saucepan, cover with lightly salted boiling water and add a strip of lemon rind. Boil until half-cooked, then pour off the water, leaving just enough to cover. Add the juice of a lemon (keeping back a squeeze or two) and finish cooking. Drain and toss in hot butter, season, and finish with chopped dill and the squeeze of lemon juice.

∗∗   Epinards Etuvés au Beurre

Braised spinach, *en branche* or roughly chopped rather than baby-food purée, is always good and keeps warm well. Do remember never to cook spinach in aluminium pots as aluminium reacts with the oxalic acid in spinach and gives that horrid teeth-edgy flavour. Except for very young true spinach (as opposed to perpetual, perennial or spinach beet), I prefer the Italian way of cooking it in plenty of water until it is just cooked, drained, refreshed in cold water, then squeezed out by the handful. If you look into Italian restaurant kitchens you will see a pile of squeezed out spinach balls just waiting to be tossed in butter and re-heated. Spinach will absorb a lot of butter so do be generous.

Ingredients
4–6 people

2–2½ lb (900g–1.15kg) fresh or 1½ lb (675g) frozen spinach
3–4 oz (75g–100g) butter

3–4 tbs cream
salt, pepper and nutmeg

Fresh Spinach. Wash really well and remove any tough stalks. Throw into plenty of boiling salted water in a non-aluminium pan, boil until just tender, drain and refresh under the cold tap; squeeze out moisture and chop roughly.

Frozen Spinach. Thaw, squeeze out only a little water and chop roughly.

Melt the butter in a non-aluminium pan until sizzling, add the spinach and season. Simmer very gently until tender (watch that it does not catch). Allow quite a lot longer for the frozen spinach than for the fresh. Remove the lid and boil up if the moisture has not all gone, add the cream and keep warm or re-heat. It seems to taste even better re-heated, and the buttery flavour really comes when all the moisture has gone.

∗∗   Petits Pois à la Française

A very good way of cooking most peas, and they will keep warm quite happily. Made with real *petits pois* it is excellent for a dinner party, though do remember they have a little rich juice which you don't want running around your plate mixing with other sauces, so serve with simply cooked dishes or separately in the French fashion.

Ingredients
4–6 people

1½ lb (675g) shelled peas or thawed deep frozen petits pois
1 large head shredded lettuce
1–2 tbs sugar
12 halved spring onions

3 oz (75g) butter
¼ pt (150ml) water
½ teasp salt
pepper

Melt the butter in a casserole, add the onions and lettuce and toss. Add all the remaining ingredients (but only half the water if you use frozen peas) and simmer gently for 20–30 minutes, tasting after 20 minutes. Add more water if it all evaporates or boil fast with the lid off if there is too much. There should be a little syrupy sauce left. This dish will keep warm very happily.

** Chou Rouge aux Marrons

Long slow cooking makes this French winter dish. Very good with tinned chestnuts or even without any when you can't get them or can't face shelling them.

Ingredients
4–6 people

2 lb (900g) red cabbage	¼ pt (150ml) strong red wine
¼ lb (100g) very thick slices of streaky bacon	¼ pt (150ml) good stock
	2–3 tbs wine vinegar
2 oz (50g) goose or pork fat or butter	2 tbs redcurrant jelly
2 large sliced onions	16–20 chestnuts
3 peeled and diced cooking apples	salt and pepper
1 clove garlic	
1 bay leaf	
nutmeg	
ground cloves	

Gently fry the diced bacon and onion in the fat in a large (preferably earthenware) casserole. Thinly slice the cabbage, removing the core, stir in and turn until every slice glistens. Add the apples, chopped garlic and bay leaf and season with pepper, nutmeg, ground cloves and plenty of salt. Pour over the wine, stock and vinegar and simmer for about 1½ hours on the stove or in a very moderate oven (325°F/170°C/Gas 3).

To skin chestnuts. I have tried every method and find this the best way. Cut halfway round the skin of the chestnuts on the rounded side and drop a few at a time into boiling water; boil for 3 minutes and remove one at a time to peel off the outer and inner skins together. If you get it just right you should be able literally to squeeze them and they will pop out of their shells.

Add the chestnuts to the cabbage with the redcurrant jelly and a little more stock if needed and cook slowly for another 1–1½ hours until the chestnuts are tender and the liquid all but gone. Correct the seasoning and serve.

This dish reheats beautifully and often tastes even better on the second occasion.

**   Choux-Fleurs Sauce Verte

Handsome and arresting from the colour point of view, this dish must be finished at the last minute or the colour goes drab. But beware of the smell of cooking if your extractor system is not up to standard.

Ingredients
4–6 people

1 firm cauliflower
2 oz (50g) butter
1½ oz (35g) flour
¾ pt (450ml) milk
2–3 tbs double cream
1 bunch watercress
salt and pepper

Melt 1½oz (35g) of the butter in a saucepan, add the flour and cook for 2–3 minutes over moderate heat. Draw the pan off the stove and when the sizzling ceases add all the milk, then return to the heat and bring to the boil, whisking hard. Season, add the cream and simmer for 2–3 minutes. Keep warm, covered, until needed.

Pick over the watercress, discarding the tough stalks, then throw into a pan of boiling salted water and blanch for 4–5 minutes. Drain into a sieve and refresh under the cold tap to set the colour. Set aside.

Wash the cauliflower and break into large florets. Boil these gently in salt water for 10–15 minutes until just tender but still crisp. Drain and arrange in a serving dish.

Liquidise the hot sauce with the watercress until it is a beautiful green, add the rest of the butter, pour over the cauliflower and serve at once.

*   Potato and Celeriac Purée

A warming winter dish that my family really enjoys.

Ingredients
4–6 people

2–3 potatoes
1–1½ lb (450–675g) celeriac root
2–4 oz (50–100g) butter

up to ¼ pt (150ml) cream or milk
salt, pepper and chopped parsley

Boil the potatoes in their skins. Slice, skin and cube the celeriac. Simmer in salt water until nearly tender (about 10 minutes), drain well and return to the pan with the butter. Leave over very gentle heat for 10 minutes or so. Peel and slice the potatoes and add to the celeriac. Mash well together, adding enough cream to make a firm texture. Season and add the parsley. Serve at once or, to keep warm, smooth the top, pour over a little cream, cover closely and stand in a pan of hot water. Beat in the cream on serving.

** Croquettes de Maïs

Crispy deep-fried croquettes with a creamy sweetcorn filling. Prepare ahead and keep warm or reheat.

Ingredients
4–6 people

To egg and breadcrumb

12 oz (350g) whole kernel sweetcorn	2 whole eggs
2 oz (50g) butter	1 tbs oil
2 oz (50g) flour	flour
¾ pt (450ml) milk (heated and infused for 10 minutes with a slice of onion, a blade of mace, 5 peppercorns, a bay leaf and several parsley stalks)	about 6 oz (175g) stale white breadcrumbs
	deep fat for frying (optional)
2 egg yolks	
1 tbs finely chopped parsley	
salt and pepper	

Fresh or frozen corn needs boiling or steaming for 10–15 minutes; tinned corn is ready to use.

Melt the butter in a saucepan, add the flour and cook gently for 2–3 minutes. Draw the pan off the stove, wait for the sizzling to cease and add the strained milk. Return to the heat, bring to the boil whisking with a wire whisk, and simmer for 1–2 minutes. Remove from the heat, beat in the egg yolks one at a time and simmer for 1 minute before stirring in the corn, parsley and seasoning. Pour into a greased 1" (2–3cm) deep dish, cover with cling film and leave to cool; chill until firm.

Beat the two whole eggs with the oil and seasoning in a soup plate, place some flour on another plate and the breadcrumbs on a third. Form the chilled mixture into cork-shaped croquettes, roll in flour, then in egg, and finally in breadcrumbs; pat the crumbs on firmly and lay on greaseproof paper. Preferably leave for an hour or so before frying.

Either deep fry a few at a time in oil heated to 360°F/180°C or shallow fry, turning once. The croquettes should be a good brown. Drain on kitchen paper and serve at once or keep hot for up to an hour. Or they can be fried in advance, then re-heated for 30–40 minutes in a moderate oven (350°F/180°C/Gas 4).

*   Watercress and Orange Salad

This crisp watercress and orange salad goes very well with or after Roast Duck or Lamb.

Ingredients
4–6 people

3 bunches good fresh watercress
2 oranges
$\frac{1}{2}$–1 oz (12–25g) toasted and skinned
   hazelnuts
1 teasp Dijon mustard
grated rind of $\frac{1}{2}$ orange
1 tbs wine vinegar
4 tbs good olive oil
salt and pepper

With a sharp knife cut off all peel, pith and skin from the oranges and cut the segments out from their skins. Place the salt, pepper, mustard and grated orange rind in a salad bowl with the vinegar, stir well to dissolve the salt and gradually beat in the oil. Combine the washed and dried watercress with the orange segments in the bowl, toss well until every leaf glistens and scatter with the very roughly chopped hazelnuts. Serve at once.

Puddings

✳✳   Hazelnut Torte

Meringue and hazelnuts combine to make this airy creation sandwiched with raspberries and cream.

Ingredients
4–6 people

4 egg whites
9 oz (250g) vanilla castor sugar
   with extra to sweeten cream
½ teasp white wine vinegar

4 oz (100g) ground hazelnuts
½ pt (300ml) cream
12 oz (350g) raspberries
icing sugar

Grease and flour two 9″ (24cm) sandwich tins and line the bases with circles of Bakewell paper. Whisk the egg whites until just holding a peak, then gradually whisk in the sugar, beating all the time until the mixture is very stiff and shiny. Fold in the vinegar and hazelnuts. Spread the mixture evenly in the tins and bake in a moderately hot oven (375°F/190°C/Gas 5) for 30–40 minutes. Turn out on to wire racks and cool.

    Whisk the cream and sweeten lightly with the vanilla sugar. Pile two-thirds of the cream on to the torte, cover with about half the raspberries and top with the second meringue layer. Sprinkle with the icing sugar and decorate with the remaining cream. Liquidise the remaining raspberries with icing sugar to sweeten, sieve and serve in a jug to pour over the torte.

    Fill the torte at least three hours before serving to make cutting easier.

𝓕 ✳✳   Extravagant Chocolate Mousse

One of the very best and richest of chocolate mousses because, let's face it, people love a really rich chocolate pudding.

Ingredients
4–6 people

6 tbs strong coffee
4 tbs brandy
8 oz (225g) best dark chocolate

2 oz (50g) castor vanilla sugar
¾ pt (450ml) cream
¼ teasp vanilla essence

Put the coffee, brandy and broken chocolate in a bowl and place over a saucepan of hot water to melt. Stir until well blended, then beat in all but 1 tbs vanilla sugar. Stir until glossy and leave to cool. Whisk the cream until thick and beat in the remaining sugar and vanilla essence. Fold in the cold chocolate mixture very carefully and thoroughly and spoon into individual glasses or a bowl. Cover and chill. This can be made 24 hours ahead.

✱✱ Strawberry Soufflé

In summer use garden-fresh berries or in winter pots of strawberry purée from the freezer.

Ingredients
4–6 people

1 lb (450g) strawberries or ½ pt (300ml)   3 tbs cold water
   purée   ½ pt (300ml) cream
3 oz (75g) castor sugar or to taste   3 egg whites
juice of ½ lemon
1 tbs (½ oz pkt) gelatine

Tie an oiled greaseproof collar round a 1 pt (600ml) soufflé dish. Sprinkle the gelatine on to the cold water in a cup, leave to soak for several minutes, then stand in a pan of hot water to melt. Purée the strawberries with the sugar and lemon juice and add the melted gelatine. Fold in the cream, whipped until just holding its shape, followed by the egg whites whipped until they too just hold a peak, and turn into the prepared soufflé dish. Chill 3–4 hours or more before serving.

   Melted gelatine added to a very cold purée can set very quickly or even go stringy, so have your cream and egg whites ready whipped, your gelatine quite warm and your strawberry purée not too icy cold (though the best flavour is achieved from barely thawed berries). If made too far ahead, the enzymes in the strawberry seem to react with the gelatine and it may thin out.

F ✱✱ Soufflé au Citron

Lemon soufflé is often served, but this does not mean that it's still not one of the very best puddings. This version is sharp and tangy and not too firmly set.

Ingredients
4–6 people

3 eggs   1 tbs (½ oz pkt) gelatine
4 oz (100g) sugar   3–4 tbs water
2 lemons (5 tbs juice)   ⅓ pt (200ml) cream
grated rind of 1 lemon   some flaked browned almonds

Sprinkle the gelatine on to the water in a cup and leave to soak 4–5 minutes. Stand in a saucepan of hot water until dissolved. Put the egg yolks, lemon juice, rind and sugar (all but one tablespoonful) in a bowl standing over a pan of hot water and whisk for 5–10 minutes, until thick, pale and golden. Remove and whisk 5 minutes more with the bowl standing in iced water. Whisk the cream until just holding its shape. Whisk the egg whites to a soft peak and beat in the remaining sugar. Add the gelatine to the yolks, then fold in the cream followed by the whites. Pour into a glass bowl or soufflé dish and chill. Decorate with flaked browned almonds.

This is just firm enough to stand up if placed in a soufflé dish with an oiled paper collar which is then peeled off when the soufflé is set. But it won't bounce round your plate like an india-rubber ball!

𝒫 ✳   **Prunes in Claret**

Do not despise a bowl of huge and shiny black prunes in a rich wine syrup for deep midwinter. These wrinkled fellows are far removed in flavour and size from our nursery memory, and are greatly appreciated with a jug of thick pouring cream.

Ingredients
4–6 people

1 lb (450g) best large prunes
¾ pt (450ml) water (approx)
1 vanilla pod
1 lemon

3 oz (75g) sugar
¼ pt (150ml) red wine (claret for choice)

Soak the prunes in the cold water with the grated rind of a lemon and the vanilla pod for 12–24 hours. Add the sugar and cook very gently for twenty minutes. Add the wine and continue to simmer until the prunes are very soft and the juice syrupy and delicious. Pour into a glass dish and serve chilled with cream.

𝓕 ✳✳   **Spiced Pears**

A pretty dish of whole pears in a spiced and lemony syrup. Pears freeze extremely well and are available most of the year.

Ingredients
4–6 people

6–8 pears
8 oz (225g) sugar
¼ pt (150ml) water

1 lemon
2 cloves
¼ stick cinnamon

Take julienne strips of lemon rind and blanch in boiling water for 10 minutes. Melt the sugar in the water and boil for 1–2 minutes; add the lemon juice, julienne strips, cloves and cinnamon. Peel the pears, leaving on the stalks, and poach in the syrup until tender. Remove the pears to a bowl, boil down the syrup until very heavy, remove the cloves and cinnamon and pour over the pears. Serve well chilled with thick cream.

✲✲   Caramel Oranges

When oranges are at their best, this makes one of my favourite late winter puddings. It is always at this season that one most enjoys these warm fruits; perhaps it's the thought of hot summers that they bring.

Ingredients
4–6 people

5–6 good juicy oranges	¼ pt (150ml) water
4 oz (100g) sugar	2 tbs Kirsch or 1 teasp orange flower water

Chill the oranges in the fridge for 1–2 hours to make peeling easier. Place the sugar and 4 tbs water in a small saucepan and heat gently, stirring until the sugar dissolves. Stop stirring, turn up the heat and boil fast until the caramel is a deep gold. Pour out a little on to greased tinfoil to crunch up when cold. Boil the remaining water and add to the rest of the caramel on the stove (beware—it splutters). Boil until all the caramel dissolves.

Peel the oranges with a very sharp knife, removing the peel, pith and skin. Slice into very thin rounds, place in a glass bowl, sprinkle with the Kirsch or orange flower water and pour over the cool caramel syrup. Leave to macerate for 1–2 hours and serve topped with the crunched up caramel.

F ✲✲   Glace aux Pruneaux

Here we use a Crème Patissière base which is quite quick to make, and the result is absolutely smooth on the tongue. The really succulent prunes (pruneaux d'Agen are best) are chopped, macerated and folded in, with some reserved to spoon over. Eaten in a converted Gothic chapel, now a restaurant, to the sound of Bach booming in the background and with a sweet dessert wine as its partner, it was something to be remembered for ever.

Ingredients
4–6 people

	Crème Patissière
¾ lb (350g) best prunes	2½ oz (60g) vanilla sugar
⅓ pt (200ml) sweet Loire wine	3 egg yolks
3–4 tbs brandy or grape ratafia from the	1 oz (25g) flour
Loire	⅓ pt (200ml) milk
⅓ pt (200ml) double cream	¼ oz (6g) butter
	1 vanilla pod
	few drops of vanilla essence.

Stone the prunes and cut into 3–4 pieces. Macerate in the brandy and wine for 3–4 hours.

Crème Patissière. Heat the milk with the vanilla pod until scalded. Beat the yolks, sugar and flour together for 3–4 minutes until thick and pale yellow. Gradually beat in the hot milk (rescue the vanilla pod, wash, dry out and pop back in your vanilla sugar jar). Pour the mixture into a heavy enamel or stainless steel pan (aluminium discolours egg sauces) and bring to the boil over moderate heat, whisking all the time. Simmer over low heat for 2–3 minutes, still whisking, to cook the flour. Remove from the heat, beat in the butter and a few drops of vanilla, turn into a bowl, cover closely with cling film and chill.

Whip the cream, whisking in a little unabsorbed syrup from the fruit, and fold into the cold Crème Patissière with half the macerated fruit. Turn into a dish and freeze. Mellow for ¾–1 hour in the fridge before serving with the remaining fruit and syrup spooned over.

F * **Brown Bread Ice Cream**

This old English recipe needs good wholemeal breadcrumbs, crisp, dried and caramelised with sugar. My grandfather used to speak of it, but it was only many years later that I found a good recipe and tasted it myself.

Ingredients
4–6 people

4 oz (100g) coarse, stale breadcrumbs from
    wholemeal or granary loaf
1½ oz (35g) butter
2 oz (50g) brown sugar
½ pt (300ml) cream

3 oz (75g) vanilla sugar
2 tbs brandy
6 tbs Crème de Cacao or Crème de Noyau
    or rum

Melt the butter in a wide frying pan, add the breadcrumbs and toss and turn over moderate heat until they begin to brown. Add the sugar and continue to fry and stir until brown and caramelised (this takes a while). Remove from the heat. Whip the cream, adding the vanilla sugar, brandy and Crème de Cacao, turn into a tinfoil container or bowl and freeze until it starts to thicken. Fold in the cooled crumbs and freeze.

    Allow up to 1 hour to mellow in the fridge before serving. Hot chopped ginger in syrup is very good with this ice cream.

T**   Tea Ice Cream

This gets everyone guessing as it has an elusive flavour that one somehow knows but can't quite place.

Ingredients
4–6 people

5 tbs tea (preferably Jackson's Earl Grey)	4 oz (100g) castor sugar
¾ pt (450ml) boiling water	½ teasp vanilla essence
½ pt (300ml) milk	½ pt (300ml) double cream
4 egg yolks	2 egg whites

Pour the boiling water over the tea and infuse for 5 minutes, then strain. Whisk the egg yolks with the sugar for 5 minutes until pale, thick and forming a ribbon. Mix the tea and milk and bring to the boil; add to the egg yolks very gradually, at first drop by drop, then in a thin stream, whisking hard. Return to a heavy stainless steel or enamel saucepan and cook very gently over low heat, stirring, until the custard coats the spoon (do not scald or boil) or cook the custard in a bowl over a pan of hot water. Add the vanilla essence, cool, and freeze to a stiff mush, whisking several times. Whip the cream and fold in. Finally whip the egg whites until just holding a peak and fold in. Freeze until firm but do not serve over-frozen.

Allow up to 1 hour to mellow in the fridge before serving.

T*   Espresso Coffee Ice

Strong dark coffee ice, bitter and refreshing at the end of a rich meal.

Ingredients
4–6 people

1 pt (600ml) boiling water	4 oz (100g) vanilla sugar
2 oz (50g) finely ground espresso coffee	
¼ pt (150ml) cream	

Put the coffee in a jug, pour on the boiling water, leave for 5 minutes and strain through a coffee filter or muslin. Alternatively make the coffee by the filter method. Add the sugar to the coffee and stir to dissolve. When cool pour into shallow dishes (tinfoil containers are good) and freeze, stirring with a fork several times.

When frozen, process in a food processor or beat until whipped very pale and mousse-like. Fold in the cream, whipped until it is just holding its shape, and spoon into glasses or a container. Freeze for several hours.

Mellow in the fridge for ½ hour before serving with little biscuits and topped with a sprinkle of fine ground coffee.

Variation. This ice can be made without any cream as a very refreshing sorbet.

128

F ∗ Elderflower Sorbet

Make this sorbet in early summer when the hedgerows are heavy with creamy elder-flowers, and have everyone guessing at the elusive flavour. You can keep it in the freezer for months without losing any of its flavour.

Ingredients
4–6 people

1 pt (600ml) water	3 lemons (rind and juice)
8 oz (225g) granulated sugar	3–4 heads of elderflower

Combine the sugar and water in a very clean pan and heat gently, stirring until the sugar dissolves. Boil hard for 5–6 minutes. Draw off the stove, throw in the elderflower heads and the pared lemon rinds and leave to infuse for 2–3 hours. Strain the liquid and add lemon juice to taste.

Freeze, beating the edges into the middle as they thicken. When the whole lot is set quite firm, process in a food processor or beat hard until soft, smooth and light. Turn into a bowl or container and re-freeze. Serve with little biscuits or slices of sponge cake.

Mellow in the fridge for ½ hour before serving.

Savouries

∗∗ Chicken Livers in Bacon

One of the very best savouries, and an easy one for the cook-hostess.

Ingredients
4–6 people

6–8 slices thin-cut streaky bacon	skewers or cocktail sticks
4–6 oz (100g–175g) chicken livers	croûtes of toast or fried bread

Pick the chicken livers over very carefully, removing any threads and green-tinged flesh, and cut each into 4–6 pieces. De-rind the bacon and stretch the rasher with the back of a knife. Cut the rashers in half if long enough and roll each piece round a bit of chicken liver, stick on to skewers or 3–4 to a cocktail stick, and lay on a rack in a small roasting tin. Cook for 10–15 minutes in a hot oven (425°F/220°C/Gas 7). Or they can be grilled, turning once or twice. Remove skewers or sticks, serve 3–4 per head, sizzling hot, on croûtes of crisp toast or fried bread, or with each one stuck with a toothpick for handing round.

** Cheese Aigrettes

Only recently did I discover that these could be deep-fried and would keep warm for a couple of hours. So into the repertoire went the recipe.

Ingredients
4–6 people

2 oz (50g) butter
¼ pt (150ml) water
4 oz (100g) 'strong' flour
4 eggs (not larger than No. 3)
4–6 oz (100–175g) strong cheese (half
    Parmesan, half Gruyère or Cheddar)
1 teasp Dijon mustard
paprika
½ teasp salt
pepper

deep fat for frying

Place the chopped-up butter, water and salt in a saucepan and heat. Once the butter has melted bring to the boil. Draw off the heat, tip in all the sifted flour at once and stir until a ball of dough forms and comes away from the side of the pan. Cook over moderate heat for 1–2 minutes, stirring, until a skin forms on the bottom of the pan. Remove from the heat and cool for 5–10 minutes. Beat in the eggs one at a time, beating hard after each addition; the mixture must remain firm enough to sit up on the spoon, so add the last egg gradually if you feel the mixture is getting too soft—it should be smooth and shiny. Or turn into a food processor, add all the eggs and process for 30–45 seconds until satiny smooth. Beat in the grated cheese, mustard and pepper.

    Heat the deep fat to 375°F/190°C or until just hazing, then add very small teaspoonfuls of the mixture, not too many at a time, and cook until puffed up and crisp and a good brown colour. Drain on kitchen paper, sprinkle with salt and paprika, spread out on a dish and keep hot until ready to serve. Serve piled up and watch them disappear like snow off a dyke. This makes plenty (the batches will take quite a long time to fry) but they always all disappear!

Informal Lunch and Supper Parties

The dishes in this section cover a wide range of entertaining, from looking after friends who come to lunch, casual parties for anything between four and twelve people, day-to-day family entertaining when you're not having to make a great impression, or late at night after the cinema or theatre. Perhaps you wish to entertain in this way because you're too busy for anything more elaborate but you still want to see your friends; or you may entertain informally because you find it easier, more relaxing and enjoyable. I certainly do, and I think it seems appropriate to the general trend of life these days.

All our informal entertaining takes place in the kitchen (or out of doors if we're lucky) because we are fortunate enough to have a large and comfortable kitchen with my grandmother's old pine kitchen table that will seat twelve at a pinch. I love the kitchen as the hub of the house. Ours has to be that because it is in the centre of the house, so one seems to find oneself in it quite naturally, and in winter the Aga makes it warm and welcoming. I like the fact that the children come in to do their homework, play trains under the table or make models on it; others may sit on a stool and pick at olives or top and tail the beans and talk to me, the cook.

Whenever I'm asked to advise on the layout of a new kitchen I design it so that wherever possible the cook is looking out into the room for most of the time as she works instead of finding herself staring at the wall or a cupboard. This allows one to cook while watching who slips their supper to the dogs or pinches the last chip from someone else's plate. It saves cutting off fingers while talking over one's shoulder to friends, and gives one an altogether more enjoyable, less trapped feeling. There can be no escaping the fact that

131

quite a lot of time must be spent in the kitchen, but if one does not feel banished or missing the party how much easier this is to bear.

Table-laying must be easy and quick, and on these occasions the effect is not achieved by polished glass and silver or precision placing but rather from bright cheerful colours and bold design. I find two candlesticks with huge fat candles that last for a couple of years save on cost and time. Orange wool mats look bright and warm on our pine table, especially with the white dishes and brown earthenware casseroles I'm so fond of. I made my mats cheaply and simply by cutting heavy woollen cloth into rectangles, fringing the edges, then machining round with a zig-zag or very small stitch. The first lot lasted for twelve years before the mice ate them.

Sometimes one is pressed for time, and the cooking of supper and table-laying must go on after the guests have arrived. I know some people hate anyone to come into the kitchen or help, but I think visitors prefer on the whole to talk to you while you make the soup if you appear to enjoy their being there; so why not get them to lay the table, wash the salad or peel the potatoes? Whatever you do, give them a positive job and the right tool to do it with.

Soft lights in the kitchen are a must for a relaxed and easy atmosphere, so if your kitchen is lit with fluorescent strips but is big enough to entertain in, find some other form of light to eat by on these occasions such as candles, camping gas lights, oil lamps or whatever. For goodness' sake don't suddenly turn on a bright light in the middle of supper and have everyone blinking like startled owls caught in the headlights of a car. Dimmers are extremely effective in kitchen and dining-room.

Suitable dishes for informal entertaining are very varied and you have far more choice than for formal dinners or buffet parties. I'm afraid I'm always experimenting on my guests and making them my guinea-pigs, but they don't really seem to mind. If we are just back from a trip abroad they may find themselves with a completely Italian, French or South African evening, and they may have to criticise a dish and give advice on how they think it could be improved and will have to say truthfully whether or not they liked it. As always, the selection of the right dish for the occasion is the key to success, and hence the need to have a large repertoire at your finger tips, including lots of dishes that can be kept ready in the freezer. Your whole meal may pivot on your use of some ingredients that you have ready for use; if your spinach patch is about to go to seed, be sure to have Oeufs Florentine instead of rushing out to buy chicken or something expensive. A carefully put together meal with something a little unusual or different can be much more successful than something conventional but more expensive. British cooking has traditionally relied on fresh and high-quality ingredients simply and carefully cooked, but because these days we cannot always find the quality we should like, or have the time to watch over the cooking, we may now have to use a different approach. But let us not depart totally from our great tradition.

Sometimes in the informal surroundings we are talking about we feel like entertaining in the French style with lots of courses, and it's not nearly as hard work as you might imagine. When we stay at our cottage in France during the summer we eat in this way, mainly to please the children, who are terrible course-snobs. So for supper I usually produce something like a *saucisson sec* with olives and radishes followed by Artichoke

Vinaigrette. Then a main course and salad, a cheese board and fruit. The same plates are kept for the first four courses and knives and forks are kept throughout in true French style. I don't find this any more work. *Saucisson* takes moments to slice, the artichokes are boiled ahead in the early morning, leaving only the vinaigrette to make, and the main course does not have to be too substantial. Dress the salad, assemble the cheese with the aid of a few fig leaves picked from outside the back door and laid on a round wicker tray and bring out the fruit basket. Lashings of bread from our wonderful old mill bakery avoids anything as banal as potatoes, and everyone feels truly on holiday, eating really well off the best that France has to offer with no great effort for the cook. To translate this to England takes a little imagination but is often very rewarding. From your summer garden you might start with Courgettes à la Grecque, then pâté, a simple main course, French beans in garlic butter served separately, a crisp salad with sorrel and herbs and a shallot dressing, cheese and fresh fruit or a pudding.

On the other hand it is also worth considering one-dish courses such as Cassoulet, Potato and Ham Gratin or Lasagne Vincigras. They need nothing but a salad to follow, and you can finish off with fruit, a sorbet or a light pudding. Simple yet satisfying, as was yet another approach I was offered the other day. This was a bowl of new potatoes, boiled in their skins, accompanied by large bowls of cottage cheese, sour cream, lots of chopped chives and sea salt. Delicious and unusual if you can only find some tasty potatoes like Fir Apple, Vanessa or Desirée.

It is often the small details that highlight a meal and lift it out of the everyday—for instance, a few slices of really good salami or *saucisson* with the apéritif. Never be fobbed off with that pink Danish substitute, for only the best with its fabulous honey flavours will do. It will keep for weeks in the fridge ready for slicing, and when produced with some good olives and crunchy radishes will set everybody off in the right frame of mind. I had some puff pastry crescents left from months before which I had despaired of ever getting rid of; heated to a crisp buttery sizzle and served with ice-cold Guacamole, they really made our supper. Heart-shaped croûtes of fried bread made by the dozen when you have a loaf of stale white bread and frozen till you need them, then reheated and served around a dish like Coq au Vin, make it that much more special, as would those same pastry crescents in a creamy sauce. Bought rolls brushed with egg and scattered with sesame or poppy seed or rock salt and caraway and heated in the oven always taste good and usually evoke appreciative comment. Better still, of course, make a big batch of your own rolls for the freezer and reheat from frozen with any of these toppings.

Sesame in particular goes well with Middle Eastern and Mediterranean dishes, while poppy seed or salt and caraway are excellent with German or Dutch dishes like Herring Salad, Dill Cucumber Salad, pâtés and sausages. The warm smell of poppy seed rolls at breakfast with hot coffee, butter and honey or jam makes the weekend worth waiting for.

Whatever tricks you use or whatever recipes you choose, the idea of informal entertaining is to make your guests happy and enable you to enjoy yourself without having to do too much hard work. Instead of the cooking perfection of haute cuisine and top-quality ingredients (although the latter should always be your aim at whatever level), we are looking for good food that is easy to cook, possibly robust and gutsy, frequently from the freezer if that makes it easier – but always enjoyable.

First Courses

T **   **Smoked Haddock Chowder**

A soup that's almost a meal; use more fish, potato and a handful of peas to make it a spoon-standing, one-course supper dish. I often make a thick version for the freezer and add more stock on thawing if I want it as a first-course soup.

Ingredients
4–6 people

1 lb (450g) smoked haddock fillet	1 teasp curry powder
2 pts (1.2l) chicken stock or water and	1 oz (25g) flour
stock-cubes	1 tbs oatmeal
1 bay leaf	½ pt (300ml) milk
a good pinch mace	¼ pt (150ml) cream (optional)
1 finely chopped onion	2 tbs parsley
1 stick diced celery	2 tbs dry sherry
2–3 peeled and diced potatoes	salt and pepper
2 oz (50g) butter	

Combine the skinned haddock in a saucepan with pepper, the bay leaf, mace and the chicken stock or water and cubes. Bring slowly to the boil and simmer for 5 minutes or until the fish will just flake. Flake the fish and set aside. In another large saucepan melt the butter and gently fry the onion and celery until golden, add the curry powder and flour and cook 2–3 minutes longer. Remove from the heat and wait for the sizzling to cease, then strain in the hot fish stock and bring to the boil, whisking hard and sprinkling on the oatmeal. Simmer for 10 minutes before adding the diced potato and flaked fish. Cook for 6–8 minutes or until the potatoes are tender. Add the milk and cream, correct the seasoning and heat through. Stir in the sherry and serve sprinkled with chopped parsley.

*   **Gazpacho**

I feel this iced soup from Spain should always be thin and refreshing with tiny cubes of the vegetables to stir in. So often recipes tell you to make a thick vegetable porridge, which may be how they make it in some provinces but I've never had it like that and it can't be so refreshing. On a beach in Northern Spain a huge and jovial Spanish family at the next table in the taverna kept passing us over huge wedges of thick potato and garlic omelette and gazpacho, pale pink and thin as water in a huge glass demijohn; my goodness, it was refreshing!

Ingredients
4–6 people

1½ lb (675g) tomatoes—unless they are
    sweet and summer-ripe use a 15-oz
    (400g) tin and 2–3 fresh tomatoes
1 cucumber
½–1 clove garlic
½ onion (preferably mild or Spanish)
1 green pepper

2 crustless slices brown bread
2 tbs wine vinegar
3 tbs olive oil
up to ¾ pt (450ml) iced water
salt and pepper

Place the bread in a food processor or liquidiser and crumb. Add the oil, vinegar, chopped onion, half the de-seeded pepper, ¾ of the cucumber, all but 2–3 tomatoes and the garlic. Process and add up to ½ pt (300ml) iced water. Strain the soup and season. Add the remaining water until the soup is light, fresh and with a good flavour. Serve very well chilled, with the remaining vegetables diced and handed in separate bowls.

F ** Spicy Walnut Soup

A most unusual soup with yoghurt, walnuts and fenugreek. It freezes well and also gives you a chance to use a sprig of curry plant should you grow it in your garden.

Ingredients
4–6 people

2 oz (50g) walnuts
2 finely chopped onions
2 oz (50g) butter
2 teasp ground fenugreek
1 clove garlic
1 oz (25g) flour

1½ pts (900ml) chicken stock
1 pt (600ml) yoghurt
1 teasp cornflour
2–3 sprigs curry plant (optional)
salt and pepper

Chop the walnuts medium fine in a food processor or liquidiser. Fry the onions in butter to a good golden brown, add the flour and fenugreek and cook for 3–4 minutes. Add the finely chopped garlic, chicken stock and walnuts and bring to the boil, whisking hard. Season. Add 2–3 sprigs aromatic curry plant if available and simmer gently for 10–15 minutes. Whisk the cornflour and yoghurt together (the cornflour stops the yoghurt from curdling). Whisk the hot soup into the yoghurt, return all to the pan (fish out the sprigs of curry plant) and bring very slowly to the simmer, stirring. Simmer for 2–3 minutes before serving.

$\mathcal{PF}$ *   # Anna's Bortsch

When Anna, a Polish friend, set out to show me how to make Bortsch, we had to tour all round Edinburgh to find the dried mushrooms she said were essential. The secret is to balance the smoky bacon flavour with the sweet beetroot and sour apples. Occasionally I have smoked some bacon rashers in my little smoker when I could not buy it smoked.

Ingredients
6 people

2½ pts (1.5l) good duck, beef or ham stock
2–3 raw grated beetroot
1 large or 2 small cooking apples, peeled, cored and chopped
1 finely chopped onion

2–3 bits of dried cèpe mushrooms soaked in tepid water for ½ hour, then chopped
2–3 oz (50–75g) diced smoked bacon
a little vinegar to taste
salt and pepper
1 small carton sour cream

Place everything, except the sour cream, in a pan (include the mushroom water, but watch out for sand) and simmer for 1½ hours or more. Rectify the flavourings; if the apples are not very sharp add more vinegar. It should be a happy blend of smoky, sweet and sour. Another beetroot grated in 20 minutes from the end keeps the colour bright. Serve strained for parties, full of bits for a rustic supper, and always topped with sour cream or cream soured with lemon juice.

$\mathcal{P}$ *   # Zeviche

This Mexican dish of fresh fish, diced and marinated in lime or lemon juice for up to twenty-four hours, produces succulent cubes of firm cooked-looking fish, and is well worth trying.

Ingredients
4–6 people

1 lb (450g) raw fresh haddock, turbot or firm white fish
2–3 lemons or 3–4 limes
3–4 large tomatoes
1 large avocado pear

1 small green pepper
1 tbs white wine vinegar
3 tbs olive oil
chopped parsley or fresh coriander leaves
salt and pepper

Skin, bone and cut the raw fish into 1" (2–3cm) cubes, season with salt and pepper, lay in a shallow earthenware, china or glass dish and cover with lemon juice. Marinate for 6–24 hours until opaque white and looking like cooked fish. Chop the green pepper small and sprinkle over the fish with the chopped parsley, oil and vinegar. Skin, de-seed and slice the tomatoes. Surround the fish with slices of tomato and slices of avocado brushed with lemon juice to prevent discolouration and serve with brown bread and butter. A little raw onion or fresh chilli can be chopped over the fish if you like.

P * ## Herring Salad

This salt herring salad from South Africa is useful because you can buy salt herrings from a delicatessen and keep them for a week or so in the fridge. The salad itself can be made up several days ahead.

Ingredients
4–6 people

2 salt herrings (filleted and soaked for 24 hours in milk)	3–4 tbs tomato ketchup
1 small mild onion	1 tbs tomato purée
2 eating apples	1 tbs wine vinegar
2 large pickled dill cucumbers	1–2 tbs sugar
	pepper

Fillet and soak the salt herring in milk for 24 hours. Drain and cut the fillets in small pieces, dice the apples and cucumber and slice the onion very finely. Combine the tomato ketchup, tomato purée, sugar, vinegar and pepper to make a dressing. Stir in the herring, apple and vegetables. Chill for 2–12 hours and serve as a first course or part of a mixed Hors d'Oeuvre. Diced potato and beetroot can also be added.

F ** ## Pâté de Foie de Volaille

A chicken liver pâté which is not harsh or too strong in flavour. It freezes well, being rich and creamy, but do thaw it really well and serve at room temperature for the maximum creaminess and full flavour. A little goes a long way, and it's well worth having a few small pots handy.

Ingredients
6 people

½ lb (225g) chicken livers	5 oz (125g) butter
1 small onion, finely chopped	¼ pt (150ml) cream
1 clove garlic	1 tbs sherry
1 tbs fresh herbs (parsley, thyme, chervil tarragon, savory or what you will)	salt, pepper and ground allspice

Pick over the livers, carefully removing any threads and green-tinged flesh. Melt 2 oz (50g) butter and gently fry the onion for 4–5 minutes. Add the chicken livers and saûté over high heat until lightly browned, stir in the chopped garlic and herbs and season well. Cover and cook gently for 4–5 minutes. Cool a little, then scrape all into a food processor or liquidiser and process; when smooth, add the remaining butter, sherry and cream and give one final quick whizz. Pour into pots and cool. Serve at room temperature.

* ## Artichoke Vinaigrette

Artichokes are thought of as luxuries but they are easily grown and look very decorative in your garden. Picking off each leaf to suck the succulent flesh with its dollop of creamy piquant dressing is fun, if always leaving one with incredible debris. Do watch out for the choke – it's a killer if you should eat it by mistake.

Ingredients
4–6 people

4–6 fine globe artichokes

Thick Vinaigrette Dressing
1 finely chopped shallot
1 tbs Dijon mustard
3 tbs lemon juice or wine vinegar
10 tbs oil
¼ teasp salt
pepper

Cook the whole artichokes in plenty of boiling salt water for about 35 minutes or until an outer leaf will pull off easily. Remove and drain, stalks uppermost, in a colander. Trim the stalks so that the artichokes will sit on a plate, and serve cold with the dressing.

Thick Vinaigrette Dressing. Place the finely chopped shallot, the mustard, salt and pepper with the lemon or vinegar in a glass jar with a well-fitting lid. Shake vigorously until well mixed, then add the oil and shake again until thick and creamy.

** ## Mushrooms or Courgettes à la Grecque

Mushrooms or baby courgettes in a syrupy, herby juice. Serve with fresh rolls or hot garlic bread or as part of a mixed Hors d'Oeuvre.

Ingredients
4–6 people

1 lb (450g) firm button mushrooms or little courgettes cut into 1" (2–3cm) fingers
½ pt (300ml) water
6 tbs olive oil
6 tbs lemon juice
2 tbs finely chopped onion

a bundle of parsley, celery and fennel (or use fennel seeds) and thyme
10 peppercorns
½ teasp coriander seeds
1 bay leaf
freshly chopped parsley
½ teasp salt

Place all the ingredients except the mushrooms or courgettes and chopped parsley in an enamel or stainless steel pan. Simmer for 8–10 minutes and then throw in the mushrooms or courgettes. Simmer for 5–8 minutes. With a slotted spoon remove the mushrooms or courgettes while still crisp to a shallow serving dish and boil down the liquid until well flavoured and about ¼ pt (150ml) is left. Remove the bundle of herbs. Pour the liquid over the vegetables, chill and sprinkle with freshly chopped parsley.

P **   Celeriac Remoulade

So often a good part of a French mixed Hors d'Oeuvre, these strips of root celery in a mustard mayonnaise make an excellent starter.

Ingredients
4–6 people

1 celeriac root (approx 1lb/450g)
juice of ½–1 lemon
salt

Remoulade Sauce
1 egg yolk
2–3 tbs Dijon mustard
¼ pt (150ml) oil
2 tbs wine vinegar
salt and pepper

Peel the celeriac, cut into small matchstick-sized pieces, sprinkle with plenty of salt and toss with lemon juice; leave to marinate for ½–1 hour, then rinse in cold water and drain well. Fold into the Remoulade Sauce and leave for 2–3 hours or overnight before serving. If time is short, blanch the cut celeriac for 1–2 minutes in boiling water, then refresh and dress.

Remoulade Sauce. Place the yolk, salt, pepper and mustard in a bowl, whisk well with a wire whisk and drop by drop beat in the oil, adding it faster as the mixture thickens. Thin with vinegar when the mixture gets very thick. When complete, check the seasoning and add more mustard if the sauce can take it, because it ought to be quite mustardy.

**   Oeufs Florentine

A classic dish with spinach, oeufs mollets and a cheese sauce. It quickly becomes a main dish by increasing the quantities and popping heart-shaped fried bread croûtes all round it.

Ingredients

4–6 people

1½ lb (675g) fresh or ¾ lb (350g) cooked
    spinach
2 oz (50g) butter
4–6 eggs
salt and pepper

Cheese Sauce

1 oz (25g) butter
1 oz (25g) flour
½ pt (300ml) milk or milk and cream
1 slice onion
1 clove garlic
1 bay leaf
1 blade mace
2–3 oz (50–75g) grated Gruyère cheese or
    mature Cheddar
salt, pepper, nutmeg

Put the eggs into boiling water and boil for 5–6 minutes. Shell, and keep them in a bowl of warm water. (Their yolks should still be soft.) Wash the fresh spinach, pull off any tough midribs and cook in plenty of boiling salt water in a non-aluminium pan. When just tender after 5–10 minutes drain and refresh under the cold tap, then squeeze dry in your hands and chop. Melt the butter until it sizzles and add the spinach. Season, and stir until dryish.

    Make a bed of the spinach in a buttered ovenproof gratin dish, place the eggs on top and cover with the sauce. Top with the grated cheese left over from the sauce. Place under the grill until heated through and the top is brown, but don't let the eggs overcook. Serve at once.

Cheese Sauce. Heat the milk or milk and cream with the slice of onion, garlic, bay leaf and mace blade and season with pepper. Melt the butter in another saucepan, add the flour and cook for 3–4 minutes over moderate heat. Draw off the stove and wait for it to cool a bit before adding the strained milk. Bring to the boil, whisking with a wire whisk, simmer for 1–2 minutes, season with salt, pepper and nutmeg, and stir in all but 2–3 tbs of the cheese which is kept for the top.

F ** **Alsatian Onion Tart**

Around Alsace you find a great variety of onion tarts; some are crispy pastry just spread with onions, others an inch or so deep with a creamy onion filling. All are delicious.

Ingredients
4–6 people

Pastry
8 oz (225g) flour
4 oz (100g) firm butter
about 4 tbs cold water
salt

Filling
4 oz (100g) thickly cut smoked bacon
1 oz (25g) butter
1½ lb (675g) onions
½ oz (12g) flour
8 fl oz (225ml) single or whipping cream
4 eggs
salt, pepper and nutmeg

Pastry. Sift the flour into a bowl or food processor with metal blade, add two pinches of salt and the firm butter in small pieces. Sprinkle over the water and mix with your fingertips or process until the pastry forms a ball. Knead briefly into a flat disc and rest for ½–2 hours in the fridge. Roll the pastry thinly to fit a 9″ (24cm) flan tin, prick the pastry and line with tinfoil and gravel or beans, and bake in a hot oven (400°F/200°C/Gas 6) for 6–8 minutes or until the pastry is set. Remove the tinfoil and gravel or beans and pour the filling into the pastry case, sprinkle over the nutmeg and place in moderately hot oven (375°F/190°C/Gas 5). Bake for 15–25 minutes until the filling is just set.

Filling. Cook the diced bacon until crisp and remove from the pan; add the butter to the pan, fry the sliced onions for about 15–20 minutes or until soft and golden and season with salt and plenty of pepper. Take the pan off the stove, return the bacon and sprinkle over the flour; add the cream and mix well. Break in the eggs one by one, season and mix thoroughly.

Main Courses

*   Baked Fish Florentine

Raw, skinned fish fillets are laid on a bed of cooked spinach and coated with a simple but delicious sauce. Then all you do is bake it to a brown and bubbling perfection.

Ingredients
4–6 people

1–1½ lb (450–675g) cod, haddock or coley fillets
about 1½ lb (675g) fresh or 12 oz (350g) cooked spinach
2 oz (50g) butter
salt, pepper and nutmeg

Sauce

1 oz (25g) butter
1 oz (25g) flour
½ pt (300ml) milk
¼ pt (150ml) cream
2–3 oz (50–75g) Gruyère cheese
salt, pepper and nutmeg

Cook the spinach until just tender in plenty of boiling salt water in a non-aluminium pan. Drain, refresh under the cold tap and squeeze out by hand. Chop roughly, toss in hot butter and season with salt, pepper and nutmeg. Place the spinach in a flat gratin dish, cover with the skinned fish fillets, pour over the sauce and sprinkle with the reserved cheese. Bake in a moderately hot oven (375°F/190°C/Gas 5) for 20–25 minutes until the top is brown and the fish is cooked.

Sauce. Melt the butter in a saucepan, add the flour and cook over moderate heat for 2–3 minutes; draw off the stove and wait for the sizzling to cease, then add the milk and bring to the boil, whisking hard. Simmer for 1–2 minutes, season with salt, pepper and nutmeg and stir in the cheese, retaining a little for the top. Add the cream to make a sauce of thick coating consistency.

☐ **   A Good Fish Pie

Good fresh fish, cooked and folded in large chunks into a parsley sauce and topped with creamy mashed potatoes. It freezes extremely well as long as you leave out the hard-boiled egg.

Ingredients
4–6 people

1–1½ lb (450–675g) cod, haddock or coley fillets
¾ pt (450ml) milk
2 oz (50g) butter
2 oz (50g) flour
2 hard-boiled eggs (optional)
2–3 tbs finely chopped parsley
1 bay leaf
mace
salt and pepper

Potato Topping
1½ lb (675g) potatoes
1–2 oz (25–50g) butter
milk
salt and pepper

Skin the fish fillets while raw (so much easier than picking over when hot), using a flexible knife and working from the tail with a horizontal sawing motion. Cover the fish with the milk, season with salt, pepper and mace and add a bay leaf. Bring to the simmer gently and cook for about 5–10 minutes until the fish will just flake. Strain, and when cool break into large flakes.

Melt the butter in a saucepan, add the flour and cook over moderate heat for 2–3 minutes. Take off the heat and leave until the sizzling has stopped. Strain in the cooking liquid from the fish, whisk well and bring to the boil. Simmer for 2–3 minutes, then carefully fold in the large flakes of fish, the roughly chopped eggs and plenty of parsley. Check the seasoning, turn into a buttered dish and top with creamy mashed potatoes. Brown under the grill or re-heat in a moderately hot oven (375°F/190°C/Gas 5) for about 35–45 minutes until brown and bubbling.

Potato Topping. Peel the potatoes and cut to even size. Boil gently in salted water until tender, drain and press through a potato ricer or crush well with a potato masher or fork. When smooth draw aside and add some milk and butter to the bottom of the pan. When warm, beat in over the heat until you have a smooth purée. Season well.

Variation. For special fish pies use prawn butter (*see page 36*) for the sauce and cook the fish in half-fish fumet, half-milk. Substitute cream for some of the milk and add prawns, scallops or mussels for extra flavour.

F ** **Home-Made Pasta and Sauce Ragù**

Once you have made your own pasta, the bought stuff never tastes quite the same. With a food processor and a pasta machine, the whole thing is child's play and the fresh pasta can be frozen. Sauce Ragù served with tagliatelle is a far cry from Spaghetti Bolognese, which the inhabitants of Bologna appear never to have heard of! It is the frying to a good brown and the careful reduction which gives these Italian sauces their full flavour.

Ingredients	4 oz (100g) braising beef
4–6 people	2 chicken livers
	1 finely diced carrot
Pasta	1 finely chopped onion
8–10 oz (225–275g) 'strong' flour	1 finely diced stick celery
2 eggs	1 clove garlic
2 teasp olive oil	2 tbs tomato purée
2 egg yolks	¼ pt (150ml) white wine
1 tbs cold water	¼ pt (150ml) good stock
½ teasp salt	3 tbs cream
	salt, pepper and nutmeg
Sauce Ragù	
2 oz (50g) sliced gammon or bacon	2 oz (50g) butter
1 oz (25g) butter	1–2 oz (25–50g) freshly grated Parmesan

Pasta. Sift the flour into a mound on a large board or work top, make a well in the centre, break in the eggs and the yolks and add the salt, oil and 1 tbs cold water. Work up to a firm dough with your fingers and knead for 10–15 minutes until silky and elastic. This is quite hard work, and it may take a little time to get the knack. Or place the eggs and yolks in the food processor bowl with metal blade and add the flour, salt and oil but no water; process for about 1 minute. The mixture should stay in polystyrene-like granules and not draw together into one lump until the end. Add more flour if it forms a sticky lump or drip in a little water if necessary. Press the dough into one lump, divide in half and roll out each half very thinly to a 15″ × 15″ (38cm × 38cm) square. The pasta should now be like a piece of chamois leather and thin enough to see the grain of the table through. Flour well and roll up loosely, cut across into ribbons of whatever width you like (or cut into squares for lasagne). Shake the ribbons out into little piles on a floured tray, sprinkle with flour and leave to dry for ½–2 hours. Or use a pasta machine!

To cook, toss into plenty of salted boiling water with 1 tbs oil and cook for about 3–5 minutes until *al dente*. Drain, toss with butter and serve with the Sauce Ragù piled on top and the Parmesan cheese handed separately.

Sauce Ragù. Dice the gammon or bacon and fry gently in the butter. Add the carrot, onion and celery and fry to a good brown. Mince the beef or chop finely in a food processor, add to the vegetables and brown. Add the diced chicken livers which have been carefully picked over to remove any green-tinged flesh, and fry lightly. Stir in the finely chopped garlic, tomato purée, wine, seasoning and stock. Turn into a saucepan or casserole and simmer gently without a lid for 40 minutes until reduced and rich. Boil fast to reduce for a few minutes if necessary and stir the cream into the sauce.

F ∗∗   # Lasagne Vincigras

This lasagne dish is very rich, unusual and delicious. Freeze only uncooked, since once cooked the cheese goes rubbery.

Ingredients
4–6 people

½ lb (225g) lasagne or home-made pasta using 6 oz (175g) flour	**White Sauce**
	2 oz (50g) butter
½–1 oz (12–25g) dried cèpe mushrooms	2 oz (50g) flour
1 finely chopped onion	1 pt (600ml) milk
4 oz (100g) chicken livers	salt and pepper
4 oz (100g) chicken breast (raw or cooked)	
2 oz (50g) butter	*Topping*
1 teasp tomato purée	¼ pt (150ml) milk
½ pt (300ml) good stock	1 oz (25g) Parmesan cheese
¼ teasp ground cinnamon	nutmeg
2 tbs Marsala	
3 oz (75g) freshly grated Parmesan cheese	
salt and pepper	

Soak the mushrooms in a little warm water for half-an-hour or so. Sauté the diced chicken breast and the diced livers, which have first been carefully picked over to remove any green-tinged flesh, in 1 oz (25g) butter and set aside. Add the remaining butter to the pan and gently fry the onion until golden. Add the chopped mushrooms (add their water to the stock but watch for sand at the bottom) and ¼ pt (150ml) stock, and simmer to reduce for 10 minutes. Stir in the tomato purée, season and add the remaining stock. Simmer for a further 15 minutes, then stir in the meat, cinnamon and Marsala. You should now have a rich syrupy brown sauce, but reduce further if necessary before adding half the white sauce. Simmer for 10 minutes.

White Sauce. Melt the butter in a saucepan and add the flour. Cook over moderate heat, stirring, for 2–3 minutes, then draw off the stove, wait until cooled a little, add the milk and bring to the boil, whisking with a wire whisk. Simmer for 2–3 minutes and season with salt and pepper.

Topping. Add the milk to the remaining white sauce together with the Parmesan cheese and nutmeg and set aside, covered, to top the dish.

To assemble. Cook the lasagne for 15–18 minutes (3–5 minutes for home-made pasta) in boiling, salted water until *al dente*. Drain and rinse with cold water. Butter a gratin dish well and layer the meat sauce, lasagne and grated Parmesan, seasoning each layer as you go. Top with the reserved white sauce, cover and set aside overnight (not essential). Bake in a moderate oven (350°F/180°C/Gas 4) for ¾–1 hour and serve when golden and bubbling.

145

PF ✳✳   Pigeon with Prunes

This one is an old English recipe, and here the prunes are used to complement the richness of the pigeon's breast.

Ingredients
4–6 people

½–1 pigeon per head (depending on size)	½ lb (225g) prunes
1½ lb (675g) onions	bay leaf
2 oz (50g) butter or dripping	sprig of thyme
4 rashers thin-cut streaky bacon per bird	¼ pt (150ml) red wine, cider or good stock
a little dripping, fat or oil	salt and pepper

Soak the prunes in tea or water overnight or for 5–6 hours (if you use those succulent Agen or Californian prunes they can go straight in). Slice the onion finely and fry gently in a casserole in the butter or dripping until soft and golden. Cut the breast, leg and wing in one piece from each pigeon. Sprinkle the pieces with pepper and bind up each piece in two rashers of bacon, impaling with a cocktail stick to secure them. Heat a little fat in a frying pan and brown the pigeon parcels on both sides. Then bury them in the golden onion, slipping in a bay leaf and sprig of thyme, season with salt and pepper and add the wine, cider or stock. Cover with tinfoil and a lid and place in a slow oven (300°F/150°C/Gas 2) for about 2 hours. Add the drained prunes and cook a further ½–1 hour till tender. Serve with mashed potatoes or buttered noodles seasoned with nutmeg.

F ✳✳   Moroccan Chicken with Prunes

Chicken, honey and prunes; unusual to us, yes, but not unlike many of the early English dishes which were brought back from the Crusades when honey was used to offset the saltiness of the meat. You will find you have to use plenty of salt to balance the flavours. Do try it; most people seem to like it, although it's a little unusual.

Ingredients
4–6 people

3½–4 lb (1.6–1.8kg) chicken	1 teasp powdered cinnamon
¼ pt (150ml) water	4 tbs thin honey
1 pkt or ¼ teasp saffron	1 oz (25g) flaked almonds
2 oz (50g) butter	1 tbs sesame seeds
1 stick cinnamon	salt and pepper
1 finely chopped onion	
a little oil	
4 oz (100g) large plump prunes	

Soak the saffron in the hot water for 30 minutes. Joint the chicken and brown the pieces in butter in a frying pan or casserole with a few drops of oil to stop the butter from burning. Remove, fry the onion, return the chicken and season with plenty of salt and pepper. Add the soaked saffron and the cinnamon stick. Cover closely and simmer gently for 35–45 minutes until the chicken is nearly cooked. Remove the chicken pieces, add the prunes to the juice and simmer for 10–15 minutes. Add the powdered cinnamon and honey and boil down until thick and syrupy; de-grease if necessary. Return the chicken to the pan and simmer all together for 10–15 minutes until hot through and the flavours are well blended.

Toast the sesame seeds in a hot, dry frying-pan, fry the flaked almonds in a speck of butter and have ready to scatter over the dish before serving with rice.

P ** Spiced Spatchcock Chicken

Fresh spices are essential for this sort of spicy but not 'hot' dish. The pounded spices are pushed under the skin and the spatchcock chicken is roasted to a succulent golden perfection, the breast staying wonderfully moist and the skin brown all over.

Ingredients
4 people

3–3½ lb (1.35–1.6kg) chicken
2 oz (50g) butter
¼ teasp whole cummin seeds
2 teasp whole coriander seeds
4 whole shelled cardamoms
½″ (1cm) grated fresh root ginger
1 clove crushed garlic
grated rind of ½ lemon
½ teasp freshly ground black pepper
1–1½ teasp sea salt

Sauce
1 finely chopped onion
2 oz (50g) butter
1 teasp turmeric
1 tbs ground almonds
1 tbs currants
2 tbs yoghurt
¼ teasp cornflour
2 tbs cream
4 tbs milk

Pound all the whole spices in a mortar until finely powdered. Cream the butter and add the spices, ginger, salt and pepper, garlic and lemon rind. Slip your fingers between the skin and flesh of the chicken breast to loosen it and also loosen the skin from the legs. Pack the spiced butter over the chicken breast and legs under the skin. Cut the chicken down the back from neck to tail, snip through the wishbone and press the chicken out flat. Leave breast upwards for the flavours to penetrate for 1–2 hours, then roast in a hot oven (425°F/220°C/Gas 7) for 35–45 minutes, basting after 15 and 25 minutes with the prepared sauce. Serve with plain boiled rice over which you spoon the buttery roasting juices.

Sauce. Melt the butter and gently fry the onion until golden brown. Add the turmeric, almonds and currants, fry 1–2 minutes, then moisten with the combined yoghurt, cornflour, cream and milk. Simmer down a little before spooning over the chicken.

F ✻✻   Poule au Pot and Saffron Rice

Classic French bourgeois cooking, simple but excellent, especially with a really good chicken. One of my favourite dishes, though I wouldn't freeze the saffron rice but only the cut-up chicken in sauce.

Ingredients
4–6 people

3½–4 lb (1.6–1.8kg) fat chicken
1 onion stuck with 2 cloves and cut in half
2 large carrots cut in half lengthways
1 stick celery
1 leek
1 clove garlic
¼ pt (150ml) white wine (optional)
4 pts (2.25l) light stock (or water and
    stock-cubes)
bouquet garni of parsley stalks, bay leaf
    and a sprig of thyme, tied up in a leek
    leaf if you like

Saffron Rice
1 oz (25g) butter
1 finely chopped small onion
½–¾ lb (225–350g) rice
¾–1¼ pt (450–750ml) of the chicken stock
1 pkt or ¼ teasp saffron
salt, pepper and nutmeg

Sauce
2 oz (50g) butter
2 oz (50g) flour
¾ pt (450ml) of the chicken stock
¼ pt (150ml) milk (approx)
squeeze of lemon
salt and pepper

Place the chicken in a saucepan or casserole with all the ingredients in the left-hand column, just cover with stock and bring very slowly to the simmer; skim and cook gently until tender. This will take anything from ½–2 hours depending on the chicken (a boiling fowl will take much longer), how long it took to come to the simmer and how gently it cooks, but the slower the better. It is done when the legs feel loose in their sockets and a prick in the thigh produces clear pinkish juices. Pour off most of the stock for the rice and sauce and keep the chicken warm in the remainder. De-grease the stock at this stage.

    Serve the chicken whole or jointed on the rice, coated with some of the sauce. Serve the remainder of the sauce separately. You can also take the chicken off the bone, dice it and fold into the sauce.

Saffron Rice. Soak the saffron for ½ hour in a little hot stock. Melt the butter in a pan, cook the onion gently until transparent, add the rice and fry and stir until each grain glistens and goes whitish, but for no more than 3 minutes. (Pre-washed and prepared rice won't go white as the starch has already been washed off.) Pour in the hot stock (the smaller quantity for the smaller amount of rice), season and add the saffron and a little grated nutmeg. Cover and simmer or cook in a moderate oven (350°F/180°C/Gas 4) for about 15–18 minutes until the rice is cooked and the stock absorbed.

Sauce. Melt the butter, add the flour and cook for 2–3 minutes, stirring. Remove from the stove and cool a little before adding the stock and milk. Bring to the boil whisking hard with a wire whisk. Simmer for 3–4 minutes, correct the seasoning, add the lemon juice and adjust to a coating consistency.

148

∗∗ Lamb Cutlets en Croûte

Delicious hot or cold and excellent for really special picnics. Try serving with a cucumber-yoghurt Tzatziki salad (*p. 155*).

Ingredients
4–6 people

8 lamb cutlets
dried mint
1 oz (25g) butter
1 tbs olive oil
egg wash
salt and pepper

Cream Cheese Pastry
4 oz (100g) soft butter
4 oz (100g) cream cheese (Eden Vale)
8 oz (225g) flour

Duxelle
½ lb (225g) finely chopped mushrooms
a few drops oil
1½ oz (35g) butter
2 tbs finely chopped shallots or spring
　onions
1 teasp fresh or ½ teasp dried mint
2 tbs yoghurt (optional)
squeeze of lemon
salt and pepper

Make the Cream Cheese Pastry and Duxelle first.

The cutlets must be of even thickness. Remove the skin and excess fat and trim all flesh from the bone end for 1–1½″ (3–4cm). Season with salt, pepper and dried mint and sauté briefly on both sides in the very hot butter and oil. Cool thoroughly.

Roll the pastry thinly and cut into 8 oblongs of 4″ × 8″ (10cm × 20cm). Lay a cold cutlet on one half of each oblong of pastry and cover with a spoonful of cold duxelle. Fold the pastry over, enclosing the meaty top of the cutlet but leaving the bone exposed so that you have a neat little parcel with a handle. Brush the edges with egg wash and seal together. Decorate with pastry trimmings, lay on a baking sheet and brush with egg wash. Cook in a very hot oven (450°F/230°C/Gas 8) for about 10 minutes, then turn down to moderately hot (375°F/190°C/Gas 5) for a final 10 minutes.

Cream Cheese Pastry. Cream the butter and cream cheese together in a food processor or by hand. Add the sifted flour and work up to a paste in the machine or with a fork. Knead into a flat disc and chill for 1–2 hours.

Duxelle. Twist the mushrooms, a few at a time, in a piece of muslin or cloth to squeeze out the juice. Heat the oil and butter in a wide frying pan and cook the onions, mushrooms and mint over fairly high heat for 6–8 minutes until the mushrooms brown a little and no longer stick together. Season with salt and pepper; add the yoghurt and lemon juice and reduce again. Set aside.

F **   Fricandeau of Beef and Sorrel Purée

An old English braise of beef, obviously evolved from the French. The sharp sorrel purée contrasts well with the rich strong gravy. Even without the larding or special herbs it's a lovely way to cook a piece of beef.

Ingredients
6–10 people

3–5 lb (1.35–2.25kg) piece of lean braising beef (topside or silverside)
3 oz (75g) streaky bacon cut in one piece or strips of pork back fat
ground cloves, mace, ground allspice
1 pt (600ml) good beef stock
¼ pt (150ml) white wine
6–8 parsley stalks
all sorts of sweet herbs – thyme, sage, mint, marjoram, savory, basil and pennyroyal (a bunch of whatever you have, preferably fresh)

1 clove garlic
1–2 shallots
4 cloves
pepper and salt

Sorrel Purée
1 lb (450g) sorrel leaves
2–3 oz (50–75g) butter

Cut the streaky bacon into long larding strips. Season with salt, pepper, cloves, mace and allspice. Lard the piece of meat, using a larding needle, or with a sharp thin knife stab the meat from both ends, then push the strips of bacon or pork fat into the holes. Tie the meat into a good shape. Place in a casserole with the wine, stock, herbs, garlic, shallots, cloves and light seasoning. Cook very gently in a slow oven (300°F/150°C/Gas 2) for 3–4 hours until very tender. Remove the meat and keep warm, covering closely. Skim the cooking liquid well, strain and reduce until very strong flavoured. Serve the meat on a bed of sorrel purée and coated with the gravy. Hand any more sauce separately.

Sorrel Purée. Wash the sorrel, removing the stalks and tough midribs. Place it 'with no more water than hangs to the leaves' in a stainless steel or enamel pan (or cook in a jar standing in a saucepan of boiling water). Cook very slowly until tender and forming a purée but don't let it catch on the pan. Beat in the butter really well and make a bed of the purée on your serving dish.

MAIN COURSES

Ham Mousse

This smooth and delicate pale pink mousse is useful for a cold lunch or supper.

Ingredients
4–6 people

½ lb (225g) lean ham diced	¼ oz (6g) gelatine (1½ level teasp)
1 teasp tomato purée	1–1½ tbs dry sherry
8 fl oz (225ml) good stock	¼ pt (150ml) cream
2 tbs dry white wine	salt, pepper, and nutmeg

Sprinkle the gelatine on to the white wine in a small cup. Leave to soak for a minute or two, then stand in a saucepan of hot water to melt. Either process the ham in a food processor until smooth, then pour on the stock, the melted gelatine and tomato purée; or place the ham, stock, melted gelatine and tomato purée in a liquidiser and process until smooth. Turn into a bowl, season well and add the sherry. Chill in the fridge, stirring from time to time until almost set, or stand in a bowl of ice and water and stir until nearly set. Beat the cream until just holding its shape and fold carefully into the mousse. Turn into a dish and chill for several hours or overnight before serving.

Civet de Lapin

A rich rabbit stew with mushrooms and fresh thyme. The sauce has dark chocolate added for a rich brown flavour.

Ingredients
4–6 people

a plump rabbit marinated for 2–4 days (several hours or 1 day would do)	4 oz (100g) mushrooms
1 tbs French mustard	1 oz (25g) flour
3 onions	3–4 cloves garlic
1 tbs red wine or sherry vinegar	a sprig of thyme
8 fl oz (225ml) red wine	2–3 tbs brandy
bouquet garni	1 oz (25g) dark chocolate
2 tbs dripping or fat	¼ pt (150ml) stock (approx)
4 oz (100g) streaky bacon	salt and pepper

Joint the rabbit and spread with the mustard. Place in a glass or china dish with one of the onions, finely chopped, the vinegar, the red wine and the bouquet garni. Season. Leave for 2–4 days in a cool larder or fridge. Drain and carefully dry the rabbit joints.

Heat the dripping or fat in a flameproof casserole and lightly brown the joints. Remove, and brown the cubed bacon, the two remaining onions, sliced, and the mushrooms. Sprinkle in the flour and brown lightly. Return the rabbit with the crushed garlic and thyme, pour over the brandy and flame. Add the marinade, the broken chocolate and a little stock barely to cover. Season, cover closely and simmer in a slow oven (300°F/150°C/ Gas 2) for three hours or until tender. Remove the sprig of thyme before serving.

Vegetables and Salads

*   **French Beans in Garlic Butter**

Toss your crisp cooked beans in garlic butter for full-flavoured succulence.

Ingredients
4–6 people

1–1½ lb (450–675g) little French beans
2–3 oz (50–75g) butter
2 cloves garlic

1–2 tbs finely chopped summer savory or
     parsley
a little grated lemon rind and juice
salt and pepper

Cook the beans in plenty of boiling salt water until just tender, then drain in a colander. Melt the butter, and when sizzling add the finely chopped garlic (but do not brown it), the beans and herbs. Toss over high heat and season with salt, pepper and a little lemon juice and rind. When hot through turn into a dish and serve at once.

**   **Braised Onions and Carrots**

The onions, little ones for choice, are gently browned, then combined and braised with the carrots, which have been barely cooked in the minimum of stock. The vegetables take a while to develop a good flavour, so give them time. This is a little too strongly flavoured to go with very delicate dishes.

Ingredients
4–6 people

¾ lb (350g) small onions
1½ oz (35g) butter
2 tbs oil
1½ lb (675g) carrots

¾ pt (450ml) stock or water and stock-
     cube
1 tbs sugar
salt and pepper
1–2 tbs finely chopped parsley

Peel the onions, keeping small pickling onions whole but cutting larger ones into quarters. Heat the butter and oil in a wide heavy pan, add the onions and sauté gently until golden brown. Peel the carrots and cut into quarters lengthways, then cut across into 2" (5cm) lengths. Put in another pan and just cover with boiling stock. Add seasoning and sugar, boil covered for about 5 minutes, then remove lid and boil fast for another 5–10 minutes. Drain, reserving the liquid, and mix with the onions. Pour over a little of the reserved liquid and simmer very gently, uncovered, for ½–¾ hour until tender and glazed in syrupy sauce. Keep quite moist if you are going to re-heat the vegetables, then boil fast at the last moment to evaporate the excess liquid. Serve sprinkled with chopped parsley.

** Winter Salad with Thousand Island Dressing

We eat so many salads that it's nice to vary the dressings. This is one I'm always being asked for.

Ingredients
4–6 people

1 small head white cabbage or Chinese leaves
3–4 sticks celery
2–3 eating apples
2–3 carrots
½ green or red pepper
1 oz (25g) sultanas plumped in a little warm water
1–2 oz (25–50g) walnuts
½ teasp carraway seeds
1–2 teasp sugar
1–2 tbs vinegar
salt and pepper

Thousand Island Dressing

1 egg
½ teasp dry mustard
2 tbs wine vinegar
8 fl oz (225ml) olive, sunflower, peanut or mixed oil
1 teasp chilli sauce
1 slice onion
1 stick celery with leaves
2 tbs chopped parsley
½" (1–2cm) slice of green pepper
1 teasp paprika
½ teasp salt
pepper

Finely slice or shred the salad ingredients, add the sultanas and broken walnuts, season with salt, pepper, carraway, a little sugar and vinegar and fold in the Thousand Island Dressing.

Thousand Island Dressing. Break the egg into a food processor or liquidiser and add mustard, salt, pepper and vinegar. Switch on and gradually add the oil to make a mayonnaise. Add the remaining ingredients with the vegetables roughly chopped. Process until fairly smooth.

P ✳✳ ## Haricots Blancs en Salade

For those who appreciate the flavour of olive oil and beans, this rich dried bean salad will not last long. But do make sure you use beans which are fresh, preferably from a quick-turnover health food shop.

Ingredients
4–6 people

½ lb (225g) best white haricot beans	1 tbs tomato purée
¼ pt (150ml) good fruity olive oil	1 lemon
2–3 cloves garlic	a few spring onions, shallots or very
bay leaf	finely chopped onion
sprig of thyme	salt and pepper

Toss the beans into a large saucepan of boiling water, boil 2 minutes, take from the stove and leave to soak for 1 hour, or else soak overnight in cold water.

Heat the oil in a saucepan or casserole, add the drained beans and simmer very gently for about ten minutes. Add the garlic, bay leaf, thyme and tomato purée. Cover by 1 inch (2–3cm) with boiling water and simmer over low heat or in a slow oven (300°F/150°C/ Gas 2) for about 3 hours until tender and the liquid has thickened to form a sauce. Squeeze over the lemon juice, season with salt and pepper, add the chopped onion and serve cold.

✳✳ ## Beetroot Orange Salad

The orange dressing seems to bring out the full flavour of the beetroot.

Ingredients
4–6 people

1 lb (450g) beetroot	2–3 tbs vinegar (sherry, cider or tarragon)
2 oranges	2–3 tbs walnut or olive oil
½–1 oz (12–25g) walnuts	sugar, salt and pepper

Boil the beetroot until tender, skin and dice. While still warm, sprinkle with the vinegar and some grated orange rind. Season with salt, pepper and sugar. When cold add the walnut or olive oil and toss. Cut off the peel, pith and skin from the oranges and cut away the segments from their skin. Add to the beetroot. Sprinkle over the roughly broken walnuts and serve.

* Dill Cucumber Salad

In Germany one so often gets this cucumber salad with a slightly sweet fresh dill and cream dressing.

Ingredients
4–6 people

1 large cucumber or several smaller garden ones
3 fl oz (75ml) cream
1 teasp chopped fresh or ¼ teasp dried dill

¾ teasp sugar
1 teasp wine vinegar
1 teasp oil
salt and pepper

Peel and slice the cucumber, not too thinly, sprinkle with salt in a colander, lay a plate on top and press with a weight for ½ hour or so to expel the juices. Place salt, pepper, most of the dill, sugar and vinegar in a bowl and stir to dissolve the salt and sugar. Add the cream and whisk until it begins to thicken. Whisk in the oil, and check the seasoning. Pat the cucumber dry with kitchen paper and mix with the dressing. Turn into a dish and serve sprinkled with the rest of the dill. The dill flavour develops after a little while.

Variation. Use sour cream instead of fresh, or yoghurt and cream mixed.

** Tzatziki

I was shown this Graeco-Turkish dish of cubed cucumber with yoghurt in Cyprus by a dear lady who was supposed to clean my house. When I discovered she was a cook the dust was left to roll up and down the corridors while she taught me authentic dishes. This one is lovely as an Hors d'Oeuvre or salad and cool on the tongue with curries and hot peppery dishes. They put no pepper in it; it is our obsession to add salt and pepper to everything.

Ingredients
4–6 people

1 large cucumber
½–¾ pt (300–450ml) yoghurt
2 tbs olive oil

1–2 cloves garlic
1 teasp dried mint (*not* fresh)
salt

Remove about half the cucumber skin lengthwise in strips and cut all the cucumber into flattish dice. Cream the garlic with salt and add the yoghurt, beat in the olive oil and mint and stir in the cucumber. Check the taste and chill. Serve with kebabs or as an Hors d'Oeuvre.

If the yoghurt is very thin, strain it in muslin for ½ hour to remove excess liquid. If the cucumbers are bitter sprinkle the dice with salt, press, and leave to drain for 30 minutes.

*   Shallot Dressing

Why can one hardly ever buy shallots? These delicately flavoured little onions, so favoured by French chefs, give a bit of a lift to many dishes, including a simple vinaigrette dressing. Try growing your own; they are not difficult, they store well, and they need only be used in very small quantities.

Ingredients
Dressing for 1 lettuce

1–2 tbs very finely chopped shallots	**1 tbs wine vinegar**
1 tbs finely chopped parsley (optional)	**3–4 tbs oil**
½ teasp Dijon mustard	**salt and pepper**

If you mix a dressing in the bottom of your wooden salad bowl it always emulsifies much better. So mix salt, pepper and mustard with the shallots, parsley and vinegar in the bottom of your bowl with a wooden salad server. When the salt has dissolved stir the oil in gradually and vigorously, and it should make a nice thick dressing.

Puddings

F *   ## Gooseberry Fool

The fruit is carefully cooked for flavour, then half-puréed and half-crushed to make an interesting texture. It's extravagant on cream, I know, but good, quick and easy.

Ingredients
4–6 people

1 lb (450g) gooseberries
4–6 oz (100–175g) sugar to taste
2 tbs water

½ pt (300ml) double cream
2–3 scented geranium leaves (optional)

Place the topped and tailed gooseberries and geranium leaves in a jar with the water and 3 oz (75g) sugar. Stand the covered jar in a pan of boiling water and let the water boil (or put in a slow oven) until the fruit pulps. Drain in a sieve. Crush one third and set it aside. Purée and sieve the remainder and combine with the crushed fruit. Sweeten and cool. Whip the cream fairly stiffly and fold in the cold gooseberry mixture. Turn into a serving dish and chill for 24 hours. Serve with Shortbread Fingers or Tuiles d'Amandes (*see page 243*).

*   ## Gooseberry and Cream Cheese Mousse

Make this when the elderflowers are blooming because they add an elusive flavour to gooseberries. Made with an unsalted curd cheese, this is not so rich as the Gooseberry Fool.

Ingredients
4–6 people

1 lb (450g) gooseberries
4–6 oz (100–175g) sugar to taste
4 oz (100g) unsalted curd or cream cheese
1 egg

¼ pt (150ml) cream
1 head elderflower (optional)

Stew the gooseberries with very little water and the sugar, adding a head of elderflower if available. Drain (juice is not needed) and purée the gooseberries, first removing the elderflower. Beat the curd or cream cheese, then beat in the egg yolk and the gooseberry purée. Fold in the cream, whipped until it will hold its shape, followed by the egg white, also whipped until it will just hold a peak. Pour into a bowl and chill before serving.

F **   Tarte Normande

Fruit tossed in hot butter, packed in a pastry case, covered with a light custard cream and baked. Delicious made with gooseberries, rhubarb, apricots or apples and eaten hot, warm or cold.

Ingredients
4–6 people

¾ lb (350g) rhubarb, gooseberries,
    apricots or apples
1 oz (25g) sugar or to taste
1 oz (25g) butter
icing sugar

Custard Cream
1 egg
1 oz (25g) castor sugar
¾ oz (20g) flour
4 fl oz (100ml) cream
1–2 tbs rum, calvados or brandy

Pastry
6 oz (175g) flour
2 tbs icing sugar
3½ oz (85g) firm butter
1 egg yolk
1 tbs cold water
pinch of salt

Pastry. Sieve the flour, salt and icing sugar into a bowl or the food processor. Add the firm butter cut up into hazelnut-sized pieces and rub in or process to the breadcrumb stage. Bind with the yolk and a very little cold water. Form into a flat disc and rest for 1–2 hours in the fridge in a plastic bag.

Roll the pastry to fit a 9″ (24cm) removable base flan tin. Prick the pastry, line with tinfoil and gravel or beans and bake in a hot oven (400°F/200°C/Gas 6) for 8–10 minutes until the pastry is set. Remove the tinfoil and cook a few minutes more.

Sauté the fruit briefly (rhubarb in thick chunks, gooseberries whole, apricots halved, apples peeled, cored and thickly sliced) in hot butter and sprinkle with sugar. Pack into the half-cooked pastry case, pour over the custard cream and cook in a moderately hot oven (375°F/190°C/Gas 5) for about 10 minutes, then sprinkle lightly with sifted icing sugar and return to the oven for about 15–20 minutes until the top has browned and the cream has set. Serve hot, warm or cold.

Custard Cream. Beat the egg with the sugar until pale and thick, beat in the sifted flour, add the cream and rum and pour over the fruit.

F ** ## Martinmas Flan

An unusual flan, good in autumn or winter and much enjoyed by children and all lovers of real English puddings.

Ingredients
4–6 people

Pastry
6 oz (175g) flour
3 oz (75g) firm butter
1 tbs icing sugar
a pinch of salt
2–3 tbs cold water

Crumble
3 oz (75g) plain flour
3 oz (75g) butter
3 oz (75g) castor sugar
1/8 teasp grated nutmeg
a pinch of salt

Filling
1 egg
grated rind and juice of 1 lemon
3 tbs golden syrup
1/4 teasp bicarbonate of soda
2 fl oz (50ml) hot water
a pinch of salt

Pastry. Sift the flour, salt and icing sugar into a bowl or the food processor and add the butter cut into hazelnut-sized pieces. Rub in or process to the breadcrumb stage, adding the cold water as you go until it forms a dough. Turn on to a board and smear down the board in egg-sized lumps with the heel of your hand to combine the butter and flour thoroughly. Rest in the fridge for 1–2 hours. Roll and line a 9″ (24cm) flan tin. Prick the base, line with tinfoil and beans or gravel and bake in a hot oven (425°F/220°C/Gas 7) for 8–10 minutes until the pastry is set. Remove the tinfoil, continue to bake for a further 3–6 minutes until the base is firm, and then pour in the filling. Carefully sprinkle over the crumble mixture and continue to bake for about 10 minutes or so until pale gold before turning down to very moderate (325°F/170°C/Gas 3) for 20–30 minutes until done. Serve hot, warm or cold.

Filling. Beat the egg with a pinch of salt, the lemon rind and juice and the syrup. Dissolve the bicarbonate in hot water, add to the egg mixture and use fairly quickly.

Crumble. Sift the flour with salt and nutmeg, rub in the butter and stir in the sugar.

** Tarte au Fromage Blanc

A crisp pastry case, filled with a cream cheese mixture and spread with jam—damson, black cherry, strawberry—or ginger or lemon marmalade.

Ingredients
4–6 people

Pastry
8 oz (225g) flour
a pinch of salt
2 egg yolks
3 tbs icing sugar
5 oz (125g) firm butter
½ teasp vanilla essence

Fromage Blanc Filling
8 oz (225g) unsalted cream cheese
2 oz (50g) butter
2 oz (50g) vanilla sugar
1 egg yolk
½ teasp vanilla essence
½ lemon
a little cream or milk
about ⅓ lb (150g) jam

Pastry. Sift the flour, icing sugar and salt into a bowl or the food processor and add the firm butter cut into hazelnut sized pieces. Rub in or process to the breadcrumb stage, then add the vanilla and yolks to bind. Turn the pastry on to a board and smear down the board in egg-sized lumps with the heel of your hand. Knead briefly into a flat disc and rest in the fridge for 1–2 hours. Roll the pastry and line a 9″ (24cm) removable base flan tin, prick the base, line with tinfoil and beans or gravel and bake in a hot oven (400°F/200°C/Gas 6) for 8–10 minutes. When the pastry is set remove the tinfoil and outer ring and continue to cook in a moderate oven (350°F/180°C/Gas 4) until completely cooked and golden.

Fromage Blanc Filling. Cream the butter and sugar, beat in the yolk and cream cheese and stir in the vanilla, a little grated lemon rind and a good squeeze of juice. If very thick, thin with milk or cream to a spreading consistency. Shortly before serving, fill the pastry shell with the mixture and spread the top with a layer of sharp marmalade, jam or jelly.

F ** Adam's Apple Flan

Another but different crisp pastry case, this time filled with caramelised apple, makes an unusual flan.

Ingredients
4–6 people

1½ lb (675g) Cox's Orange Pippins
8 oz (225g) granulated sugar
¼ pt (150ml) cold water
2 teasp Camp coffee
1 oz (25g) butter

Pastry
6 oz (175g) plain flour
a pinch of salt
4 oz (100g) firm butter
1 tbs icing sugar
1 egg yolk
2–3 tbs cold water

Pastry. Sift the flour, salt and icing sugar into a bowl or the food processor with metal blade, add the firm butter cut into hazelnut sized pieces, and rub in or process to the breadcrumb stage. Add the yolk and water to bind and draw into one lump. Smear down the board in egg-sized lumps with the heel of your hand, form a flat disc and chill for 1–2 hours. Roll and line a 9″ (24cm) removable base flan tin, prick and line with tinfoil and beans or gravel and bake blind in a hot oven (425°F/220°C/Gas 7) for 8–10 minutes until the pastry is set. Remove the tinfoil and outer ring and continue baking in a moderately hot oven (375°F/190°C/Gas 5) for 15–20 minutes until the pastry is cooked and golden.

Peel, core and thickly slice the apples. Dissolve the sugar in the water in a large clean saucepan, and when every grain of sugar has dissolved boil fast without stirring until the syrup is a good brown caramel colour. Add the prepared apples all at once, cover and turn heat down low. After 4–5 minutes the caramel will have dissolved with the apple juices. Turn up the heat and boil fast to cook the apples and evaporate the juices. Add the butter and coffee and cook for about 10–15 minutes until the apple is tender but unbroken and a small quantity of syrupy juices remain. Turn into the cooked pastry shell and serve warm or cold.

F ✳✳   Apple Chartreuse

Masses of apple slices baked for an unusually long time in a soufflé dish are then turned out to make an amber-coloured gâteau. Simple but unusual, and nice when you want a pure fruit sweet.

Ingredients
4–6 people

**3 lb (1.35kg) apples (cookers, or eaters
    that keep their shape)
about 5–6 oz (125–175g) sugar to taste
¼ teasp mixed spice
4–5 tbs quince jelly or apricot jam**

Caramel
**4 oz (100g) granulated sugar
3 tbs cold water**

Caramel. Dissolve the sugar in the water in a small pan over gentle heat, stirring. Once every grain of sugar has dissolved stop stirring, turn up the heat and boil fast to a good brown caramel. Pour at once into a warmed 1½–2 pt (900ml–1.1l) soufflé dish and coat the bottom and sides with the caramel.

Peel, core, quarter and slice the apples. Layer them with the mixed sugar and spice in the soufflé dish until full, pressing well down. Cover with a butter paper and bake (standing the dish in a pan of hot water to come halfway up) in a hot oven (400°F/200°C/Gas 6) for 2½–3 hours. Cool, and when lukewarm turn out on to a serving dish and spoon over the jelly or jam. Serve cold with cream.

PF ** ## Summer Pudding Special

When fresh fruit is plentiful and good, what better than a real Summer Pudding with a little kirsch or fruit liqueur to make it a bit special? Stale bread is essential, for if you use fresh the outside can be very soggy. Make two and freeze one to treat yourself with in winter. Use a mixture of several or all of the following fruits, though in my family some blackcurrants and plenty of raspberries are considered essential – not too many of the former, however, as they are rather overpowering in flavour.

Ingredients
4–6 people

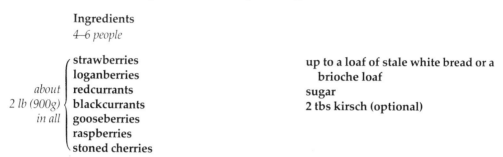

| *about* 2 lb (900g) *in all* | strawberries
loganberries
redcurrants
blackcurrants
gooseberries
raspberries
stoned cherries | up to a loaf of stale white bread or a
  brioche loaf
sugar
2 tbs kirsch (optional) |

Line a 2–3 pt (1.2–1.8l) pudding bowl or soufflé dish with crustless ⅜" (1cm) slices of bread or brioche. Very gently simmer the mixed summer fruit with sugar to taste and very little water until the juices run. Stand the bread-lined bowl on a large plate to catch drips and fill with the fruit, juice and kirsch until tightly packed. Cover the top with more bread and over this lay a plate or saucer that just fits the top. Weight with a brick and keep in a cool larder or fridge for 24 hours. Turn out the beautiful firm red pudding and serve, cut in slices like a cake, with plenty of thick cream.

** ## Cherry Almond Pudding

A classic steamed pudding which one rarely gets a chance to eat these days.

Ingredients
4–6 people

2 eggs and their weight in soft butter,
  castor sugar and self-raising flour
2–3 tbs milk
½ teasp almond essence

4–5 tbs cherry jam (or use damson or plum)
grated rind of ½ orange
a good pinch of cinnamon, nutmeg and
  cloves

Break the eggs into a bowl, whisk lightly and leave over a pan of warm water for about 10 minutes. Cream the butter well, gradually beat in the sugar, and cream until white and fluffy, or use a food processor with plastic blade. Gradually add the whisked eggs, then fold in the sifted flour and almond essence and mix to a dropping consistency with milk (or process just long enough to incorporate the flour and milk).

Mix the jam with the grated orange rind and spices and put in the bottom of a greased 2 pint (1.2l) pudding basin, spoon in the mixture and cover the top with buttered paper and tinfoil or a cloth tied on with string. Place in a steamer or saucepan with boiling water to come halfway up the bowl. Cover tightly and steam or boil for 2 hours. Replenish the pan with boiling water and keep boiling all the time. Turn out and serve with cream or custard.

* Pain Perdu

This age-old recipe, found in many countries to use up stale bread, is perhaps nicest if you use a light milk loaf or a fruit bun. All ages enjoy it.

Ingredients
4–6 people

6–8 ½" slices of stale milk, currant or
    white loaf
a few almonds
a little candied peel
2 eggs
4 tbs single cream or milk
¼ teasp cinnamon
2–3 oz (50–75g) butter
salt and pepper

Butterscotch Sauce
3 oz (75g) butter
4 oz (100g) golden syrup
½ lemon

Remove the crusts from the bread, cut into squares, fingers or triangles, and into these press a few slivered almonds and bits of peel. Whisk the egg and cream with the cinnamon, a pinch of salt and a little pepper. Dip the bread briefly into the egg on both sides and fry gently in butter until brown, first on one side and then on the other. Drain on kitchen paper, pour over the butterscotch sauce and serve at once, preferably with pouring or clotted cream.

Butterscotch Sauce. Combine the chopped-up butter, syrup and lemon juice in a saucepan. The moment the butter melts, whisk with a wire whisk while the mixture boils for 2–3 minutes only; any longer and you have toffee!

$\mathcal{F}$ **   **Baklava**

Made with bought filo paste (those tissue-paper layers of strudel pastry which can be bought from a good delicatessen), this classic Middle Eastern pastry and nut sweet is so good that it has anyone with a sweet tooth absolutely drooling. It can be frozen (that's about the only way to keep it safe from nibbling fingers); it thaws very rapidly. The orange flower water and rosewater can also be bought from a good delicatessen or chemist.

Ingredients
6–8 people

8 oz (225g) filo paste
6 oz (175g) unsalted or lightly salted
    butter
3 oz (75g) blanched almonds
3 oz (75g) walnuts
a good pinch of cinnamon
orange flower water
rosewater
3 tbs castor sugar

Syrup
8 oz (225g) granulated sugar
¼ pt (150ml) water
½ lemon
orange flower water
rosewater

Make the syrup first to have it chilled by the time the baklava comes out of the oven.

Melt the butter gently in a saucepan. Chop the nuts separately in the food processor until they are like coarse breadcrumbs, or put through the mincer. Combine the nuts with the castor sugar, cinnamon and enough orange flower water and rosewater to taste and stir until the mixture just clings together. Take a 10″ × 12″ (25cm × 30cm) deep baking or roasting tin and brush lavishly with melted butter. Place a layer of filo paste in the tin, turning in the edges to fit. Brush with more butter and continue with layers of paste and butter until about one third of the pastry has been used (if left out in the air the pastry will very quickly dry up and crumble to pieces). Spread the nut filling all over the paste and continue layering paste and butter until all is used, but do not use all the white sediment of the butter. With a sharp knife cut the baklava into lengthways strips about 1½″ (4cm) wide then cut diagonally to form diamonds. Bake in a moderately hot oven (375°F/190°C/Gas 5) for 30–40 minutes until cooked and a good brown.

    As it comes out of the oven pour the cold syrup all over the baklava; using well chilled syrup on the hot pastry keeps the whole thing crisp. Serve cold. Baklava will keep 2–3 days in fridge or larder.

Syrup. Melt the sugar in the water over low heat, simmer for about 10 minutes until syrupy, then add the lemon juice and a few drops of orange flower water and rosewater until it is lightly perfumed. Chill really well.

Khoshaf

A winter fruit salad using all those succulent dried fruits. A little goes a long way as it's very rich-tasting. The orange flower water and rosewater are available at a good delicatessen or chemist.

Ingredients
4–6 people

8 oz (225g) succulent dried apricots
4 oz (100g) best prunes
4 oz (100g) dried peaches
4 oz (100g) dried pears
2 oz (50g) seedless raisins
2 oz (50g) halved blanched almonds
a sprinkle of pistachio nuts (optional)
1½ pts (900ml) cold water (approx)
3 tbs rosepetal, apricot or plum jam
2 teasp orange flower water
1 tbs rosewater or 1½ tbs kirsch

Place the washed fruit in a bowl with the almonds and jam, cover with the water and sprinkle with orange flower water and rosewater (sometimes these are very concentrated, so add gradually). Macerate for 48 hours. Sprinkle with pistachio nuts and serve with thick pouring cream and sponge fingers.

SECTION 5

Special Occasions

For anyone who enjoys cooking there must be some escape from the humdrum three meals a day and as-cheap-as-possible syndrome that quickly kills the pleasure of it. So one needs occasionally to tackle some complicated or rather special dish for the immense satisfaction of producing a masterpiece, and of course there must be someone to appreciate and share it with you. When better than the Special Occasion?

There are many different special occasions when for one reason or another we want to do something distinctly out of the ordinary and take just that extra bit of trouble. Maybe it's your mother's birthday and you want to give her a surprise sit-down dinner for twenty of her best friends. Perhaps you've just won a bet on the National and want to celebrate. Long-lost friends may be coming to see you, or it may be an important family anniversary. For some reason we wish to show our thanks, admiration, love or appreciation, and we do it in the timeless and primeval way by providing a feast.

The party can be large or small, rather grand or quite informal, and the dishes can be expensive or otherwise; if they are good that is enough, and our guests don't have to work out exactly how much we've spent on them before they can enjoy themselves. I have included a few of my favourite recipes which suit this philosophy: I will admit to a small stab of pride and pleasure as I serve them.

But it isn't always like this. Frequently the occasion presents itself but you may have neither the time nor the inclination to spread yourself. Then you have to get the purse out! A reliable supplier of good smoked salmon by post within twenty-four hours is something to have up your sleeve. This is also the moment when your love affair with the butcher is tested to the full; can he find you fresh fillet or rump steak, Scotch beef or best English lamb? Can he lay his hands on veal escalopes or a brace of young partridges? A good butcher is to be treasured.

Perhaps the occasion is created by the food itself, something rather special and dying to be eaten at its best. You may want to ask a few appreciative souls to the first cutting of your asparagus, one of the few commodities to defy modern living and the freezer and retain its cachet and a season. You might (if you're very clever indeed) have grown enough basil to indulge in home-made pasta (so special in itself) with Pesto Sauce and fresh Parmesan or Pecorino. Should salmon, lobster, grouse or partridge come your way they also deserve a special occasion, though, sadly, they seem to be slipping out of our reach as the rest of the world discovers (not for the first time) our superb natural food resources. In any event these rare ingredients should be treated in the simplest, most classic way unless you have a surfeit of them and just have to find a new way to use caviar! No, I'm confining myself to the more accessible and normally-priced of our fine foods and to some dishes which are just rather special or which have become traditional for some reason or other.

Some of the best times are the informal evenings with perhaps only a couple of friends when you can make some of the special dishes that are difficult to do for larger numbers or need last-minute cooking. What a wealth of them there are, if you're relaxed, and happy to cook the blinis or pop the soufflé into the oven while everybody chats and has another glass. I enjoy making Veal St Simon, Venison Steaks or Crêpes Suzette in the dim warmth of the kitchen, missing none of the conversation and knowing that my visitors will enjoy the results.

Great family celebrations, Christmas, Easter, christenings, weddings, birthdays and other anniversaries, each is a special occasion and needs the appropriate food. So, of course, do the first night of the holidays and the last night of the holidays. Children are great creatures of habit and love ritual (though often pretending not to), so build on this and instigate family traditions. I think we should have a strike on our hands and the children would refuse to go to school if we didn't have Snails in Garlic Butter on the last evening.

Whatever your special occasion, family or friends, formal or informal, I hope this chapter will give you some ideas to make it a *really* special one.

First Courses

*   Creamed Mushroom Consommé

When time is at a premium this mixture of tinned consommé, cream and wafers of fresh baby mushrooms is well worth knowing.

Ingredients
4–6 people

2 tins Campbell's condensed beef
   consommé
2 teasp dried tarragon
2 oz (50g) button mushrooms
½ pt (300ml) whipping cream
½–1 teasp potato flour

squeeze of lemon juice
finely chopped chervil or parsley
salt and pepper

Heat the consommé with the tarragon and infuse for 10–15 minutes. Strain, add the very finely sliced mushrooms and simmer for 3–4 minutes. Mix the potato flour with a little cream, add and boil to thicken. Pour in the rest of the cream and heat through. Correct the seasoning, add a squeeze of lemon juice and serve scattered with chopped chervil or parsley.

**   Potage Germiny

This wickedly rich smooth soup with its chiffonnade of sorrel is from the realms of haute cuisine but is not difficult to make.

Ingredients
4–6 people

2 pts (1.2l) very good chicken stock
4 egg yolks
6 fl oz (175ml) double cream
1–1½ oz (25–35g) butter
finely chopped chervil or parsley
salt and pepper

Chiffonnade of Sorrel
20–30 large sorrel leaves
1 oz (25g) butter

Heat the stock, add 2 tbs sorrel chiffonnade and continue to heat for 5 minutes or so. Whisk the egg yolks in a bowl for about 1 minute. Whisk in the cream, then gradually, drop by drop, beat in ½ pt (300ml) soup and return the mixture to the pan. Cook, stirring, over very gentle heat until the yolks thicken. *DO NOT LET THE SOUP BOIL.* Check the seasoning, and when ready to serve draw off the stove and add the butter in flakes and the chervil. Stir and shake until dissolved into the soup. Keep hot in a *bain marie* so that it cannot boil and as the best way of thickening the yolks slowly in order that the flavour may mature.

Chiffonnade of Sorrel. Wash and dry the sorrel and remove any tough midribs, pile it up like the leaves of a book and shred into fine strips (a 'chiffonnade'). Melt the butter in a small stainless steel or enamel pan (not aluminium which reacts with sorrel), add the sorrel and cook gently until it softens and the moisture has all gone but it still remains in shreds.

* Asparagus with Melted Butter Sauce

I never find the French or German white asparagus as good as the best green English varieties, which, especially when cut from the garden as the water comes to the boil, are superlative. Simple melted butter, or this melted butter sauce prepared with the same care our ancestors took, makes this one of the greatest seasonal dishes still obtainable.

Ingredients
4–6 people

2–3 lb (900g–1.35kg) fresh asparagus

Melted Butter Sauce
8–12 oz (225–350g) best butter
squeeze of lemon juice
1½–2 teasp flour
3–4 tbs milk or water

Trim and wash the asparagus, peeling any tough stems with a potato peeler. In the absence of a proper upright asparagus boiler, tie in small bunches with two strings to each bunch and boil gently in lightly salted water for about 12–20 minutes until just tender. Lift out by the strings, using two forks, and drain well. Serve at once with the melted butter sauce.

Asparagus used to be served on a folded linen napkin or a special asparagus plate with a drainer in the bottom. A shallow saucer or plate upside down in the bottom of your serving dish will successfully act as a drainer, any water from the asparagus draining underneath it.

Melted Butter Sauce. Chop up the butter and mix in the flour. Put in a small pan to melt with the milk. Bring to the boil, shaking all the time, and boil for a moment only. Serve at once. Or chop up the butter, melt it very gently and serve it just as it is.

✱✱   Jubilee Seafood Starter

The raw diced smoked haddock in this has everyone guessing; is it smoked salmon or perhaps smoked eel? Most people don't realise that you can eat good smoked haddock raw; it's delicious and keeps down the price of this pretty dish of a jellied tomato chartreuse topped with seafood cocktail. Invented for Jubilee Year, we consider it one of our specialities.

Ingredients
4–6 people

6 oz (175g) raw smoked haddock fillet
2–3 oz (50–75g) peeled prawns
1 tbs tomato ketchup
½ teasp chilli sauce
3–4 tbs whipped cream (using 2–3 fl oz
   (50–75ml) of cream)
½ teasp wine vinegar
1 tbs chopped chives or a slice of onion
   put through a garlic press
1 teasp chopped fresh or ¼ teasp dried
   basil
1 tbs chopped parsley
lemon juice
salt and pepper

Tomato Chartreuse
1 × 14 oz (425g) can tomatoes and liquid
2 teasp gelatine
2 tbs cold water
¼ bay leaf
slice of onion
2″ (5cm) stick celery
very small slice of green pepper (optional)
grated rind of ½ orange
squeeze of lemon juice
salt, pepper and sugar

Mayonnaise
1 egg yolk
¼ teasp mustard
¼ pt (150ml) mixed olive oil and
   sunflower or safflower oil
lemon juice to taste
salt and pepper

Tomato Chartreuse. Sprinkle the gelatine on to the cold water in a small bowl, soak for several minutes, and then stand in a saucepan of hot water to melt. Liquidise and sieve the remaining ingredients for Tomato Chartreuse, add the gelatine, check the seasoning and pour into 4–6 glasses or individual serving dishes to come about halfway up. Put aside to set.

Mayonnaise. Beat the egg yolk with salt, pepper and mustard in a bowl for 1 minute until thick and sticky. Gradually, drop by drop to start with, beat in the oils and finish with a squeeze of lemon juice to taste.

Combine the mayonnaise with the tomato ketchup, chilli sauce (beware—this is hot and gets hotter!), vinegar, chives or onion, parsley, basil and whipped cream. Skin the raw smoked haddock and cut into cubes. Combine with the prawns and squeeze over some lemon juice. Mix with the mayonnaise sauce, and preferably leave to mature for several hours. Spoon on top of the Tomato Chartreuse, sprinkle with parsley and serve with Sesame Fingers (*see page 242*).

F ✳   Smoked Salmon Pâté

Quick, easy and light as air, this delicate pâté does nothing to detract from the flavour of the salmon.

Ingredients
4 people

4 oz (100g) smoked salmon bits	**2½ fl oz (60ml) cream**
3 oz (75g) butter	**lemon juice**
	salt, pepper and paprika

Melt the butter. Place the roughly chopped smoked salmon in a food processor or liquidiser, turn on and add the butter in a thin stream. Process until very smooth, season and cool. Whip the cream and fold into the cold salmon mixture with lemon juice to taste. Check the seasoning and turn into a pot. Serve at room temperature with hot toast, brioche toast or fresh bread.

P ✳   Kippered Salmon

The boss could never say no to this old Scots recipe from my great-great-grandmother's book. We prefer it to smoked salmon but most people can't tell it apart. So if you ever get a fine fresh salmon (or use other fresh, firm-textured fish), do treat yourself to it.

Ingredients

A fine side or a whole fresh salmon

Per pound boned fish weight
1½ tbs coarse sea salt
1½ tbs Barbados sugar
a pinch of saltpetre
1 teasp brandy

Allow 3–4 oz (75–100g) sliced kippered salmon per person

Take the side of salmon off the bone, wipe clean with a wet cloth and then a dry one. Mix the salt, sugar and saltpetre together. Sprinkle a little of this mixture on a deep dish and lay the salmon on it skin-side down. Cover with another layer of the mixture and sprinkle the brandy over it. If you are doing a whole salmon, prepare the second side as the first and lay it skin-side up on top of the first side. Sprinkle with more of the mixture and cover with a dish (for one side I cover with greaseproof paper first) and heavy weights. Keep in a cool larder or the fridge and let it lie for 24 hours to 3 days, then remove and wipe down. Slice and serve as smoked salmon with lemon and brown bread and butter.

You can place fresh dill on the salmon with the salt mixture, which makes Gravad Lax. It's very good, but I prefer the natural taste of the salmon. You can also mix the juices which run from the fish with sweet German mustard and Barbados sugar; it makes a delicious sauce, but again I think detracts from the salmon.

T *   Smoked Trout Mousse

Simple and quick to make, this delicious mousse is a firm favourite.

Ingredients
4–6 people

8 oz (225g) smoked trout
6 oz (175g) cream cheese (Eden Vale
    Somerset soft cream cheese for choice)
¼ pt (150ml) plain yoghurt
2 teasp gelatine
2 tbs white wine

½ teasp horseradish sauce
a squeeze of lemon juice
¼ pt (150ml) cream
¼ cucumber
salt, pepper and nutmeg

Sprinkle the gelatine on to the white wine in a cup, soak for several minutes, then stand in a saucepan of hot water to dissolve. Skin and bone the smoked trout and flake into a food processor or liquidiser. Process until finely chopped, then add the cream cheese and yoghurt. Season with salt, pepper and nutmeg and add the horseradish, the melted gelatine and lemon juice to taste. Turn into a bowl. Fold in the cream, whipped until just holding its shape. Put in a 1 pt (600ml) soufflé dish and chill. Decorate with sliced cucumber and serve with thin brown bread and butter.

***   Millefeuilles aux Fruits de Mer

A hot breath of puff pastry split and filled with seafood in a beautiful cream sauce. Fill the pastries at the last moment on individual plates as the sauce is unthickened and oozes out from the pastry, and it's too good to waste a drop.

Ingredients
4–6 people

Puff Pastry
5 oz (125g) 'strong' flour
5 oz (125g) butter
a pinch of salt
3–4 fl oz (75–100ml) iced water (approx)
squeeze of lemon juice
egg wash

Filling and Sauce
6–8 oz (175–225g) shelled unbreaded
    scampi
8 oz (225g) prawns (in their shells)
6 tbs olive oil
3 tbs brandy
2 oz (50g) diced carrot

½ finely chopped onion
1 small clove garlic
3 parsley stalks, a sprig of thyme and ½
    bay leaf
3 tbs port
8 fl oz (225ml) dry white wine
1 tbs tomato purée
½ pt (300ml) double cream
1 teasp fresh or ½ teasp dried tarragon
lemon juice
salt and pepper
2 oz (50g) very finely chopped mild or
    spring onion
a bunch of chives

172

Puff Pastry. Sift the flour and salt into a bowl and add a third of the butter, diced, and a squeeze of lemon juice. Rub in the butter, then add water to make a medium firm dough known as *la détrempe*. Do not overwork the dough or it will become elastic. The remaining butter should be of the same consistency as *la détrempe*, firm but spreadable; make it into a square flat cake. Roll the pastry into a rectangle, place the butter on one half and fold the other over to encase it, sealing the edges. Roll carefully to a rectangle (stop at once and chill if the butter shows signs of coming through), dust off flour, then fold up the bottom third of the pastry and fold the top third over it. Press the edges together and rest for 20 minutes in a plastic bag in the fridge. Replace on the floured board, with the folded edge to your left, and roll out into a neat rectangle. Fold in thirds as before and give the pastry a half-turn to the right so that the folded edge is again on your left. Roll again, fold, and rest for 20 minutes. Repeat two more 'rolls' and 'turns', rolling only in a lengthwise direction as slantwise rolling will produce an uneven rise, and rest again for 20 minutes. Repeat this process once more so that the pastry has seven 'turns' and four rests in all. The pastry is now ready to be kept until needed.

When you want to use it, roll to a rectangle of just over 10½" x 11" (27cm × 28cm); with a large knife trim all round the edges, then cut into 6 rectangles 3½" × 5½" (9cm × 14cm). Brush a baking sheet lightly with water. Turn each pastry rectangle on to the sheet and glaze carefully with egg wash, remembering that puff pastry will only rise from a cut edge and if the egg gets on that edge it cannot rise. Bake in a hot oven (425°F/220°C/Gas 7) for 12–15 minutes until brown, crisp and very well risen. Keep warm until needed (or if necessary you can rewarm in a slow oven). Split the pastries in half and place the lower halves straight on to the plates. Spoon over the seafood and sauce (which will be quite runny), sprinkle with the raw onion and a little chopped chives, pop on the pastry tops and serve at once.

Filling and Sauce. Shell the prawns but reserve the shells. Heat the oil in a frying pan or sauté pan, and when hot add the thawed and drained scampi and toss over high heat for about 1 minute. Add the brandy and flame. Remove the scampi and set aside with the prawns. Add the carrot and onion to the pan, together with the prawn shells, garlic and herbs, and cook gently without browning until the vegetables are softened. Add the port, cover and boil up until reduced by half; then add the wine, tomato purée and seasoning. Boil uncovered for about 10 minutes until reduced by one-third. Add the cream and tarragon and simmer gently for 10 minutes or so. Strain the sauce through muslin, pressing the debris well. Combine the sauce with the scampi and prawns, heat and keep warm in a *bain marie* or reheat when needed. Check the seasoning and finish with a squeeze of lemon juice.

***   Pâté en Croûte Truffé

For Christmas (or at any other time) this lovely pâté in a light, cheesy pastry crust, truffled or untruffled, is fun to make, looks very professional and is a joy to eat.

Ingredients
8–10 people

Pâté
8 oz (225g) back pork fat
4 oz (100g) cooked sliced ham
1 lb (450g) lean pork
1 small finely chopped onion
1 oz (25g) butter
2 tbs brandy
2 tbs Marsala or sherry
½ teasp fresh chopped thyme or lemon thyme
1 small clove garlic
1 tbs finely chopped parsley
½ teasp quatre épices or allspice
2 eggs
½ teasp salt (approx)
pepper

Pastry
12 oz (350g) flour
½ teasp dry mustard
3 oz (75g) grated mature Cheddar cheese
9 oz (250g) firm butter
4 tbs iced water (approx)
a good pinch of salt

To Assemble
1 raw chicken breast
1 tbs finely chopped parsley
1 small fresh or tinned truffle or 2 teasp green peppercorns
egg wash

Pastry. Sieve the flour, salt and mustard into a bowl or the food processor, add the grated cheese and the cold butter in hazelnut-sized lumps and rub in or process. Bind with the water, knead briefly into a lump and roll out on a floured board to a 10″ × 5″ (25cm × 12cm) rectangle. Fold the top third down and the bottom third up, press the edges together and give the pastry a turn to the right. Roll and fold pastry twice more, then rest for 2 hours.

Pâté. Fry the onions gently in the butter until soft and golden, add the brandy and Marsala or sherry and reduce by half. Cut half the pork fat into little dice and the ham into matchstick strips. Mince or chop the lean pork and remaining pork fat quite finely in a food processor. With the food processor change to the plastic blade. Beat in the onion mixture, crushed garlic, lemon thyme, parsley, seasoning, spices, diced pork fat and ham strips. Bind with the eggs and fry a little bit to check the seasoning.

To Assemble. Take a 2–3 pt (1.2–1.7l) hinged pâté mould or loaf tin and grease well. Line with two-thirds of the pastry rolled about ⅜″ (1cm) thick. Press well into the corners but don't let the pastry become too thin, and leave a 1″ (2cm) overhang all round the top of the mould. Pack the pastry-lined mould with half the pâté mixture. Cut the chicken breast into long fillets, roll heavily in the parsley, and lay down the middle of the pâté mixture, embedding them well together with the precious slivers of truffles or a scatter of green peppercorns. Cover with the remaining pâté mixture, domed slightly in the centre: if the mould is too full juices bubble out during cooking. Cover with the remaining pastry rolled to fit the top and nearly ½″ (1cm) thick. Turn up the overhang of pastry over the pastry top and seal with egg wash. Cover the joint with pastry leaves and decorate. Make two holes and insert tinfoil 'chimneys' for the steam to escape. Brush the top with egg wash and insert a meat thermometer if used.

Bake in a moderately hot oven (375°F/190°C/Gas 5) for 20–30 minutes until the crust sets and browns, then turn down to moderate (350°F/180°C/Gas 4) for a further 1–1½ hours until the meat is cooked (170°F/75°C on a meat thermometer) and the pastry is a good golden brown. Cover with tinfoil or paper if it gets too brown and remove any fat that accumulates in the baking sheet. Leave to cool completely before unmoulding.

Setting aspic can be poured through a funnel into the pâté to fill any empty corners but I don't feel it's really necessary and it must be of very good flavour. Keep the pâté for 2–3 days before serving for the flavour to mature.

Snails in Garlic Butter

Classic garlic butter, freshly made and packed on top of the snails in their shells. Served with plenty of French bread, this brings you restaurant luxury at home prices.

Ingredients
4–6 people

**48 large tinned snails and their shells
(allowing 8 or 12 per head)**

Garlic Butter
**10–12 oz (275–350g) butter
4–6 cloves garlic
8 tbs finely chopped parsley
finely grated lemon rind and a good
squeeze of juice
3 tbs white breadcrumbs
2 teasp finely chopped fennel or several
crushed fennel seeds (optional)
salt, pepper and nutmeg**

Open the tins and rinse the snails. Press one well down into each shell and pack the shell with garlic butter. Set the snails carefully upright on snail plates or ovenproof plates, using a few bread crusts to keep them straight. Heat in a hot oven (425°F/220°C/Gas 7) for 10–12 minutes until bubbling and sizzling. Serve at once.

Garlic Butter. Cream the softened butter and beat in the very finely chopped garlic, parsley, fennel (if used), breadcrumbs, lemon rind and juice and seasoning.

P *** Boned Stuffed Duck

I suppose this is the dish I have demonstrated more than any other. It's much easier to tackle once you have seen it done but is well worth learning, for it looks and tastes wonderful and goes a long way. It is also a good choice for a main course.

Ingredients

15–20 people as a first course
10–12 people as a main course

5 lb (2.5kg) duck
2 tbs brandy
2 tbs dry vermouth
2 tbs Marsala or sherry
2 oranges
3 tbs finely chopped parsley
1 teasp fresh finely chopped lemon thyme
   or thyme
1½ teasp crushed coriander seeds
salt and pepper
lettuce leaves or watercress

Pâté Mixture

1 oz (25g) butter
1 small finely chopped onion
1 lb (450g) lean pork
4 oz (100g) cooked sliced ham
8 oz (225g) back pork fat
4 oz (100g) duck or chicken livers
2 eggs
1 small clove garlic
2 tbs pistachio nuts
1½ teasp salt (approx)
pepper

Bone out the duck, starting by cutting straight down the back with a sharp boning knife; then carefully work your way round to the breast bone, cutting the skin and flesh off the carcass and easing the legs and wings from their sockets. When the flesh is detached on both sides except along the breast bone, pick up the carcass so that the weight of the flesh hangs down and cut along the breastbone, being careful not to pierce the skin or leave a gristly strip of breastbone in the meat. Cut off the two end wing joints from each wing and bone out the third; cut carefully round the joint to detach the ligaments and tendons and then you should be able to pull out the bone quite easily, drawing the wing skin through to the inside. Remove the thigh bones but leave the drumsticks in so as to have a good ducky shape. Leave a bit of the lower leg bone on or the flesh will draw up the drumstick, making it look naked. Should there be any holes in the skin do not despair but sew them up, leaving a generous end of thread to pull out later.

Combine the grated rind of 1 orange with 4 tbs orange juice and the brandy, vermouth and Marsala. Season the duck on the inside with salt, pepper and some of the parsley, lemon thyme and coriander; sprinkle over some of the orange-brandy mixture. Fold the duck up and leave in the fridge while you prepare the filling. I sometimes leave it overnight, in which case add the duck livers to the orange-brandy mixture to marinate overnight also.

To stuff the duck, unfold it and place a layer of pâté mixture down the centre (get plenty between the duck's legs or you will end up with something looking like a tadpole with its legs dangling behind it!). Press the seasoned duck livers (which have been carefully picked over, removing any threads and green-tinged flesh) into the pâté mixture down the centre and cover with the remaining pâté. Re-form the duck. Do not have it too tightly filled but cut off the excess skin at the tail and neck if necessary. With a large, long darning needle and button thread, take one stitch through the skin at the tail end and tie a knot leaving a long thread to pull out later; sew up with a hefty oversewing stitch. Turn over, pat into shape (don't worry if it doesn't look good, because it will pull into shape during the cooking) and lay on a rack in a roasting tin. Wrap the bone ends of the drumstick in tinfoil so that they don't burn, and if you are using a meat thermometer insert into the centre of the duck. Roast in a moderately hot oven (375°F/190°C/Gas 5) for 1¼–1¾ hours (to a meat thermometer reading of 170°F/75°C), covering loosely with tinfoil if getting too brown. You can test with a skewer pushed into the thickest part from the tail end; the juices should be clear but not pink or bloody, but it's a pity to do this as it lets out some of the luscious juices. Cool, and preferably keep for 1–2 days for the flavour to mature before serving. Carefully pull out the thread plus any little darns you may have had to do. For a buffet, I often decorate it with orange slices, blanched strips of green pepper, black olives, etc., and glaze it with aspic. Set on a dish of lettuce leaves or watercress bunches. Serve cut across into even slices, and you will find you get twenty or more slices from one duck.

Pâté Mixture. Fry the onion gently in butter until tender and golden, add the remaining orange-brandy mixture, and boil until reduced to a few syrupy tablespoonfuls. Cut half the pork fat into small dice. Chop the lean pork and remaining pork fat in the food processor (with metal blade), or mince it. With a food processor change to the plastic blade. Beat in the diced fat, the ham cut into matchstick strips, the eggs, orange-brandy syrup, crushed garlic, salt, pepper and the remaining parsley, lemon thyme and coriander. Beat all really well together to achieve a nice light mixture and fold in the pistachio nuts. Fry a small spoonful and taste; it must be perfectly flavoured and balanced. Keep covered in the fridge if not required at once.

Blinis with Sour Cream and Smoked Salmon or Kipper Fillets

$\mathcal{P}$ **

More of an experience than simply a dish! The blinis are best cooked just before you eat, and you will find yourself jumping up to cook some more very quickly. Everyone loves these do-it-yourself dishes, dripping on the butter, spooning on the cream and topping with your chosen goody. Don't forget the finely chopped onion—it's essential. I think one should really have Blini Parties, or at least make whatever follows very light and insubstantial.

Ingredients
4–6 people

Blinis
3 oz (75g) 'strong' white flour
3 oz (75g) buckwheat or wholemeal flour
approx 8 fl oz (225ml) milk or 6 fl oz
   (175ml) milk and 2 fl oz (50ml) cream
2 oz (50g) butter
2 eggs
½ oz (25g) fresh yeast
½ teasp salt
pinch of sugar

Topping
2–3 oz (50–75g) smoked salmon per head
   or 2–3 filleted kippers of the very best
   quality
1 small carton sour cream
2–3 tbs cream
1–2 very finely chopped onions
2 lemons
3–4 oz (75–100g) melted butter
salt and pepper

Blinis. These take 2½–3 hours' preparation time and must then be cooked within ½ hour or the yeast over-rises, though they may be cooked in advance and re-warmed.

Dissolve the yeast in 5 fl oz (150ml) tepid milk, mix with the 'strong' white flour to make a dough and leave in a warm place, covered, for 1 hour. Gradually add the buckwheat or wholemeal flour, the salt, sugar, yolks, melted butter, and enough milk or milk and cream to make a fairly thick batter. Beat well and rest for a further hour. Beat again and fold in the whites of egg whisked until just holding a peak. Rest a further ½ hour.

Heat a lightly oiled frying pan and drop spoonfuls of the mixture to make 3" (8cm) drop-scones about ½" (1cm) thick. Turn when brown but the top is still unset and cook the other side; keep warm in a folded cloth in a low oven.

To make ahead, cook the blinis, cover with a damp cloth and cool on a wire rack then slip into a plastic bag. Freeze if not using the same day. Re-warm in a slow oven in a tightly-covered container or tinfoil parcel so that they don't dry out. Serve in a folded cloth.

Topping. While the blinis are rising prepare the topping ingredients. Slice the smoked salmon wafer-thin, or cut the filleted kippers into 3" (8cm) strips, sprinkle with lemon juice and season with pepper. Arrange on a dish. Whip the cream, fold into the sour cream and turn into a bowl. Melt the butter gently in a jug, quarter the lemons, and put the onion in a small bowl.

Blinis are served warm. Everyone pours liberal quantities of melted butter over them, then ladles on a blob of sour cream, then some salmon or kipper, a sprinkle of raw onion, a turn of pepper and finally a squeeze of lemon juice. Very rich and absolutely scrumptious, bound to make any party a huge success—but have lots, as they are very more-ish!

Main Courses

✳✳ Poached Salmon with Sorrel Sauce

A wonderful treat these days. Try your salmon hot with this simple but delicious sorrel cream sauce or cold with a really good mayonnaise.

Ingredients
4–6 people

**4–6 lb (1.8–2.7kg) sea trout (salmon trout)
  or salmon**
a bunch watercress or parsley

Chiffonnade of Sorrel
10–20 sorrel leaves
¹⁄₂ oz (12g) butter

Sorrel Sauce
5 oz (125g) unsalted butter
¹⁄₄ pt (150ml) double cream
a squeeze of lemon juice
salt and pepper

Poach the salmon in gently simmering salt water for 4-6 minutes to the pound. Draw the pan off the stove and leave for ¹⁄₂ hour before removing from the water. Alternatively, you can parcel the salmon in buttered tinfoil with ¹⁄₂ glass of white wine, salt, peppercorns and several slices of lemon and bake in a moderate oven (350°F/180°C/Gas 4) for ³⁄₄ hour; don't unwrap for 10 minutes or so after removing from the oven.

Skin the salmon, dish up on a large plate and decorate with a fine bunch of fresh parsley or watercress.

Chiffonnade of Sorrel. Take a handful of sorrel leaves, wash, shake, remove the tough midribs and shred finely. Melt the butter in a small saucepan (not aluminium) and add the sorrel. Cover and cook gently until the sorrel is soft but still in strips and the moisture has gone.

Sorrel Sauce. Chop the butter and heat gently to melt (it must oil but not separate), add the cream and heat, but not to boiling. Draw off the stove and beat in a good squeeze of lemon (this thickens and binds it), a teaspoon or so of sorrel chiffonnade and seasoning. Serve hot.

✳✳✳ Seafood au Gratin

The Prawn Butter used in this dish ensures that you get every scrap of flavour and value from the prawns in their shells.

Ingredients
4–6 people

¾ lb (350g) prawns in their shells
1–1½ lb (450–675g) filleted turbot,
    monkfish, haddock or cod
3–4 fresh scallops
1 lb (450g) fresh mussels in their shells
approx ¾ pt (450ml) prawn fumet (see
    p. 37)

Sauce
2½ oz (60g) prawn butter (see p. 36)
1 finely chopped shallot or small onion
2 oz (50g) flour

½ pt (300ml) of fish cooking liquid
¼ pt (150ml) milk
¼ pt (150ml) double cream
½ teasp tomato purée (optional)
a squeeze of lemon juice
salt and pepper

Topping or Garnish
4–6 tbs stale white breadcrumbs and
    1 oz (25g) butter in flakes *or*
8–12 fleurons (crescents) of puff or flaky
    pastry and finely chopped parsley

First peel the prawns and use the shells to make the Prawn Butter and the Prawn Fumet. Wash, scrape and beard the mussels, discarding any open shells. Steam open in a covered saucepan over high heat, shaking; remove mussels from their shells and strain the liquid. This is added to the prawn fumet unless it is too salty. Set the mussels aside.

Wash the scallops, remove the brown intestine thread, separate the coral and cut the white flesh of each into 3–4 pieces. Skin the fish, barely cover with prawn fumet and poach until just cooked, adding the scallop white for 3–4 minutes and the coral for 2–3 minutes at the end. Remove the fish and scallops and set aside. Strain the liquid to use for the sauce.

Sauce. Melt most of the prawn butter in a saucepan, add the shallot or onion and cook very gently until transparent and tender; add the flour and cook gently for 3–4 minutes, stirring. Remove the pan from the stove, wait for the sizzling to cease and add the milk and ½ pt (300ml) of the reserved liquid. Bring to the boil, whisking hard with a wire whisk. Simmer for 3–4 minutes, then add most of the cream, the seasoning and a speck of tomato purée to colour the sauce if you feel it is necessary. Cover and keep warm in a *bain marie* or on a heat diffuser for the flavour to mature.

Fold large flakes of fish, scallops, prawns and mussels into the sauce, correct the seasoning and consistency with the remaining cream and finish with a squeeze of lemon and stir in the rest of the prawn butter. Turn into a buttered gratin dish and top with breadcrumbs and butter flakes; brown under the grill and serve.

The sauce will be all the better for being made in advance and matured in a *bain marie*, as the flavour always seems to develop. The whole dish can be prepared a day ahead if you have really good fresh fish. Instead of breadcrumbs and butter flakes, cover closely with tinfoil and reheat in a moderately hot oven (375°F/190°C/Gas 5) for 30–40 minutes. Serve sprinkled with parsley and garnished with fleurons.

**   Truite Sauce Aurore

Good trout are not so easy to come by now the trout farm has proliferated in rather the same way as the broiler chicken house. But if you can find firm-fleshed, fine-tasting trout, this Hollandaise-based sauce with the reduced cooking liquid added is superb.

Ingredients
4–6 people

	Sauce Aurore
4–6 good trout	3 egg yolks
1 small very finely chopped onion	4–6 oz (100–175g) unsalted butter
8 fl oz (225ml) good white wine	½ lemon
1 tomato, peeled, de-seeded and cut into tiny dice	1 tbs cold water
	tomato purée
1 tbs double cream (optional)	salt and pepper
some finely chopped parsley	
salt and pepper	
8–12 fleurons (crescents) of cooked puff pastry	

Place the cleaned and seasoned trout in a shallow buttered baking dish, add the onion and wine, cover with butter papers and bake in a moderate oven (350°F/180°C/Gas 4) for 15–20 minutes until just done and the eye goes white. When the fish are cooked remove to a serving dish and keep warm. Boil the juices down to two tablespoonfuls (this takes a little while), cool, and strain into the Sauce Aurore. Add the thick cream if used, the dice of tomato, and a little more lemon juice if necessary. Pour a little sauce over the fish and serve sprinkled with parsley and surrounded by warm puff pastry fleurons, serving the remaining sauce separately.

Sauce Aurore. Keep 1 oz (25g) of the butter ice-cold but chop up the rest and melt in a small pan over low heat. Whip the egg yolks well in a bowl with a wire whisk and beat in 1 tbs lemon juice and the cold water. Add half the cold butter, place the bowl over a pan of hot, not boiling, water so that the water does not touch the bowl, and stir until the butter melts and the yolks thicken enough for you to see the bottom of the bowl when you draw the whisk across it—no longer, or you will have scrambled eggs. Add the remaining cold butter to arrest the cooking and take the bowl off the heat. Whisk in, and when the butter has melted gradually drip in the melted butter, whisking the while. Season with salt and pepper and add a mere whisper of tomato purée for a delicate rose colour. The sauce can now be kept warm by standing the closely covered bowl in a pan of *lukewarm* water in a warm (not hot) place for up to 4 hours.

*   Poulet Gros Sel à ma Façon

In Hong Kong a Chinese friend gave us chicken baked in salt. Paul Bocuse does it with truffles under the skin, but in my version I use a mushroom duxelle. Everything depends on having a really good chicken, and you must use coarse sea salt which can be stored and used again for general cooking.

Ingredients
4–6 people

3½ lb (1.6kg) chicken
6 lb (2.7kg) sea salt

Duxelle
1 oz (25g) butter
1 tbs chopped shallot or spring onion
4 oz (100g) finely chopped mushrooms
salt and pepper

Duxelle. Melt the butter in a frying pan and gently cook the onion. Squeeze the moisture from the mushrooms, using a muslin cloth. Add to the pan and cook over a brisk heat for 6–8 minutes until the mushrooms begin to brown and crumble apart. Season with salt and pepper and freeze the mixture in 4 flat little cakes for 10 minutes or so.

Season the inside of the chicken with pepper only. Slip your fingers between the skin and flesh of the chicken breast to loosen it, and also loosen the skin from the legs. Now slip the little frozen mushroom cakes under the skin over the breast and legs. Sew the chicken up so that no salt can fall in. In a deep casserole, lay a bed of 2 lb (900g) of the sea salt. On this lay the chicken and pour the remaining salt all round and over until the bird is completely encased (you can do this in a tinfoil parcel if you have no suitable dish). Cook in a hot oven (425°F/220°C/Gas 7) for 1¾ hours. Break open the salt, remove the chicken and very carefully brush off every speck of salt. The skin should be pale brown and the bird succulent, perfumed with mushrooms and perfectly salted.

**   Chicken à la Kiev

Always a huge success, but only when you can cope with the last-minute frying.

Ingredients
4 people

4 fresh chicken breasts with wing
   attached
3 oz (75g) soft butter
½ lemon
salt, pepper and mace
flour

1–2 eggs
few drops olive oil
plenty of stale white breadcrumbs

deep fat for frying

Cream the butter with a good squeeze of lemon juice and the seasoning. Shape into four oblongs and chill in the fridge.

Remove all the breast bone from the chicken joints, leaving only the wing bones. Then cut off two end wing joints and push the flesh towards the breast on the third to expose the bone. Separate the breast from the fillet, remove the whitish tendons, and gently flatten the meat with a rolling-pin. Tuck the iced butter into a pocket in the breast well up towards the bone, cover carefully with the fillet and pat and roll into a neat shape.

Dust with flour and dip in egg beaten with olive oil (this makes a crispier finish) and then in the breadcrumbs; pat on well. Chill for at least 2 hours before cooking. Deep fry in hot fat (360°F/185°C) for 5–6 minutes until cooked and a good golden brown, then drain on kitchen paper and pop into a hot oven (400°F/200°C/Gas 6) for 2–3 minutes. Serve at once.

** Chicken Sauté 77

A Jubilee Year dish in the modern haute cuisine style based on a Poulet au Vinaigre dish we ate with Paul Bocuse. Careful reduction is the secret, so give yourself plenty of time to complete the dish.

Ingredients
4–6 people

3½–4 lb (1.6–1.8kg) chicken	½ pt (300ml) best chicken stock
1 tbs oil	3–4 wafer-thin slices of lemon
4 oz (100g) butter	salt and pepper
2–3 fl oz (50–75ml) white wine vinegar	finely chopped parsley
3 fl oz (75ml) dry white wine	fleurons (crescents) of puff pastry or
4 oz (100g) skinned, de-seeded and diced	heart-shaped croûtes of fried bread
tomatoes	

Joint the chicken into four or eight and season with salt and pepper. In a frying or sauté pan heat the oil with 2 oz (50g) butter; when the frothing subsides add the chicken joints in one layer and sauté to a good brown on all sides. Add the vinegar, wine, tomato dice (keeping a few back to scatter over at the end), lemon slices (with white pith removed if it is at all thick and bitter) and a light seasoning. Cover and cook gently for about 30–40 minutes until just tender. Or turn the browned chicken into a casserole, deglaze the pan with the wine and vinegar, pour over the chicken with the tomato, lemon, etc., and cook well covered in a moderately hot oven (375°F/190°C/Gas 5) for 30–40 minutes. Remove the chicken and keep warm.

Reduce the sauce by fast boiling, adding the stock little by little until you have about 8 fl oz (225ml) well-flavoured sauce left. Sieve and return to the pan, or leave unsieved if you prefer. Correct the seasoning, and off the stove whisk in the remaining butter in little pieces to thicken and enrich the sauce. Pour over the chicken joints, sprinkle with tomato dice and chopped parsley and surround with fleurons of puff pastry or croûtes of fried bread.

The chicken can be kept warm in the reduced sauce before the butter is added; then remove the portions to a serving dish, boil up the sauce, whisk in the butter and serve at once. If you don't have good jellied stock and the sauce does not become rich and syrupy, you may like to thicken it with a tiny bit of *beurre manié* or arrowroot.

*** Pot au Feu

A Sunday lunch with a difference. You start with the delicate bouillon with the marrow eaten on dry toast to accompany it. Then the main feast of boiled meats and vegetables with several sauces. Don't waste this on the uninitiated!

Ingredients
10–12 people

4 lb (1.8kg) piece rolled brisket, silverside or topside	8 leeks
2 lb (900g) piece shin of beef (optional)	8 carrots
3 lb (1.35kg) veal knuckle with lots of meat (optional)	4 large onions
1–2 boiling fowl or roasters	1 small piece turnip or parsnip (if you must!)
1½ lb (675g) piece ham or boiling bacon (optional)	1 thick slice celeriac or 3 sticks celery
4–6 lengths sawn marrow-bones	3 cloves garlic
3–4 lb (1.35–1.8kg) well-washed meaty beef bones	8–10 bruised peppercorns
6 oz (175g) ox liver (optional)	1 tomato
chicken necks, giblets (and feet if you can get them!)	large bouquet garni of 2 bay leaves, bunch of parsley stalks, fresh thyme
	12–14 pts (7–8l) cold water
	1 tbs gros sel or salt
	10–12 slices stale French bread

Tie all meats into a good shape, leaving a length of string on each to attach to the pan handle. Tie the marrow bones in individual pieces of muslin so that the marrow will not fall out (leave these on strings too), or if you really cannot be bothered dip the ends in salt, which *helps* to keep the marrow in. Put the water into the pot, add the meats, boiling fowl, ox liver, bones and giblets (but not the marrow-bones or roasting chicken, as they only go in for the last hour) and bring to the boil quickly. Meanwhile clean and prepare the vegetables, leaving the leeks and carrots whole and the skins on the onions as they help to colour the broth. Before adding the tomato cut it in half, sprinkle with sugar and grill deep brown, as this also helps the colour.

As the Pot au Feu comes to the boil skim off all the grey-brown scum with a slotted spoon (it will rise thickly for 10–15 minutes), and also wipe round the edges of the pot. Add a small glass of cold water and give the pot a good shake to help bring up the scum; once this is white and frothy you can leave it. If you do not skim adequately you will get a cloudy stock with poor flavour. Add the vegetables, bouquet and peppercorns. Skim again when it comes back to the boil, then add salt. Cover the pot, with the lid half off for the steam to escape, and simmer at a *tremble* for 3½–4 hours, skimming from time to time and removing the meat as it cooks. Add the roasting chicken and marrow-bones 1 hour before serving. Bake the French bread golden in a low oven.

It is also nice to draw off some of the stock and cook more and different vegetables in it—carrots, cabbage cut in quarters, turnips, onions or celery. Steam or boil potatoes in their skins.

Serving. This dish will keep hot for up to 1 hour before serving. First have a bowl of de-fatted bouillon, served with the toasted French bread spread with the bone-marrow and salt. Next, with the drained meat and vegetables, serve the potatoes, with a choice of gherkins, creamed horseradish, and mustard or a mayonnaise sauce. *Gros sel* is an essential accompaniment. Either have a bit of everything or set some things aside for another meal. For later, the chicken can be served with rice cooked in the stock and a velouté sauce, or as creamed chicken, croquettes or chicken pie. The beef is delicious cold; try it sliced and layered with sliced boiled potatoes, dressed with a thick parsley and shallot vinaigrette. The veal can be used for Vitello Tonnato, veal and ham pie or creamed veal, ham and mushroom filling. The stock is wonderful for soups, and can be concentrated for consommé or sauces. All the bones can be re-boiled for soup stock.

**   Boeuf Stroganoff

Correctly done this is a last-minute dish for not too many people, but it is a real classic.

Ingredients
4–6 people

1½–2 lb (675–900g) fillet of beef (end bits will do; allow approx 6 oz (175g) a head)
2 finely chopped onions
8 oz (225g) button mushrooms
4 oz (100g) butter
1 teasp oil

½ pt (300ml) double cream soured with lemon juice
1–2 tbs tomato purée
nutmeg, mace and paprika
salt and pepper

Cut the meat into thin strips 1″ × ⅜″ (3cm × 1cm). Sauté the onions gently in 2 oz (50g) butter until soft and golden. Add the sliced mushrooms and cook for 2–3 minutes over high heat until just firm. Stir in the tomato purée, then remove the onions and mushrooms to a plate. Add 1 teasp oil to the pan and then the remaining butter (the oil allows the butter to heat to a higher temperature without burning), and as the foam subsides toss in the meat. Sauté over high heat for 3–4 minutes until just cooked. Return the onion and mushroom mixture, season and sauté 1 minute more. Add the cream, boil up a minute or so and serve *at once*.

✳✳   Veal St Simon

This is the dish which I created for the *Sunday Times* Cook of Britain competition. Rather a last-minute dish, but it can wait a little while. It is rather good.

Ingredients
4–6 people

4–6 veal escalopes, about 4–6 oz (100–175g) each
4 tbs Madeira or half-and-half Marsala and dry sherry
4–5 skinned, de-seeded and chopped tomatoes

4 oz (100g) finely sliced fresh button mushrooms
4 oz (100g) butter
½ pt (300ml) double cream
1 teasp paprika
8–12 fleurons (crescents) of cooked puff pastry
salt and pepper

Trim the escalopes and bat them out very thin. Lay in a flat dish and spoon over the Madeira. Leave to marinate for 2 to 4 hours.

Melt the butter in a frying pan, and when hot and frothing lay the drained escalopes in it and cook quite quickly for about 4 minutes, turning once. Take them from the pan and keep warm. Add the tomatoes to the pan and cook down to a pulp; this tomato purée helps to thicken the sauce, which has no flour in it. Add the finely sliced mushrooms and cook for 4 to 5 minutes longer. When the mushrooms are cooked pour in the cream, season with salt, pepper and paprika and reduce over brisk heat for about 3 minutes, stirring in the pan juices and crusty bits. When you have a luxurious creamy sauce, return the escalopes to it for a few minutes to heat through and allow the flavours to meld. Dish up and spoon over the sauce, surround with fleurons of puff pastry and serve at once.

A dish like this should be served the moment it is made, but I have quite successfully kept it warm, the escalopes left covered in the reduced sauce. On serving remove the escalopes to a serving dish, boil up the sauce, whisking, pour over and serve.

**   Venison Steaks with Farthinghoe Sauce

If you can get hold of a loin of venison, fallow or roe deer for choice, ruthlessly bone it out and prepare as steaks, it is a revelation of what venison can be. As a dark meat you can serve it very rare.

Ingredients
4–6 people

a complete 3–4 lb (1.35–1.8kg) best end or
    loin of venison (we use young fallow
    deer)
2 tbs olive oil
3–4 tbs port, wine or stock
a good bunch watercress
salt and pepper

Farthinghoe Sauce
5 good tbs redcurrant jelly
1 lemon
½ stick cinnamon
2 tbs port
2 oz (50g) butter

Bone out the meat carefully, removing every vestige of skin and fat so that you are left with only the noix of meat. Cut this fillet into steaks ½"–¾" (1–2cm) thick and season with pepper. You should have approximately 4–6 oz (100–175g) per head.

Heat the pan until very hot, add a little oil, and cook the venison steaks very fast for about 1½–2 minutes on each side. Season with salt and dish up on a heated dish. Add the port to the pan, swirl round to remove the tasty juices, and pour over the steaks. Garnish with watercress and serve at once, the Farthinghoe sauce handed separately.

Farthinghoe Sauce. Take julienne strips from half the lemon, place in plenty of cold water in a saucepan, bring to the boil and blanch for 5–10 minutes until no longer bitter; drain and refresh under the cold tap to set the colour. Gently melt and heat the jelly, port, cinnamon, julienne strips and a long strip of thinly pared lemon rind. Simmer for 5–10 minutes, then add the juice of ½ lemon, remove the long lemon strip and cinnamon stick and whisk in the butter in little bits. Turn into a sauceboat and keep warm.

P ✳✳✳   Raised Game Pie

With a waisted mould or a removable base cake tin you can make this sensational game pie. It's not really difficult, but it will give you a flutter of pride to produce and it tastes good too. A splendid Christmas-time dish.

Ingredients
10–12 people

1 pheasant's breasts or 8 oz (225g) game
   fillets kept whole

Pastry
1 lb (450g) flour
8 oz (225g) butter
2 egg yolks
3 fl oz (75ml) cold water (approx)
1 teasp salt

Pâté Mixture
8 oz (225g) boned flesh of pheasant,
   partridge, rabbit, hare or grouse, etc.
4 oz (100g) lean pie veal ⎫ *or use all pork*
4 oz (100g) lean pork ⎭
8 oz (225g) back pork fat
4 oz (100g) streaky bacon
2 eggs
½ teasp allspice or quatre épices
4 tbs brandy
1½ teasp salt
black pepper

Pastry. Sift the flour and salt into a bowl, rub in the butter and work up to a stiff paste with the egg yolks and some water (in a food processor make half at a time). Rest, preferably for 12–24 hours.

Pâté Mixture. Mince, or chop finely in a food processor with the metal blade, the game, veal, pork, pork fat and streaky bacon and beat in the seasoning, brandy and eggs. Fry a little to check the seasoning.

Grease well a 2–3 pt (1.2–1.7l) hinged pâté mould or removable base cake tin. Take three-quarters of the pastry and roll out, keeping the middle thicker than the edges. Flour well and fold in half, edges towards you. Roll into a bag shape by drawing the edges towards you and rolling out the thicker centre. Fit into the mould, pressing well into all the corners and making sure no holes appear. Leave 1" (2–3cm) overhang all round the mould. Pack with half the pâté mixture, then lay in strips of the pheasant breast or game fillets. Cover with the remaining pâté mixture, doming slightly in the centre; if the mould is too full juices bubble out during cooking. Cover with the remaining pastry rolled to fit the top and nearly ½" (1cm) thick. Seal the edges with water. Decorate and brush with beaten egg. Make a hole and insert a tinfoil 'chimney' for steam to escape. Also a meat thermometer if used. Bake in a moderately hot oven (375°F/190°C/Gas 5) for 20–30 minutes until the crust sets and colours, then turn down to moderate (350°F/180°C/Gas 4) for 1–1½ hours until the meat is cooked (160°F/70°C on a meat thermometer). Cover with tinfoil or brown paper if it is getting too brown. Leave to cool completely before unmoulding.

Setting aspic can be poured through a funnel into the pâté to fill any empty corners and helps to keep it moist, but to my mind it is not really necessary.

Keep 2–3 days for the flavour to mature before serving.

Roast Wild Duck with Fruit and Green Peppercorn Stuffing

P **

Teal or mallard (if you can be sure they have not fed by the sea, when they can occasionally be disgustingly fishy) are superb. Their dark meat can afford to be rare like a steak, and the sharp fruity stuffing contrasts well with the rich meat. Serve with home-made noodles tossed in pan juices and green peppercorns. Save this for yourself and your best friends. This dish can also be made with domestic duck, though the flavour is blander.

Ingredients
4 people

2 mallard or 4 plump teal	2 oz (50g) butter
4 oz (100g) plump dried apricots	1 teasp green peppercorns
¼ pt (150ml) white wine or water (approx)	1 batch of home-made pasta or 1 lb (450g)
1 oz (25g) walnuts	tagliatelle
2 lemons	salt and pepper

Soak the apricots in the minimum of white wine or water overnight. Cut out the preen glands from either side of the duck's tail as they give the birds a strong musky taste. Take tiny julienne strips of rind from 1 lemon and blanch in boiling water for 4–5 minutes. Cut the pith and skin from this lemon and remove the flesh in segments. Mix with the drained chopped apricots (reserve the liquid), the chopped walnuts and the julienne lemon strips. Add ½ teasp green peppercorns and stuff the ducks. Prick the mallard (not the teal) all over with a fork and place in a roasting tin. Roast in a hot oven (425°F/220°C/Gas 7) for 5 minutes without basting to seal in the juices, then turn down to moderately hot (375°F/190°C/Gas 5). Cover the breast with butter and add 4 tbs of the apricot soaking juice and the remaining peppercorns to the pan. Roast teal for 20–25 minutes in all or mallard for 30–40 minutes; this should give quite pink meat. Baste frequently with buttery juices and see that they don't burn (add more liquid if the fat seems to be over-browning). Remove the duck and keep warm. Rest for at least 10 minutes before carving.

    Cook the tagliatelle in plenty of boiling salt water and drain. Mix 3–4 tbs of the buttery juices with the cooked noodles (serve the remaining juices separately). Toss well and heap on a serving dish. Carve the mallard or arrange the teal on the tagliatelle with the spooned-out stuffing. Cut the remaining lemon into wedges for squeezing over the ducks. Serve at once.

Rice, Vegetables and Salads

P **   **Wild Rice Risotto**

I despatched Simon to London to buy me wild rice. 'Get a pound,' I said. At £3.60 a half-pound he nearly died, but dutifully bought it. Goodness, we did enjoy it, but I'll seldom be allowed it again. Of course, it's not really a rice at all but an aquatic grass which grows wild in the great lakes of Canada and North America; harvested by Indians and parched, it does have a certain cachet. It swells enormously, and 1 oz per head is ample. It has a lovely taste and an unusual crunchy texture. Serve it with game; especially wild duck, or try the Brown Rice with Almonds and Raisins in Section 3 if you're feeling mean!

Ingredients
4–6 people

4 oz (100g) wild rice (soaked overnight)	3 tbs flaked almonds
1 finely chopped onion	2 tbs sultanas
2 oz (50g) butter	salt and pepper
4 oz (100g) mushrooms	

Place the wild rice in a saucepan and cover with water by about 3" (7–8cm). Simmer for about 30 minutes until just tender. Drain into a sieve, cover with a tea-towel and steam over a saucepan of boiling water for 10–15 minutes.

Melt the butter in a casserole and gently fry the onion until golden. Add the sliced mushrooms and fry until brown, adding the almonds and sultanas. Stir in the rice, toss until heated through and season with salt and pepper.

This can be reheated in the oven or on the stove, tossing carefully.

*   **Mushrooms with Garlic and Thyme**

Fine whole mushrooms sautéd in olive oil and scattered with chopped garlic and thyme. Full flavoured and splendid with a steak or roast.

Ingredients
4–6 people

¾–1 lb (350g–450g) button mushrooms	2–3 cloves finely chopped garlic
3–4 tbs olive oil	salt and pepper
1–2 teasp freshly chopped thyme	

Wash and drain the mushrooms. Heat the oil in a frying pan until just smoking, add the mushrooms, shake, cover with a lid to fit and heat for 5–10 minutes. Remove the lid and continue to cook over high heat until all the liquid has evaporated and the mushrooms are frying again. Sprinkle with the thyme and garlic, heat, season and serve.

**   # Concombres au Poivre à la Crème

Cooked cucumbers, delicate in flavour and always available, mixed into a creamy sauce with green peppercorns.

Ingredients
4–6 people

2 large cucumbers
some chopped fresh or a pinch of dried
    tarragon or some chives

Sauce
1 oz (25g) butter
1 oz (25g) flour
½ pt (300ml) milk
¼ pt (150ml) double cream
2–3 teasp green peppercorns
salt and pepper

Remove narrow strips of skin lengthways from the cucumber all the way round, leaving on half the skin (use a cannelling knife or potato peeler). Cut the cucumber into 2″ (5cm) slices, then cut these into four lengthways, removing any seeds. Toss into boiling salt water and simmer for about 5–10 minutes until just tender but still crisp. Drain, refresh under the cold tap to set the colour, drain well and add to the sauce. Heat through, turn into a dish and serve sprinkled with chopped tarragon or chives.

Sauce. Melt the butter in a saucepan, add the flour and cook gently for 2–3 minutes over moderate heat. Draw the saucepan off the stove, wait for the sizzling to cease and add the milk. Bring to the boil whisking hard, simmer for 1–2 minutes, then add the cream, salt, a very little ground pepper and the green peppercorns.

*   # Glazed Baby Carrots

Little carrots (though it's a nice way to cook all carrots) cooked in sweet salty water and dressed with an old-fashioned butter sauce.

Ingredients
4–6 people

1½ lb (675g) baby carrots
2 teasp sugar
very finely chopped parsley

½ teasp flour
2 oz (50g) butter
2 tbs milk
salt and pepper

Cook the carrots with the sugar in boiling salt water until just tender. Drain. Mix the butter and flour together and add to the saucepan with the milk. Heat until boiling, shaking the pan all the time until a creamy sauce forms. Add the well-drained carrots, seasoning and chopped parsley, and shake to coat the carrots.

**   Timbales d'Epinards

Creamed spinach mixed with egg yolks and baked in ramekins until set. This makes an elegant vegetable or an unusual starter when topped with Béarnaise sauce (*see page 43*).

Ingredients
4–6 people

2½ lb (1.15kg) fresh or 1½ lb (675g)
   frozen spinach
3 oz (75g) butter
2 egg yolks

salt, pepper and nutmeg

4–6 slices stale white bread
butter and olive oil for frying

Throw the washed and de-stalked fresh spinach into a large non-aluminium pan of boiling salt water. Boil until just tender, drain, refresh under the cold tap to set the colour, then squeeze out the excess moisture with your hands. With frozen spinach you thaw it, squeeze out the excess moisture and add to the melted butter in a non-aluminium pan; cover and braise until done, boiling fast uncovered if there is too much moisture.

Purée the spinach in a food processor, adding the egg yolks and melted butter (if not used for cooking frozen spinach), season well and turn into 4–6 buttered ramekin dishes. Set these in a pan of boiling water to come halfway up and bake in a moderate oven (350°F/180°C/Gas 4) for 15–20 minutes until set.

Cut circles of bread the same size as the ramekin dishes and fry to golden in butter and oil. Keep warm. Turn out the timbales on to the fried bread rounds and serve around a main dish.

*   Pear and Spinach Purée

The clean taste of spinach and the freshness of pear combine in an unusual mixture which sets people guessing.

Ingredients
4–6 people

1½ lb (675g) fresh spinach
2 eating pears

2 oz (50g) butter
salt and pepper

Peel, core and quarter the pears and poach in boiling water for 15 minutes. Toss the washed, de-stalked spinach into a large non-aluminium pan of boiling salted water and cook until just tender. Drain in a colander and refresh under the cold tap to set the colour. Squeeze out excess moisture with your hands. Process the pears and spinach in a food processor with metal blade, or purée, and season with salt and pepper. Add the butter, re-heat and serve at once for a good green colour.

*   Salade des Gourmets

Tiny fresh French beans bathed in a vinaigrette with chopped shallot and wafer-sliced pink baby mushrooms. A mouthful of a first course or a salad.

Ingredients
4 people

½ lb (225g) very young French beans
2 oz (50g) firm button mushrooms

Dressing
1 tbs finely chopped shallots
1 tbs white wine vinegar
3 tbs olive oil
salt and pepper

Toss the whole beans into a saucepan of boiling salt water, cook until still very crisp to the teeth, drain and refresh under the cold tap to set the colour. Combine the cold drained beans and very finely sliced mushrooms. Toss well with the dressing and serve well chilled.

Dressing. Mix together the salt, pepper, shallots and vinegar. Stir well and gradually beat in the oil.

**   Tomato, Bean and Pine-Kernel Salad

Summer-grown tomatoes which really taste of tomato, French beans blanched so that they still snap, and richly textured pine-kernels make this colourful salad.

Ingredients
4–6 people

1 lb (450g) firm tasty tomatoes
½ lb (225g) young French beans
1–2 tbs pine-kernels
a little fresh chopped basil

Dressing
½ teasp Dijon mustard
2 tbs lemon juice
6 tbs rich fruity olive oil
salt and pepper

Toss the beans, broken into 2" (5cm) lengths, into a saucepan of boiling salt water and cook until still very crisp to the teeth. Drain and refresh under the cold tap to set the colour. Drain well. Peel the tomatoes by pouring boiling water over them; leave for 30 seconds or so, then drain and plunge into cold water so that they don't start to cook and go mushy under the skin. Skin and slice, mix with the beans, season with salt and pepper and add the dressing. Sprinkle with chopped basil and pine-kernels.

Dressing. Combine the salt, pepper, mustard and lemon juice. Stir well, then gradually stir in the olive oil.

** Fresh Pesto Sauce for Pasta

Try making your own pasta (*see page 144*). It's better than anything you can buy, and should you ever succeed in growing enough fresh basil, blow the expense, buy pine-kernels and Pecorino and treat yourself. A real Genoese would insist on your using a pestle and mortar.

Ingredients
With 1–2 batches of fresh pasta for 4–6 people

2 oz (50g) fresh basil leaves
1 oz (25g) pine-kernels
1 oz (25g) shelled walnuts
1–2 cloves garlic

2 oz (50g) freshly grated Pecorino or 3 oz
  (75g) freshly grated Parmesan cheese
4–5 tbs fruity olive oil
salt and pepper

Place the basil, pine-kernels, walnuts, garlic and grated cheese in a food processor or liquidiser. Process until smooth and drip in the olive oil to make a creamed butter-like sauce. Season with very little salt and some pepper. Keep for at least 1 hour before using, then thin with several spoonfuls of the hot pasta cooking water before serving on top of the cooked and drained pasta with a knob of butter and cheese handed separately. Or you can toss the pasta with butter and seasoning and hand the sauce separately, or toss the pasta with half the sauce and hand the remainder separately.

Opposite: Rose-petal Sorbet, Bombe aux Marrons et au Café, Tuiles d'Amandes

Puddings

F * ### Lemon Posset

Also called Lemon Solid. A very old English pudding, and I use a recipe from my great-great-grandmother which is very simple to make and very rich to eat, but with a sharp lemony tang.

Ingredients
4–6 people

1 pt (600ml) double cream
2 lemons
5 oz (125g) castor sugar

2–3 tbs good brandy (optional)
4–6 macaroons or a packet of ratafias

Combine the cream, the grated lemon rinds and the sugar in a saucepan. Stir over the stove for ten minutes, just bringing to the simmer. Cool, stirring from time to time so that a skin does not form, and when almost cold add the strained juice of the lemons and the brandy (if used). Pour over the macaroons or ratafias arranged in a glass bowl or little individual pots. Leave this dish in a cool larder or fridge for 24 hours before serving.

** ### Pears in Raspberry Sauce

Whole pears poached, then covered in a raspberry purée. Serve with a little sprig of scented geranium leaf on each pear stalk. The colours are breathtaking and the taste clean and fresh.

Ingredients
4–6 people

4–6 large pears
4 oz (100g) vanilla sugar
5 fl oz (150ml) water

8 oz (225g) raspberries
juice of ½ lemon
4–6 scented geranium leaves (optional)

Dissolve the sugar in the water and boil for 2–3 minutes to form a syrup. Peel the pears but keep them whole with the stalk on. Poach them very gently in the syrup until tender and remove to a serving dish. Liquidise the raspberries with a little of the syrup, sharpen with lemon juice and sieve. Spoon this thick sauce over the pears and serve well chilled.

**   Marsala Oranges

Sliced oranges covered in a caramel Marsala syrup make a fine end to any meal.

Ingredients
4–6 people

4–6 good juicy oranges (placed in the fridge for 3–4 hours to make peeling easier)	4 fl oz (100ml) cold water
	5 fl oz (150ml) boiling water
	5 fl oz (150ml) Marsala
8 oz (225g) granulated sugar	1 lemon

Take julienne strips of rind from 1–2 of the oranges, using a julienne stripper or potato peeler and a knife to cut the pithless rind into matchsticks. Place in plenty of cold water and bring to the boil. Boil for 5–10 minutes until no longer bitter, then drain and refresh under the cold tap to set the colour.

In a heavy pan combine the sugar and cold water. Stir over gentle heat until the sugar has quite dissolved, then turn up the heat and boil without stirring to a good caramel brown. Still on the fire, add the boiling water but stand back—it spits like mad! The caramel will dissolve in water, giving you a caramel syrup. Add the Marsala, lemon juice and orange julienne and simmer down until you have a heavy syrup. Cool.

Cut the peel, pith and skin from all the oranges with a very sharp or serrated knife. Slice the oranges, removing any pips, and either re-form and stick together with a toothpick or place the slices in a serving dish. Add to the syrup any orange juice that has escaped, and pour over the oranges. Serve well chilled.

P *   Petits Coeurs à la Crème

In summer, eaten with fresh raspberries or strawberries, these little heart-shapes of airy cream cheese and cream are exquisite, but you must have a good unsalted curd cheese. In winter use home-made jams or jellies. I find redcurrant or damson especially good.

The china heart-shaped moulds pierced with draining holes are not always easy to obtain, but you can improvise by making your own, using shallow plastic tubs pierced with half-a-dozen holes.

Ingredients
4–6 people

	To Serve
6 oz (175g) fromage blanc or cream cheese	¼ pt (150ml) cream
6 fl oz (175ml) cream	1 lb (450g) fresh raspberries,
1 tbs castor or vanilla sugar	strawberries or redcurrants, or really
2 egg whites	good jam (optional)
	granulated sugar

Beat the cheese smooth or put through a sieve; if it is very stiff thin with a little milk so that you can fold in the cream and egg whites. Whip the cream carefully with the sugar until it is just holding its shape, then fold into the cheese, followed by the egg whites, which are whipped until they too just hold a peak. Turn the mixture into the muslin-lined moulds or plastic pots and leave in a cool larder for 4–12 hours. If you keep them in the fridge, beware that they don't pick up a fridgy taste.

Unmould on to plates, pour the unwhipped cream round them and serve sprinkled with sugar—for you must have crunch—and accompanied by the fruit or jam if you wish.

**   Crème Brûlée or Burnt Cream

Another old English pudding, rich in cream and egg yolks and with a caramel top.

Ingredients
4–6 people

¾ pt (450ml) double or whipping cream	½ vanilla pod
5 egg yolks	a few drops vanilla essence
1½ oz (35g) vanilla sugar	castor sugar

Place the cream and vanilla pod in an enamel or stainless steel saucepan and bring very gently to the simmer, stirring occasionally to prevent scorching. Beat the vanilla sugar gradually into the egg yolks and continue to beat for 4–5 minutes until thick, pale and forming a 'ribbon'. Very slowly, drop by drop, beat the hot cream into the yolks. Add a few drops of vanilla essence and strain the custard into a 1-pt (600ml) soufflé dish, place the dish in a tin of hot water and bake in a very moderate oven (325°F/170°C/Gas 3) for about 45 minutes until set. Cool thoroughly and chill, then clean carefully round the edges.

Several hours before serving, heat the grill until very hot. Sprinkle ¼" (½cm) layer of castor sugar evenly over the top of the cream, especially up to the edges, and place high under the grill until the sugar has browned and turned to caramel; watch that it does not burn. Serve cold. It should have a hard shiny brown top.

Many household cookers simply will not heat evenly or hot enough, even when pre-heated for ½–¾ hour, to caramelise the sugar to a good brown without beginning to melt the cream. So the answer is to make a little caramel separately in a pan, using about 4 oz (100g) sugar and 2–3 tbs cold water, and pour it carefully over the top. It will harden very quickly.

𝒫 ✳✳✳   Gâteau Millefeuilles

Such a marvellous sweet that it deserves to be eaten from time to time. Home-made puff pastry has a light buttery flavour.

Ingredients
6–8 people

½–¾ lb (225–350g) fresh raspberries, strawberries, sliced peaches or frozen raspberries or strawberry or black cherry jam
⅓ pt (200ml) double cream
vanilla sugar
1 teasp orange flower water
½ egg white
icing sugar

Puff Pastry
6 oz (175g) 'strong' flour
6 oz (175g) best unsalted or lightly salted butter
¼ pt (150ml) iced water (approx)
a squeeze of lemon juice
a pinch of salt

Puff Pastry. Sift the flour and salt into a bowl and add a third of the butter, diced, and a squeeze of lemon juice. Rub in the butter, then add the water to make a medium firm dough known as *la détrempe*. Do not overwork the dough or it will become elastic. The remaining butter should be of the same consistency as *la détrempe*, firm but spreadable. Make it into a square flat cake. Roll the pastry into a rectangle, place the butter on one half and fold the other over to encase the butter, sealing the edges. Roll carefully to a rectangle (stop at once if the butter shows signs of coming through), then fold up the bottom third of the pastry and fold down the top third over it. Press the edges together and rest for 20 minutes in a plastic bag in the fridge. Replace on the floured board, with the folded edge to your left, and roll out into a neat rectangle. Fold in thirds as before and give the pastry a half-turn to the right so that the folded edge is again on your left. Roll again, fold, and rest for 20 minutes. Repeat two more 'rolls' and 'turns', rolling only in a lengthwise direction as slantwise rolling will produce an uneven rise, and rest again for 20 minutes. Repeat this process once more so that the pastry has seven 'turns' and four rests in all. The pastry is now ready to be kept until needed.

Roll the pastry into a rectangle of approx 12″ × 18″ (30cm × 46cm). Trim all the edges, then carefully roll on to your rolling pin and unroll on to a large greased baking sheet. Prick the pastry all over at ¼″ (½cm) intervals and bake in a hot oven (425°F/220°C/Gas 7) for about 10 minutes. Look at it after 5 minutes, and if any pastry is bubbling up press it down with a baking tin. Turn oven down to moderate (375°F/190°C/Gas 5) and continue to bake until crisp and golden brown right through. While still warm trim the edges, then cut the pastry into three equal strips (use a ruler and serrated knife) and cool on a rack.

    Slowly whip the cream, adding the orange flower water and vanilla sugar to taste. When the cream is quite stiff fold in the white of egg whipped until just holding a peak and the fruit or beaten jam. If you are using frozen fruit it should be barely thawed.

    Layer one strip of pastry with half the fruit and cream, top with the second strip, layer with the rest of the mixture and cover with the remaining strip, smooth side uppermost.

Press lightly but firmly together and dredge the top with sifted icing sugar (or glacé icing). Cut into slices with a sharp knife held almost perpendicular and used with a brisk up and down action. It is best put together not more than 1 hour before you eat it or the cream may soften the pastry.

**   Crêpes Suzette

Prepare the pancakes ahead and then have the fun of making this dish in front of a few guests. It is impressive and tastes wickedly decadent, though I'm not sure quite why.

Ingredients
4 people

Crêpes (8–10 pancakes)	*Sauce*
3 oz (75g) flour	**4 sugar lumps**
a pinch of salt	**2 oranges and 1 lemon squeezed to make**
1 egg	**¼ pt (150ml) juice**
1 egg yolk	**3 oz (75g) butter**
8 fl oz (225ml) milk	**3 oz (75g) castor sugar**
1 oz (25g) unsalted butter	**2 tbs Grand Marnier or Orange Curaçao**
a little lard or oil	**2 tbs brandy**

Crêpes. Place the eggs and half the milk in a food processor or liquidiser and add the flour and salt. Process until smooth and well beaten and add the remaining milk and the gently melted butter (or make by hand, beating the eggs and milk gradually into the flour). Rest for ½–1 hour, then make very thin pancakes.

Heat a 6″–8″ (15cm–20cm) frying pan and lightly grease with lard or oil. Pour in just enough batter to cover the bottom of the pan and swirl it around. Cook until lightly brown, turn and cook the other side. Turn out and pile up ready to use (or the pancakes will keep wrapped in the fridge for a day or two). Remember to cool the base of the pan in cold water before making each pancake. You should not need to grease it after the first time as there is enough butter in the mixture to keep it greased. Should your first pancake stick, scrape it out and clean the pan with salt and kitchen paper but do *not* wash it. Heat it, grease it and try again; after two or three times the most stubborn pan should comply!

Sauce. Rub the sugar lumps over the orange and lemon rind until they are saturated in zest (or use a little grated orange and lemon rind). Crush the lumps. Sprinkle the castor sugar evenly in the frying pan and heat until it starts to melt. Add the butter cut in little pieces and heat until very hot but not burning before adding the orange and lemon juice. Allow to bubble up to dissolve the caramel before stirring, then boil until the sauce is thickening.

Take the crêpes one at a time and turn them in the sauce. Fold into four and push to the edge of the pan. Bubble all up and add the Grand Marnier or Curaçao and brandy. Flame and serve at once.

✱✱   Hot Rum Soufflé

The simple base is prepared ahead, but it doesn't take long to finish off the soufflé and then into the oven it goes. This has been a never-fail recipe that always draws the oohs and ahs!

Ingredients
4 people

a little butter and sugar to prepare the soufflé dish	½ oz (12g) butter
4 fl oz (100ml) milk	2 egg yolks
2 tbs sugar	3 egg whites
a pinch of salt	3 tbs rum
1 oz (25g) flour mixed with a little cold milk	sifted icing sugar

Generously butter a 1-pt (600ml) soufflé dish and sprinkle with castor sugar. Place the milk, sugar and salt in a small pan and bring to the boil, dissolving the sugar. Off the stove stir in the flour and milk mixture. Boil, stirring, for 2–3 minutes until smooth and thick. Set aside covered. When ready to cook re-warm the sauce, beat in the butter, egg yolks and rum, then fold in the whites, whisked until they just hold a peak. Turn into the prepared soufflé dish and smooth the surface of the soufflé. Cook in a hot oven (400°F/200°C/Gas 6) for about 14–16 minutes until well risen, golden and just trembling when you move the dish. Sprinkle with icing sugar and serve *AT ONCE*.

ℱ ✱✱   My Mince Pies

These are filled with a bought mincemeat souped up—preferably some weeks ahead—to taste like home-made. The crisp pastry, which is so easy to handle, makes them very light and melting.

Ingredients
3–4 dozen pies

	Pastry
1 lb (450g) good mincemeat	8 oz (225g) plain flour
2–3 tbs Grand Marnier, brandy or sherry	5 oz (125g) firm butter
2 oz (50g) best chopped candied peel	3 tbs icing sugar
2 oz (50g) chopped flaked almonds	1 egg yolk
2 oz (50g) best raisins	2–3 tbs iced water
grated rind and juice of ½ lemon	a pinch of salt
1 peeled, cored and chopped sharp apple	
a pinch of salt, a grind of pepper and some freshly grated nutmeg	

Mix together all the ingredients in the left-hand column.

Pastry. Sift the flour, icing sugar and salt into a bowl or the food processor and add the firm butter cut into hazelnut-sized pieces. Rub in or process to the breadcrumb stage and bind with the yolk and water until it draws into a lump. Knead briefly into a flat disc and rest for 1–2 hours in the fridge.

Roll the pastry very thin and cut circles to line little bun tins. Prick the base lightly and fill with a teaspoonful of mincemeat; moisten the edges with cold water and top with a slightly smaller round of pastry. Press the edges together and prick the tops. Bake in a hot oven (400°F/200°C/Gas 6) for about 10 minutes until lightly browned, then turn down to moderate (350°F/180°C/Gas 4) for about 15–20 minutes until the mince-pies are beautifully golden in colour and cooked underneath. Cool on racks and store in tins. Warm through before serving with brandy butter.

F ✱✱   Bombe aux Marrons et au Café

A delicious chestnut ice cream, hollowed out and filled with coffee water-ice. A lovely blend of colour, flavour and texture.

Ingredients
4–6 people

Marron Ice Cream
3 eggs
3 oz (75g) castor sugar
4 oz (100g) unsweetened tinned chestnut
   purée
⅓ pt (200ml) cream
2 tbs rum
a few drops vanilla essence
1–2 marrons glacés (optional)

Coffee Water-Ice Filling
½ pt (300ml) water
1 oz (25g) strong, very finely ground
   continental coffee
2 oz (50g) vanilla sugar

To Finish
¼ pt (150ml) cream
4 or 5 marrons glacés or grated chocolate

Marron Ice Cream. Separate the eggs. Beat the yolks with the sugar until very pale, thick and mousse-like. Whip the cream until it just holds its shape. Stir the rum and vanilla essence into the chestnut purée, fold in the egg 'mousse', then the whipped cream and the marrons glacés in pieces (if used). Finally fold in the whites of eggs, whipped until just holding a peak. Turn into a chilled 2-pt (1.2l) bombe mould or pudding basin and freeze. When nearly firm, hollow out a hole in the middle and fill with the frozen coffee water-ice. Freeze until firm. Mellow in the fridge before turning out and decorating with whipped cream and marrons glacés or grated chocolate. Serve cut in slices like a cake.

Coffee Water-Ice Filling. Pour boiling water over the coffee, leave for 5 minutes, filter and add the vanilla sugar; stir to dissolve. Freeze in a flat dish, stirring in the crystals with a fork once or twice. When nearly frozen process in the food processor or liquidiser until light and smooth.

201

$\mathcal{PF}$ ✳✳✳   Frozen Plum Pudding with Iced Brandy Sauce

Macerated fruits in a rich ice cream topped with a sharp sorbet sauce. One of great-great-grandmother's which shows how well they ate.

Ingredients
6–8 people

1 oz (25g) chopped crystallised orange or citron peel
1 oz (25g) chopped crystallised pineapple
¾ oz (20g) rinsed and diced crystallised (glacé) cherries
1 oz (25g) chopped pistachio nuts or almonds
¾ oz (20g) sultanas
2tbs brandy
2tbs Marsala, Curaçao or Crème de Cacao
10 fl oz (300ml) single cream
a strip of lemon peel
3 egg yolks
3 oz (75g) castor sugar
8 fl oz (225ml) cream
1 egg white

Caramel Syrup
4 oz (100g) granulated sugar
3 tbs water
2–3 fl oz (50–75ml) boiling water

Iced Brandy Sauce
6 oz (175g) sugar
¼ pt (150ml) water
1 orange
1 lemon
4 tbs white wine
4 tbs brandy

Soak together for 3 hours the orange or citron peel, the crystallised pineapple and cherries, the pistachio nuts, sultanas, brandy, and Marsala, Curaçao or Crème de Cacao.

Make the Caramel Syrup and leave to cool.

Heat the single cream and lemon peel to boiling point in an enamel or stainless steel pan. Remove the lemon peel. Beat the egg yolks and sugar for 3–4 minutes until thick and pale and gradually, drop by drop, beat in the hot cream. Place the bowl over a saucepan of hot water and cook, stirring, until thickened, when the custard should coat the back of the spoon. Add the Caramel Syrup and cool. Freeze to a snowy mush.

When nearly frozen beat well and stir in the drained macerated fruit. Beat the whipping cream, whisking in any remaining liqueur from the fruit. Fold in. Finally fold in the white of egg, beaten until just holding a peak. Pack into a mould and freeze for 3–4 hours or until required. Turn out, mellow in the fridge for about ¾ hour and serve topped with the Iced Brandy Sauce, which should be like melting snow.

Caramel Syrup. Dissolve the sugar in 3 tbs water over gentle heat. When the sugar has completely melted, boil without stirring to a good brown, then add enough boiling water (between 2–3 fl oz) to make ¼ pt (150ml) syrup. Watch out, for it spits like mad as you add the water. Shake the pan to dissolve the caramel. If you add too much water boil down to ¼ pt (150ml).

Iced Brandy Sauce. Dissolve the sugar in the water, boil for 5 minutes and chill. Add the grated rind of ½ orange and ½ lemon to the syrup with the squeezed juice of the whole orange and lemon, add the wine and brandy and freeze to a mush. Stir once or twice.

F * ## Rose-petal Sorbet

I know this is not possible for everyone, but you don't have to live in the country to have an old-fashioned scented rose in your garden. We planted a Guinée climbing rose five years ago and in June its deep velvet red flowers and heavy scent intoxicate the senses. Scented mints, scented geranium or elderflower also make wonderfully refreshing sorbets.

Ingredients
4–6 people

1 pt (600ml) water
8 oz (225g) granulated sugar
2 good handfuls sweetly scented
   rose-petals
2 lemons

Combine the sugar and water in a very clean pan and heat gently, stirring until the sugar dissolves; boil hard for 5–6 minutes. Remove from the heat, throw in the rose-petals and the thinly pared rind from 1 lemon and leave to infuse for 2–3 hours. Strain the liquid and add lemon juice to taste. Freeze in a shallow container, beating the edges into the middle as they freeze. When the whole lot is set quite firm process in a food processor or liquidiser until smooth and light. Pack into a chilled serving dish or container and re-freeze.

This sorbet will need mellowing in the fridge for ½–¾ hour before serving. Serve with little biscuits or slices of sponge cake.

SECTION 6

Spontaneous Entertaining

This means different things to different people. In my experience it can mean fifteen friends asked back to supper after a cocktail party or just someone dropping in to lunch. Sometimes the children like to ask their chums to stay on or friends will ring up and say they are staying in the next village and I reply, without giving it a thought, 'Well, why don't you all come to lunch tomorrow?' Or you may just decide to give a party, perhaps for no reason at all. Some husbands are uncontrollably gregarious with no idea how meals arrive on the table and, bumping into old friends at a party when the excitement of the moment is overwhelming, ask up to twenty people, probably can't remember how many, to come to supper. Whether this sort of thing throws you into confusion or whether you take it in your stride usually depends on how confident you are of your ability to cope. This means having a few plans up your sleeve.

Don't worry about the confusion; it's bound to occur, but the secret is how to control it and get it under wraps in the time available. This is why I always bless the friends who ring before dropping in, even if it's only ten minutes before they arrive, for it gives me time to mobilise the forces. Children rally round when time is short, and I have a few moments to find the necessary food, clear a path through the accumulated chaos and whisk away the week-old dead flowers!

With this sort of entertaining it is difficult to be too specific with menus or recipes: it's more a question of having a wide repertoire of recipes tucked away in your mind's computer with a retrieval system that works, the knowledge of what flavour goes with which (and this only comes with experience) and the willingness to be adventurous and inventive. But what I can do is to give you ideas of how to make things go a bit further,

204

suggest useful items for the store cupboard, mention a number of my favourite quick and easy dishes and tell you about some of the things I keep in my freezer for moments such as these.

Sometimes the idea is to feed more people with the same dish; if the children beg that all their friends may stay to lunch this may only mean emptying a tin of beans and a tin of tomatoes into the mince to turn it into the famous Alligator Stew. Or maybe you rustle up a crumble topping for your mince, or satisfy teenage appetites by adding suet dumplings to your stew.

Unfortunately not all problems can be solved so simply; you may be just about to grill your pork chops for supper when the telephone rings, in which case you can usually turn your chops for two into Sweet Sour Pork for three or four; your Grilled Kidneys may become Kidneys in Mustard or your Fillet Steak metamorphose into Boeuf Stroganoff. But what about the poor girl who was just about to fry her cod steaks? How could she make another? Quick thinking made her cut a slice of bread to the right size, egg and breadcrumb it and fry it with the rest of the fish. The important thing was to make sure she served it to herself, though I think I am too greedy to make such an unselfish sacrifice.

What is often needed is only the ability to make more tasty juice or gravy to stretch the meat further. A revelation to me was my dear grandmama, a good and inventive cook, who came to stay with us in Germany and helped me to make a Steak and Kidney Pie. She made so much good gravy, by frying the onions really brown first, browning the flour gently, using boiled carrot water for flavour, then mushroom ketchup and Worcester sauce, a lot of this and a bit of the other, that we ended up with such a lot that I had to use a far larger pie dish. One goes on learning!

So have in your store cupboard the necessities for making a bit of taste, such as curry powder, tomato purée, authentic French and English mustards, mushroom ketchup, Worcester sauce, herbs, stock cubes and green peppercorns. I also keep wine dregs handy, a little real stock and tasty things like duck, chicken or pork fats. All help to add flavour, and don't forget that it is by reduction that one intensifies a flavour and gives it depth. You ought to have a few items to help dress up a dish and make it a bit more of an occasion. A tin of artichoke hearts in the Chicken Casserole or lychees in the Sweet Sour Pork may do the trick. Italian Tomato Sauce will heat up in the time it takes to cook the pasta, and combined with a tin of tuna or clams or fried chicken livers makes a hearty pasta dish. Down the scale again to children's favourites, I am never without a few tins of rice pudding for an instant Rice Pudding Brûlé, delicious with bottled or tinned plums. A tin of peaches can also be turned into Spiced Peach Crumble almost as soon as this takes to say.

Very quickly made soups like Sweetcorn and Tuna or Curried Pea call for ingredients you can always have around. A spread like Tapenade, made with olives and anchovies, Tuna Pâté, Sardine Pâté or Tachina, the sesame seed dip, can keep everyone going while your main dish cooks in the oven. If you have the cheese, Fondue takes very little time to prepare and your guests can enjoy cooking it at the table while you heat the French loaf from the freezer and wash the fresh green salad from the garden. Other instant dishes include steaks, chops, escalopes; some of my favourites are Lamb Kidneys with Mustard or pork fillets as Medaillons à la Savoyard or with green peppercorns. These are only suitable if there is time to pop out to the butcher, and shouldn't be attempted if you have more than a few visitors.

Freezers provide many of the answers. Sardine Croissants or Spinach Beureks lie ready to be popped into a hot oven for ten minutes to produce a sizzling hot first course. The Sardine Dartois can also be slid from freezer to oven to make a delicious supper main course, on the table in half an hour; never mind if you have no cream or lemon for the sauce, it's good without if better with. For other instantly cookable main courses there are Fillet of Pork en Croûte and Suprême de Volaille en Papillote, the advantage of the latter being that you can take out the exact number you need for the invasion. For puddings, the freezer can offer instant rescue; individual Crêpes Suzette (not quite authentic, so we call them Crêpes Suzanne) or Mincemeat Pancakes can be ready to hit the table in seven to ten minutes from the freezer via a hot oven. Various ice creams take only half an hour to mellow in the fridge, and the Chocolate Icebox Gâteau can be cut into slices while still frozen, for it thaws in a few minutes on a plate, while a bunch of bananas gives you Banana Flambé in five minutes.

Some Emergency Stand-bys

Anchovies. As part of a mixed Hors d'Oeuvre (steeped in milk for 15 minutes or so to plump them up), for Stuffed Eggs, Salade Niçoise or other salads. Also for pâtés, for dips like Tapenade, for Anchoiade or in sauces.

Artichoke Hearts (tinned). Add to chicken dishes or to salads or use as a base for Baked Eggs.

Baked Beans. For filling up teenage tums, for adding to mince or stew or for a 'cheating' Bean Salad.

Bread, etc. Frozen for instant use such as:
    French loaves for many uses or for turning into Garlic Bread (remember the crust crumbles off if left in the freezer for more than a week or two).
    Rolls to heat up with a poppy or sesame seed topping.
    Crumpets for nostalgic winter teas.
    Sliced bread which can be prized apart to make toast.
    Wholemeal or granary loaves to cut into hearty hot chunks.

Clams (or vongole). For quick pasta dishes or seafood salads.

Dill Cucumbers. These pickled cucumbers will keep in a large jar in the fridge for months.

French Beans. Frozen to add to soups or stews, or for a good vegetable try Haricots Verts à la Crème.

Olives. Buy the best in tins or bottles, or else loose and keep them in oil in a jar. They are something to nibble while your meal cooks, and help in mixed Hors d'Oeuvres, risottos, salads or Tapenade Dip.

Peas. Preferably frozen but, at a pinch, tinned for soups, quicky Peas à la Française or in salads and risottos.

Sardines. To serve as part of a mixed Hors d'Oeuvre or as a savoury, turned into a pâté or used as a filling for pastry or eggs or even for a quiche.

Spinach (frozen or tinned). Use in vegetable soups, in sauces or frittatas.

Sweetcorn. For a quick soup, gratin or vegetable.

Tahini. Sesame paste which can be found in Cypriot stores and health food shops. It makes a delicious dip with lemon, garlic and water. Use bread, biscuits or bits of fresh vegetable like cauliflower or carrot for dipping, or make into a Middle Eastern mezé with olives, cheese cubes and nuts to nibble with your apéritif.

Tinned Consommé. Campbell's or Sainsbury's. For Creamed Mushroom Consommé or adding depth and texture to Quick Onion Soup.

Tinned Peaches. For Spiced Peach Crumble or Peach Délice.

Tinned Pears. For Chocolate Baked Pears, Pear Délice or Spiced Pears.

Tinned or Bottled Plums. To serve as they are or with rum and quince jelly added for the sophisticates.

Tinned Rice Pudding. For Rice Pudding Brûlé or just to keep the smalls happy.

Tinned Tomatoes. To eke out or jazz up stews; to make Gazpacho or an Italian Tomato Sauce or as a vegetable with seasoning, herbs and a breadcrumb topping.

Tuna. Invaluable for Mixed Hors d'Oeuvres, Salade Niçoise, Tomato and Rice Salad, pâtés, pasta dishes, gratins, sauces or soups.

First Courses

Ŧ ∗   Sweetcorn and Tuna Soup

Quickly made with a couple of tins, and a useful stand-by.

Ingredients
4–6 people

12 oz (350g) tin sweetcorn
3 oz (75g) tin tuna
2 oz (50g) butter
½ teasp curry powder
1½ oz (35g) flour
1 pt (600ml) chicken stock or water and
   stock-cubes
½ pt (300ml) milk

2 tbs sherry
finely chopped parsley
salt and pepper

Melt the butter and gently cook the curry powder and flour for 2–3 minutes. Off the stove add the chicken stock and milk, bring to the boil whisking hard and simmer 1–2 minutes. Stir in the sweetcorn and shredded tuna, season and heat through. Add the sherry and serve sprinkled with chopped parsley.

Ŧ ∗   Curried Pea Soup

Pop it all in a pot, simmer and whizz; easy but good.

Ingredients
4–6 people

8 oz (225g) fresh or frozen peas
1 chopped onion
1 chopped carrot
1 chopped stick celery
1 large diced potato
1 teasp curry powder

½ teasp sugar
1½pt (900ml) chicken stock or water and
   stock-cubes
½ pt (300ml) milk
¼ pt (150ml) cream
fresh chopped dill or mint
croûtons
salt and pepper

Place the peas, onion, carrot, celery and potato in a saucepan, add the curry powder, sugar, salt, pepper and stock, cover and simmer for 15–20 minutes. Liquidise the soup until very smooth and add the milk and cream. Pass through a sieve and serve hot with a sprinkle of finely chopped mint or dill, and croûtons.

L *   # Quick French Onion Soup

One should take ages to brown the onions gently, but it's surprising how you can speed it all up when you have to, and it's a good dish for a sudden late-night invasion. Cheddar cheese will do on top, but you will bless having some Gruyère in the freezer.

Ingredients
4–6 people

1 lb (450g) quite thickly sliced onions
3 oz (75g) dripping or butter and oil
2 teasp sugar
1 oz (25g) flour
2½ pts (1.5l) beef stock (or 1 beef cube,
    2 pts (1.2l) water and a 10 fl oz (300ml)
    tin Campbell's Consommé)

4–6 slices stale French bread
4–6 tbs grated Gruyère or Cheddar cheese
1 egg yolk
3–4 tbs port or white wine } *optional*
salt and pepper

Heat the fat in a large frying pan or heavy casserole, add the sliced onions and sugar and fry fast for 10 minutes or so to a good brown; sprinkle on the flour and cook gently until lightly brown. Turn into a saucepan if necessary, add the stock (or cube, water and consommé) and bring to the boil, whisking. Season with a little salt and plenty of pepper and simmer for 5 minutes–1 hour depending on available time.

Place the bread in a soup tureen or individual bowls, ladle on the soup and scatter with cheese. Serve as it is, or brown under the grill, or pop in a hot oven (425°F/220°C/Gas 7) for about 10 minutes until golden brown and bubbling. If you are using the egg yolk and port or wine, whisk the yolk well and add the port. Slip a spoon under the cheesy crust and stir this mixture carefully into the soup just before serving.

*   # Sardine Pâté

A tasty sardine spread which will do well in an emergency.

Ingredients
4–6 people

2 tins sardines
3 oz (75g) butter
1–2 tbs green peppercorns

⅛ teasp mace
1 lemon
salt

Cream the butter well, beat in the drained sardines and season with salt, a good sprinkle of mace, a little grated lemon rind and the green peppercorns. Beat well and add a good squeeze of lemon juice (this can all be done very quickly in the food processor with metal blade). Pack into a pot or mound on to a dish and chill. Serve with toast, bread, buns or biscuits. Also very nice for open sandwiches, spread thickly on crustless brown bread and garnished with slices of hard-boiled egg, olives and strips of dill cucumber.

*   Tuna, Clam and Prawn Cocktail

When time allows you to make some mayonnaise this is a good, if rather extravagant, starter or main course salad.

Ingredients
4–6 people

7 oz (200g) tin tuna in oil
10 oz (300g) tin clams in brine
4–6 oz (100g–175g) frozen prawns
1 grapefruit or orange or some melon or
   cucumber (whichever is available)
a few lettuce leaves if available

Sauce
1 egg   *or ¼ pt (150ml)*
1 teasp vinegar   *ready-made*
¼ pt (150ml) oil   *mayonnaise*
salt, pepper and mustard
1½ tbs tomato ketchup
¾ teasp curry paste or powder
1 teasp dried tarragon
1½ teasp Worcester sauce
1 teasp sugar
good squeeze of lemon

Fold into the sauce the drained flaked tuna, the drained clams, the thawed prawns and the half segments of grapefruit or orange or the diced melon or cucumber. Serve on lettuce leaves in individual glasses.

Sauce. Either place everything but the oil in the food processor with metal blade or the liquidiser and process, dripping in the oil to make a mayonnaise sauce, or else beat the flavourings into the ready-made mayonnaise.

*   Tachina

With a jar of tahini (sesame paste) and a lemon or two you can quickly make this Middle Eastern dip. All you need is the bread or vegetables to dunk in it. A great addition to sitting and sipping in summertime or useful as part of an Hors d'Oeuvre.

Ingredients
4–6 people

6 tbs tahini
1–2 cloves garlic
3 tbs olive oil

6 tbs water
3 tbs lemon juice or to taste
chopped parsley
salt and pepper

Crush and cream the garlic in a bowl with a wooden spoon, add the tahini, then gradually add the oil, water and lemon juice alternately as if making mayonnaise. Or make in the food processor, which takes a few seconds. If it should separate add water until the tachina combines again. Season with salt and pepper and stir in the finely chopped parsley.

Opposite: Wholemeal Bread, Brioche Loaf, Terrine de Campagne

* Tapenade

This Provençal spread or dip does not take long to make (once you've stoned the olives!). All the ingredients can be kept in stock, and I'm often surprised because olive-haters seem to love it.

Ingredients
4–6 people

2 oz (50g) stoned black olives	8–12 tbs fruity olive oil
1 oz (25g) tin anchovy fillets	lemon juice to taste
1 teasp Dijon mustard	freshly ground black pepper
1 oz (25g) capers	

Place the stoned olives, anchovies, capers and mustard in a liquidiser or food processor and process until smooth. Gradually add the oil to make a mayonnaise-like purée. Finish with lemon juice and ground black pepper. A tasty dip for raw vegetables or to eat on bread, toast or biscuits, or mashed with egg yolks as a hard-boiled egg filling.

* Cape Mushroom Salad

This salad or first course needs to be made ahead but does not take long; it's a recipe I evolved after tasting something very like it in Cape Town.

Ingredients
4–6 people

¾ lb (350g) fresh button mushrooms	1–1½ teasp lime pickle
3–4 chopped spring onions or 2–3 shallots or a good bunch of chives	1½ tbs lemon juice
	4–6 tbs olive oil
2 pickled dill cucumbers (approx 3" (8cm) each)	salt, pepper and mustard

Wash the mushrooms and drain. Stir together the salt, pepper, mustard, chopped lime pickle and lemon juice in a bowl; beat in the onions and oil to make a dressing. Quarter or thickly slice the mushrooms, depending on size. Fold in the cubed dill cucumber and mushroom and turn until thoroughly coated in dressing. Turn into a dish and serve well chilled as an Hors d'Oeuvre or salad.

F ✳✳   Spinach Beureks

These little crisp parcels of filo paste (tissue paper layers of strudel dough) are found all over the Middle and Far East with a variety of fillings. Lovely freshly made, but they can be frozen uncooked and deep fried straight from the freezer successfully. You can buy the filo paste from good delicatessens.

Ingredients
24 pieces for approx 4–6 people

1 lb (450g) fresh spinach or ¾ lb (350g)
    frozen
3 tbs olive oil
1 finely chopped onion
½ lb (225g) ricotta or cream cheese

1 egg
½ lb (225g) filo paste
2–3 oz (50–75g) melted butter
salt, pepper and nutmeg
oil for deep frying

Plunge the fresh, washed and de-stalked spinach into plenty of boiling salted water in a non-aluminium pan. Cook until barely done, then drain and refresh under the cold tap; squeeze out the excess moisture with your hands and chop roughly. Fry the finely chopped onion in the oil until brown, add the chopped spinach and cook for several minutes more until dry. With frozen spinach you need to thaw, squeeze and chop it, then add it to the browned onions and cook very gently, covered, until tender.

Remove from the stove and beat in the cream cheese and egg; season highly with salt, pepper and nutmeg and set aside to cool. Take sheets of filo paste and cut into three lengthways to make 3″ (8cm)-wide strips; brush each with melted butter, place a spoonful of filling near one end, turn over the corner to make a triangle the width of the strip, then keep folding over and over to make a triangular wrapped parcel. Deep fry in hot oil until a good brown and drain on kitchen paper. If you are deep frying them from frozen, finish in a hot oven (400°F/200°C/Gas 6) for 4–5 minutes to make sure the filling heats through. Serve at once.

F ✳✳   Sardine Croissants

These are adapted from one of Robert Carrier's recipes. They are a useful stand-by in the freezer, either uncooked or cooked. They can go straight from freezer to oven and be on the table within fifteen minutes.

Ingredients
24 croissants for 4–6 people

Cream Cheese Pastry
6 oz (175g) soft butter
6 oz (175g) curd or cream cheese
10 oz (275g) flour
¼ teasp salt

Sardine Filling
1 tin sardines
¼ teasp curry paste or powder
1 tbs finely chopped parsley
½ lemon
salt and pepper

Cream Cheese Pastry. Cream the butter and cheese well, using a wooden spoon or the food processor, then sift in the flour and salt and mix to a dough. Knead briefly into a flat disc and chill for 1 hour.

Roll the pastry thinly and cut into 4″ (10cm) squares, then across into triangles. Put a teaspoonful of sardine filling in the centre of each triangle and roll up from base to point. Twist the ends to form into a crescent shape. Bake in a moderate oven (350°F/180°C/Gas 4) for 10–15 minutes until golden brown. Serve sizzling hot or take cold on picnics.

Sardine Filling. Add the curry, seasoning and parsley to the drained sardines and mash well, adding lemon juice to taste.

✲✲ Frittata alla Genovese

Egg and spinach fritters. Into the pan and on to the plate, or served cold with a herby vinaigrette as I found them in a Genoese grocer.

Ingredients
4–6 people

3–4 eggs	**1 tbs freshly grated Parmesan**
½ eggshell cold water	**salt, pepper and nutmeg**
4–6 oz (100–175g) spinach, cooked,	**a little oil for frying**
squeezed and chopped	
chopped parsley, lemon thyme or	
marjoram	

Beat the eggs with the cold water and add the chopped spinach, herbs and seasoning. Heat a little oil in a frying pan and place large spoonfuls of the mixture (which should be stiff enough to hold its shape) in the pan to make 3″–4″ (8cm–10cm) pancakes. Cook to a light brown on both sides. Eat at once, perhaps slipped inside a fresh buttered bap or served with Italian Tomato Sauce, or leave to cool and serve sprinkled with a herby vinaigrette dressing at a summer meal or picnic.

**   Baked Eggs with Mustard Hollandaise

Baked eggs are tricky to do because they need very careful timing. Don't forget they will go on cooking as you take them from the oven to the table. But a useful stand-by, and with a spoonful of mustardy Hollandaise they become quite special. Even better with a tinned artichoke heart underneath.

Ingredients
4–6 people

4–6 eggs
1 oz (25g) butter or a little cream
4–6 tinned artichoke hearts (optional)
salt and pepper

Mustard Hollandaise
2 egg yolks
4 oz (100g) butter
2 teasp Dijon mustard
½ lemon
1 tbs cold water
½ teasp fresh or a good pinch dried
   tarragon
salt and pepper

Butter 4–6 ramekin dishes and set in a pan of boiling water. Pop into a moderately hot oven (375°F/190°C/Gas 5) for a moment to heat the dishes, then break an egg into each, season and top with a dab of butter (or cream). Set in the middle of the oven and bake for 6–9 minutes. The eggs should be just set and tremble in the dish. Top with a spoonful of Mustard Hollandaise and serve.

Mustard Hollandaise. Melt 3 oz (75g) of the butter, keeping the remainder chilled in two bits. Whisk the yolks for 1 minute in a bowl, then add the mustard, tarragon, 1 tbs lemon juice and 1 tbs cold water and set the bowl over a pan of hot, not boiling, water so that the bowl does not touch the water. Add one piece of the cold butter and stir with a wire whisk until the yolks thicken. Remove the bowl quickly from the saucepan and add the remaining cold butter to check the cooking and stop the yolks from curdling. Once this has melted gradually whisk in the melted butter as if making mayonnaise. Season very lightly with salt and pepper, adjust the mustard and lemon and keep warm, covered, standing in a pan of lukewarm water in a warm, not hot, place. It will keep for 3–4 hours.

Main Courses

F **   **Sardine Dartois with Lemon Cream Sauce**

Freshly made or ready in the freezer to slip straight into the oven, this makes a supper party dish with a difference. It's nice even without its lemon cream sauce, but better with it. Good cold too. Cook direct from the freezer.

Ingredients
4–6 people

Flaky Pastry
5 oz (125g) 'strong' white flour
3½ oz (85g) butter
squeeze of lemon juice
2–3 fl oz (50–75ml) iced water
good pinch of salt
egg wash

Lemon Cream Sauce
1½ oz (35g) butter
¼ pt (150ml) double cream
½–1 lemon
salt and pepper

Filling
3 tins sardines
2–3 oz (50–75g) cream cheese
1½ oz (35g) butter
3 oz (75g) cooked rice
1 egg yolk
1 teasp green peppercorns
1 tbs chopped parsley
little grated lemon rind
salt and pepper

Flaky Pastry. Sieve the flour and salt into a bowl or food processor with metal blade and add a squeeze of lemon juice. Divide the firm but spreadable butter into quarters and rub or process one quarter into the flour until the mixture is like breadcrumbs. Add enough iced water to form a medium firm dough. Knead briefly until smooth and roll into an oblong ¼" (½cm) thick. Take a second quarter of the butter and with the point of a knife place dabs on the top two-thirds of the pastry, leaving a margin all round. Sprinkle lightly with flour and fold the bottom third up and the top third down, press the edges to seal, and give the pastry one turn to your right. Repeat the process with the remaining portions of butter. Refrigerate if the pastry becomes too soft. Finally roll into a 12" (30cm) square; trim off the edges and cut into two rectangles. Place one on a greased baking sheet and spread the filling over it, leaving a border all round. Damp the edges with water, cover with the other rectangle of pastry and press the edges together. Decorate with pastry leaves and make a hole in the top. Bake in a hot oven (400°F/200°C/Gas 6) for 20 minutes. Cover if getting too brown. Serve very hot with Lemon Cream Sauce.

Filling. Cream the butter with the cream cheese, beat in the drained sardines, parsley, peppercorns and rice, bind with the egg yolk and season with salt, pepper and lemon rind.

Lemon Cream Sauce. Melt the butter very gently, stir in the cream and heat without boiling. Season and add the juice of ½–1 lemon.

F * # Haddock Monte Carlo

A delicious dish for any entertaining, but as it is quick to make I am putting it here. Freeze only unbaked, or your cheese will go rubbery.

Ingredients
4–6 people

1–1½ lb (450–675g) smoked haddock
    fillets
½ lb (225g) tomatoes
pepper

Sauce
1 oz (25g) butter
1 oz (25g) flour
¼ pt (150ml) milk
¼ pt (150ml) single or whipping cream
2–3 oz (50–75g) grated Gruyère cheese
salt, pepper and mace

Skin the haddock fillets and lay in one layer in a well buttered shallow baking dish. Skin, de-seed and dice the tomatoes and scatter over the fish. Season with pepper only. Pour the sauce over. Sprinkle with the grated cheese and bake uncovered in a moderately hot oven (375°F/190°C/Gas 5) for about 20 minutes. Brown under the grill if necessary.

Sauce. Melt the butter, add the flour and cook for 2–3 minutes over moderate heat, stirring. Draw off the stove, wait for the sizzling to cease and add the milk and cream. Bring to the boil, whisking with a wire whisk, and simmer for 1–2 minutes. Season with pepper, mace and very little salt. It should be a fairly thick coating sauce as some moisture will come out of the fish in the cooking.

F ** # Suprême de Volaille en Papillote

Another rather super dish to prepare ahead for freezer-to-oven simplicity. But if you freeze the dish don't leave it frozen for too long, and start with fresh chicken.

Ingredients
4 people

4 chicken breasts
4 slices cooked ham
2 oz (50g) butter
salt and pepper

Duxelle
8 oz (225g) finely chopped mushrooms
2 tbs finely chopped shallots or spring
    onions
1½ oz (35g) butter
a few drops of oil
2 fl oz (50ml) strong stock (optional)
2 fl oz (50ml) Marsala or sherry
1 teasp fresh chopped or ½ teasp dried
    tarragon
salt and pepper

Remove the skin and cut off the wings from the chicken breasts to make suprêmes. Bat out gently between sheets of cling film. Heat the butter and gently fry the breasts until very lightly browned, turning once. Oil four pieces of tinfoil of about 8″ × 10″ (20 × 25cm). Place a slice of ham on each piece, then a chicken breast covered by one quarter of the duxelle, and close up the parcel. Place all the parcels on a baking sheet and bake in a hot oven (400°F/200°C/Gas 6) for about 20 minutes (30–40 minutes from freezing). Serve in the packets so that everyone opens his own and smells the trapped aroma. Have a plate handy for the tinfoil.

Duxelle. Twist the finely chopped mushrooms a few at a time in a piece of muslin or cloth to squeeze out as much juice as possible. Heat the butter and oil in a large frying pan and fry the onions and mushrooms over fairly high heat for about 6–8 minutes until the mushrooms brown a little and no longer stick together. Season, add the stock, Marsala and tarragon, then reduce over high heat until the mushrooms are nearly dry again. Set aside.

F ** Sweet Sour Pork with Red Peppers and Lychees

Not authentic Chinese but a surefire favourite that freezes beautifully.

Ingredients
4–6 people

	Sweet and Sour Sauce
1½ lb (675g) lean leg or shoulder of pork, cut into ½″ (1cm) cubes	2½ tbs sugar
½ teasp salt	2 tbs wine vinegar
1 teasp soy sauce	1 tbs cornflour
¾″ (2cm) fresh root ginger	1½ tbs soy sauce
a little grated orange rind	1 tbs tomato purée
small tin lychees	1 tbs sherry or red wine
1 red pepper	½ teasp chilli sauce
1 onion	grated rind of ½ orange
2 tbs oil or lard	lychee juice made up to ¾ pt (450ml) with orange juice or water

Place the pork cubes in a bowl with the salt, soy and half the grated or chopped ginger (you can grate it straight from the freezer) and a little grated orange rind. Toss and rub the seasoning well into the meat. Leave for 1 hour if possible. Slice the onion finely lengthways and cut the seeded red pepper into even strips.

Heat the oil in a large frying pan over high heat until just smoking. Toss in the meat and stir-fry until well browned (about 3–3½ minutes). Remove, add the onion to the pan and stir-fry 1 minute; add the red pepper and fry 1 minute more. Lower the heat and add the well-stirred sauce mixture to the pan, bring to the boil, stirring all the time, and simmer for 2–3 minutes until thick and clear. Return the meat, add most of the lychees and the remaining grated ginger and heat through. Serve at once with rice, or it will keep warm very happily.

Sweet and Sour Sauce. Mix all the sauce ingredients together in a bowl.

F **   # Filet de Porc en Croûte

A good recipe for pork fillet, stuffed and wrapped in cheesy pastry. It's lovely hot for entertaining at any time, and even better cold. It also makes a grand picnic dish. Have it ready in the freezer for unexpected guests when it can go straight into the oven to cook, allowing 10 minutes extra time. For best results don't freeze for more than a month or so.

Ingredients
3–4 people

1–1½ lb (450–675g) pork fillet (fresh if you are going to freeze it)
3 oz (75g) grated mature Cheddar
1 egg
2 tbs finely chopped parsley
½ teasp finely chopped lemon thyme, rosemary or tarragon
4–5 rashers very thin streaky bacon or prosciutto
a shake of Tabasco
salt and pepper

Pastry
6 oz (175g) flour
4½ oz (110g) firm butter
1½ oz (35g) grated mature Cheddar
½ teasp dry mustard
2–3 tbs iced water
salt and pepper

Pastry. Sieve the flour with salt, pepper and mustard into a bowl or food processor and add the grated cheese and firm butter cut in hazelnut-sized pieces. Rub in or process, adding iced water as you go and stopping as the mixture draws together. Knead briefly into a ball and roll to a 5″ × 10″ (12cm × 25cm) rectangle. Fold the bottom third up and the top third down, press the edges together and give the pastry a turn to the right. Roll and fold pastry twice more, then rest in a plastic bag in the fridge for 1–2 hours.

Trim the fillet, removing all sinews, skin and fat. Carefully cut the fillet nearly in half lengthways, cut lightly down the middle of each half, then bat out flat under cling film. Beat the egg and set half aside to seal and glaze the pastry; to the remaining half add the grated cheese, herbs, Tabasco and seasoning. Spread this filling all over the meat and roll up widthways to make a long roll. Spread and flatten the streaky bacon under the blade of a knife and wind around the fillet in a spiral.

Roll the pastry and set the fillet in the middle, bring up the pastry sides and seal together with egg like a Cornish pasty; decorate the top with pastry leaves, etc., and make a hole for steam to escape. Brush with the remaining egg and bake in a hot oven (425°F/220°C/Gas 7) for 35–45 minutes, depending on the thickness of the fillet (170°F/75°C on a meat thermometer); cover lightly when a good brown. Serve cut into slanting slices. This is delicious with a creamy horseradish sauce.

*   # Medaillons de Porc aux Poivres Verts

A last-minute quicky for a few people; you can ring all sorts of changes on this theme. Pork fillets are not always easy to find because they have to come from the bacon factories. I try always to have one or two in the freezer.

218

Ingredients
4–6 people

1½–2 lb (675–900g) pork fillet	¼ teasp potato flour, arrowroot or
1 tbs olive oil	cornflour
2 oz (50g) butter	2–3 teasp green peppercorns
2–3 tbs wine, stock or water	a squeeze of lemon juice
¼ pt (150ml) mixed yoghurt and cream	salt and pepper

Trim the fillets, removing all sinews, skin and fat. Cut on the slant into 1″ (3cm) wide slices, bat out gently under cling film and season when ready to cook. Stir the potato flour into the yoghurt and cream to stabilise it so that it won't curdle when boiled. Heat the butter and oil in a large frying pan and when the frothing subsides add the medaillons of pork and sauté briskly for 1–2 minutes on each side; remove to a serving dish. Add a dash of wine to the pan and stir in any brown tasty bits, then cool the pan for a moment before adding the yoghurt and cream and green peppercorns. Bring to the boil, whisking well. Simmer a moment, then correct the seasoning, add a squeeze of lemon and pour over the pork medaillons. Serve at once.

* Potato and Ham Gratin

Layers of sliced potato and chopped ham topped with cheese make this an easy bake which will wait for you.

Ingredients
4–6 people

2–2½ lb (900g–1.15kg) potatoes	½ pt (300ml) milk
¾–1 lb (350–450g) cooked ham	¼ pt (150ml) cream
¼ lb (100g) button mushrooms	2–3 oz (50–75g) Gruyère or strong Ched-
1 clove garlic	dar cheese
2 oz (50g) butter	salt, pepper and nutmeg

Rub a flat gratin dish, preferably earthenware, with a cut clove of garlic and butter liberally.

Place the crushed garlic in a saucepan with the milk and bring to the simmer. Grate the cheese and put on one side. Slice the mushrooms and set aside. Cut the ham into small slices or strips. Slice the potatoes thinly (a food processor makes this child's play). Layer the potatoes in the prepared dish with the ham, the mushrooms, a seasoning of very little salt, pepper and a scrape of nutmeg; dot with butter and sprinkle with a little grated cheese. Continue these layers, finishing with potato. Pour over the hot milk (without the garlic) and the cream and top with grated cheese and dabs of butter. Bake for about 40 minutes in a hot oven (400°F/200°C/Gas 6) until golden and tender.

* Lambs' Kidneys with Mustard

A lovely supper for two to four people, quickly made at the last minute. No good for too many as the kidneys exude juice in the pan and boil rather than sauté, and this toughens them.

Ingredients
3–4 people

10–14 lambs' kidneys
4 oz (100g) butter
1–2 tbs Dijon mustard

6 tbs port, red wine or stock
¼ teasp potato flour, arrowroot or
   cornflour
2 tbs finely chopped parsley
squeeze of lemon juice
salt and pepper

Skin, halve and core each kidney and slice into about three pieces. Heat about 3 oz (75g) of the butter in a large frying pan. When the frothing subsides but before the butter burns, throw in the kidneys and toss and sauté over high heat until they are just firm and lightly browned (do them in batches if you have not got a large pan and fierce heat). Season, add the port mixed with the potato flour, reduce the heat and simmer very gently for 2–3 minutes (if the sauce is too thin remove the kidneys and boil hard to reduce), then add the mustard and a good squeeze of lemon juice. Finish the sauce off the stove by stirring in the remaining butter in little pieces. Sprinkle with parsley and serve at once.

F * Mince with Herby Cheese Crumble

A great favourite, this freezes well ready-made but unbaked, or it can be whipped up fairly quickly from scratch. Freeze your mince in thin layers the size of a handkerchief, separated by cling film, and they will prise apart and thaw quite quickly.

Ingredients
4–6 people

1–1½ lb (450–675g) mince
2 oz (50g) dripping
1 finely chopped onion
2 diced carrots
1 finely chopped stick celery
1½ oz (35g) flour
½ pt (300ml) stock
2 teasp Worcester sauce
1 teasp mushroom ketchup
salt and pepper

Herby Cheese Crumble
6 oz (175g) flour
1½ oz (35g) butter
1½ oz (35g) grated cheese
plenty of freshly chopped parsley and
   other herbs
salt, pepper and paprika

Melt half the dripping in a casserole or saucepan and gently cook the finely chopped vegetables. Heat the remaining dripping in a frying pan and brown the mince fast over high heat (cook in several batches). Add to the vegetables and stir in the flour, seasoning and stock. Cook for ½–1 hour (depending on your mince) in a moderate oven (350°F/ 180°C/Gas 4) until tender. Or it can simmer on top of the stove. Turn into a pie dish and cover with the crumble. Bake for 30 minutes in a moderately hot oven (375°F/190°C/Gas 5) until the top is brown.

Herby Cheese Crumble. Rub the butter into the flour. Add the grated cheese, chopped herbs and seasoning.

✳✳   Nasi Goreng

This Indonesian speciality can be made with all the proper ingredients, in which case don't hesitate to entertain your friends with it; or cheat with a few left-overs which will make a tasty meal for the family.

Ingredients
4–6 people

12 oz (350g) long grain rice
8 oz (225g) cooked and diced chicken,
    roast pork or veal
8 oz (225g) prawns
8 oz (225g) cooked and diced ham
4 onions
5–6 tbs peanut or vegetable oil or pork fat
2–3 large garlic cloves

1–2 red chillies or 1 teasp chilli powder
4 eggs
2–4 tbs soy sauce
juice of ½ lemon
salt and pepper

Boil the rice in plenty of salted water until just tender, drain and refresh with cold water.
    Heat a little oil in a small frying pan. Beat two eggs in a bowl with seasoning, pour just enough of the egg into the pan to cover the base and cook over medium heat until set; turn out, roll up loosely and cut across into strips. Make several omelettes in this way until the egg is used up. Heat the remaining oil in a large frying pan and fry the sliced onion for about 15 minutes until a good brown; add the chopped garlic and the chillies or chilli powder, then stir in the chicken, ham, prawns and rice. Toss and heat, adding the soy sauce and lemon juice. Salt and pepper may be added if necessary but the soy and chilli should do. When really hot and glistening make two little nests and break in the remaining eggs. Cover with the hot rice and leave over low heat until the eggs are nearly cooked, then tear apart and mix in with two forks. Turn on to a hot plate and garnish with the omelette strips.
    This is often served with a side dish of crisp fried onion and peanuts. Chopped parsley, cubed tomato, peas and hard-boiled eggs look and taste good but may not be altogether authentic.

✳✳   Tagliatelle San Bernardo

This is based on one of Vernon Jarratt's legion of pasta dishes and is easy to make using stored ingredients. It is even better if you have home-made pasta in the freezer.

Ingredients
4–6 people

1–1½ lb (450–675g) packet tagliatelle or
   1–2 batches of home-made pasta
   (page 144), depending on appetites

Sauce
1 lb (450g) tinned tomatoes
1 oz (25g) butter
8 oz (225g) fresh or frozen petits pois
a little sugar
1 clove garlic
6 tbs olive oil
8 oz (225g) tin tuna fish
finely chopped parsley
salt and pepper

Cook the tagliatelle in plenty of boiling salted water for 10–15 minutes (3–5 minutes for home-made) or until *al dente*, just firm to the tooth. Drain and turn into a serving dish, pour the sauce over and sprinkle with parsley. Serve at once.

Sauce. Squeeze the juice and seeds from the tomatoes and pass through a food mill or process in food processor and sieve. Season with a little salt and simmer uncovered in a pan for 30 minutes or so until thick. Melt the butter in a saucepan, add the petits pois, salt, pepper and a little sugar, cover and cook slowly until tender. While the pasta is cooking heat the oil and garlic clove in a large frying pan; discard the garlic once it turns golden. Add the tomato pulp, petits pois and flaked tuna fish; leave over a very low heat to heat through.

* **Cheese Fondue**

Be it Gruyère, Emmenthal or mature Cheddar, it's extravagant on cheese, but by itself makes a good party and with no work beforehand.

Ingredients
4–6 people

Swiss Fondue
1 lb (450g) Gruyère or Emmenthal
10 fl oz (300ml) very dry white wine
2 teasp potato flour
2 tbs kirsch
grated nutmeg
1 clove garlic
plenty of cubed crusty French bread
ground pepper

British Fondue
1 lb (450g) strong Cheddar
8 fl oz (225ml) cider
2 teasp potato flour
2 tbs brandy
grated nutmeg
1 clove garlic
plenty of cubed crusty French bread
ground pepper

Rub an earthenware dish with a cut clove of garlic, pour in the wine (or cider) and place over moderate heat. Grate the cheese and add, with a grating of nutmeg and some pepper. As the mixture heats, stir with a wire whisk or wooden spoon until simmering. Add the potato flour mixed with kirsch (brandy) and simmer for 5–6 minutes more, whisking all the time until smooth and tasting mellow. Allow to simmer until thick enough to adhere to bread. Place it on a hot-plate where it must just simmer. Everyone has a fork and a pile of cubed crusty French bread. Spear the bread, dunk into the cheese to coat, then eat. A glass of chilled white wine (cider) should be near at hand!

The gentlemen who lose their bread in the fondue have to buy the next bottle. The ladies have to give a kiss all round. It can be a good party!

Vegetables, Salads and Other Good Things

* Quick Jade Courgettes

This Chinese method of cooking is good with young vegetables; the courgettes come out a beautiful jade green. They take only a few moments in the pan but must be eaten at once.

Ingredients
4–6 people

1–1½ lb (450–675g) fresh little courgettes
½–1 oz (12–25g) butter
2 tbs water

salt and pepper
finely chopped parsley

Cut the courgettes (which should be not more than 1" (2–3cm) in diameter) into quarters lengthways, then across into 1½" (3–4cm) wedges. Heat the butter in a wide frying pan with a lid and when very hot toss in the courgettes and stir-fry for about 2 minutes. Season with salt and pepper, and as the edges just begin to brown add about 2 tbs water and cover at once. Cook over high heat, shaking hard from time to time, for 2–3 minutes, then remove the lid (re-cover quickly if not quite done or you lose the colour). The courgettes should be a bright jade green, cooked but still very crisp, and the moisture all but gone. If there is moisture left boil fast with the lid off to evaporate the excess liquid. Serve at once, sprinkled with very finely chopped parsley.

* Stir-Fried Cabbage

Again the cooking time is negligible for the finely sliced cabbage, which is given an oriental flavour with soy, ginger and garlic.

Ingredients
4–6 people

1–1½ lb (450–675g) sliced white cabbage
1 oz (25g) lard or oil
1 clove garlic
2 tbs water

1" (2–3cm) piece of fresh root ginger
3 tbs soy sauce
salt and pepper

Heat the lard in a very large frying pan or wide casserole with a lid. Add the lightly crushed clove of garlic and half the ginger and fry until light brown. Discard. When the fat is just smoking throw in the cabbage; grate over it the remaining ginger and stir-fry for about 2 minutes until every piece glistens, is very hot and just beginning to brown. Now add 2 tbs water, cover and cook over high heat, shaking hard from time to time, for about 2–3 minutes. Uncover and add the soy sauce and seasoning. Toss and boil fast to evaporate any excess moisture. Serve at once whilst still crisp and crunchy.

* Sweet and Sour Red Cabbage

This quickly cooked red cabbage is dressed with a sweet sour sauce and is another that needs instant eating.

Ingredients
4–6 people

1–1½ lb (450–675g) finely sliced red cabbage
1 oz (25g) lard or oil
1 clove garlic
½″ (1cm) piece peeled fresh root ginger
2 tbs water

Sweet Sour Sauce
1 teasp cornflour
1 tbs sugar
3 tbs wine vinegar
1 tbs soy sauce
a few drops chilli sauce or Tabasco
3 tbs undiluted orange or lemon squash

Heat the lard in a very large frying pan with a lid, add the lightly crushed garlic clove and piece of ginger; fry until light brown, then discard. When the fat is just smoking throw in the cabbage and stir-fry for about 2 minutes until it is very hot, glistening and just beginning to brown. Now add 2 tbs water, cover and cook over high heat, shaking hard from time to time, for 2–3 minutes. Turn down the heat, remove the lid and add the sauce off the stove; simmer and stir for 2–3 minutes before serving. The cabbage should be crisp and crunchy, have kept a nice bright colour and be coated in a glistening sauce.

Sweet Sour Sauce. Mix all the sauce ingredients together.

* Baked Bean Salad

Vinaigrette added to baked beans; instant, cheaty, but quite useful and surprisingly good.

Ingredients
4–6 people

2 × 15 oz (425g) tins baked beans
1 tbs Dijon mustard
1 tbs wine vinegar
½ crushed clove garlic
1 tbs very finely chopped shallot or spring onion

4 tbs oil
salt and pepper
1–2 skinned and roughly diced tomatoes (optional)
2–3 tbs finely chopped parsley or mixed herbs

Empty the tins into a large sieve or colander to drain a little while you make the dressing. Stir the salt, pepper, mustard, garlic, onion and vinegar together in a wooden salad bowl to dissolve the salt. Gradually beat in the oil to make a thick dressing, stir in the beans, discarding the tomato sauce, and scatter the diced tomato and herbs over it.

*   Salade Niçoise

This Provençal speciality can be assembled very quickly and merits being dressed with a good fruity olive oil.

Ingredients
4–6 people

1 crisp lettuce
1 small tin anchovies
¾ lb (350g) firm tomatoes
4 hard-boiled eggs
12–24 black olives (depending on size, but they should be the little olives of Provence)

Optional extras
8 oz (225g) French beans
3 oz (75g) tin tuna fish in oil
1 small thinly sliced shallot or mild onion
a few sliced boiled potatoes
sliced green or red pepper

Dressing
2 tbs wine or tarragon vinegar
1 clove garlic
8 tbs fruity olive oil
a little chopped chervil and tarragon (optional)
salt and pepper

If you are using French beans, blanch them in boiling water until done but still crisp; drain and refresh under the cold tap. Drain.

Place the lettuce in a large salad bowl or in individual bowls, rubbed with garlic, and arrange on it the quartered eggs and tomatoes (and beans, onion, pepper and potato if used). Scatter over the anchovies and olives and chunks of tuna (if used).

Dressing. Either flatten the clove of garlic under the blade of a knife, mix with the salt, pepper and vinegar, then beat in the oil and herbs and hand this dressing on serving the salad. Or add the herbs to the salad and let everyone season and drip over vinegar and oil to their taste. The main thing is that the salad must not be dressed or tossed until just before being eaten.

**   French Tomato and Rice Salad

Rice cooked and dressed while warm with a vinaigrette and with lots of chopped tomatoes added. It makes a lovely summer salad, but do not overdress or it becomes oily. When I lived with a French family it was always a picnic dish, taken along in a huge wooden bowl. I've always found it a great favourite.

Ingredients
4–6 people

8 oz (225g) long grain rice
1 lb (450g) firm ripe tomatoes
1–2 tbs chopped chives
1–2 tbs chopped tarragon or parsley

Dressing
2 tbs tarragon vinegar
6 tbs olive oil
salt, pepper and French mustard

Boil the rice in plenty of boiling salted water until just cooked but with some bite in it. Drain in a colander and rinse with cold water. Shake out all the surplus water and dress while still warm with some of the dressing. Pour boiling water over the tomatoes and leave for thirty seconds or until the skins are loosened; plunge into cold water, skin and chop roughly. Stir into the rice with the finely chopped fresh herbs and season well with salt and pepper, adding more dressing as necessary.

Dressing. Mix the salt, pepper and mustard with the vinegar, stir well to dissolve the salt, then beat in the oil.

* # Mushroom Salad with Almonds

A good winter salad when other salad vegetables are not around; or serve it as part of a mixed Hors d'Oeuvre.

Ingredients
4–6 people

½–¾ lb (225–350g) firm button
    mushrooms
1 tbs chopped chives, spring onion or leek
2–3 tbs yoghurt
½ lemon
4–6 tbs olive oil

a good pinch of dried mint
salt, pepper and paprika
2–3 tbs flaked browned almonds

Wash the mushrooms in a colander and drain. Place the chopped chives and yoghurt in a wooden salad bowl, add the salt, pepper, paprika and mint and stir well with a wooden spoon. Gradually beat in the oil and add lemon to taste. Slice the mushrooms, fold in and serve within ½ hour if possible. Sprinkle with browned almonds on serving.

**   Champignons Farcis

You need big flat mushrooms for this dish, which goes well with game or grills or makes a hot first course when topped with cheese.

Ingredients
4–6 people

8–12 large mushrooms 3"–4" (8cm–10cm)
    across
2 oz (50g) butter
1 finely chopped onion
3–4 tbs whole oat or wheat flakes or
    breadcrumbs

3 tbs chopped parsley
salt and pepper
3 oz (75g) Gruyère (optional)
a few flakes of butter

Remove the mushroom stalks and set aside. Melt 1½ oz (35g) butter in a frying pan and dip each mushroom cap into it; place the mushrooms in one layer in a shallow gratin dish. Add the remaining butter to the frying pan, gently sauté the onion until translucent, add the finely chopped mushroom stalks and sauté until all the moisture has gone. Toss in the oat or wheatflakes or breadcrumbs and sauté to absorb the butter. Season and add the parsley and 2 oz (50g) grated cheese (this can be omitted if the mushrooms are to accompany a meat dish). Spoon the mixture into the mushroom caps and top with the remaining grated cheese (if used) and a flake of butter. Bake in a moderately hot oven (375°F/190°C/Gas 5) for 15–20 minutes until the topping is browned and mushrooms are cooked.

**   Pickled Mushrooms

Once made these will keep in the fridge for several months; fish them out to go with cold meat, as part of a mixed Hors d'Oeuvre or to nibble with drinks. A good way of using fresh field mushrooms.

Ingredients
4–6 people

1 lb (450g) or more button or field
    mushrooms
¼ pt (150ml) wine or cider vinegar
8–10 coriander seeds
2 sprigs thyme

olive oil
1 bay leaf
salt and pepper

Wash the mushrooms and drain well. Place the vinegar, coriander, thyme, 4 tbs olive oil, salt, pepper and a bay leaf in an enamel or stainless steel saucepan (aluminium reacts with vinegar and mushrooms). Bring to the boil and toss in some mushrooms; cover and cook for 5–6 minutes until the mushrooms are just cooked. Remove with a slotted spoon and drain in a sieve. Cook further batches of mushrooms, returning any strained juice to the pan. When really well drained put the mushrooms into a pot or glass jar, boil down the liquid until very strong and pour over the mushrooms; there should be just enough to cover. Cool and pour on enough olive oil to cover mushrooms by ¾" (2cm). Keep the jar in the fridge and remove the mushrooms as required. They must always remain covered by the oil.

* Italian Tomato Sauce

A very simple sauce that I came across when we once stopped in a tiny village in the Italian Alps out of season. Yes, they could put us up but we should have to wait while they cooked something; would we like some home-made salami to be going on with? Yes, please! I watched the Signora make the sauce: onions fried in oil, then the tomato purée fried and then the whole lot left to simmer for about an hour. It's a great standby, it freezes well, and you can add other good things to the pasta as you serve it, such as fried bacon or chicken livers.

Ingredients
4–6 people

1 finely chopped onion	½ pt (300ml) stock
3–4 tbs olive oil	1 slice lemon
6 tbs tomato purée	1 bay leaf
1 clove garlic	1 teasp sugar
	1 teasp dried basil
	salt and pepper

Fry the onion in the oil in a saucepan. When soft and transparent add the tomato purée and fry 3–4 minutes. Add the finely chopped garlic, stock, lemon, seasoning, sugar and basil. Simmer for 1 hour until quite thick, rich and of good flavour. Fish out the slice of lemon and bay leaf.

Serve with pasta, gnocchi, fritters, vegetables, etc.

*   Cheddar Cheese with Walnuts

We make this with Cheddar cheese from the freezer, and even when I'm offering a good cheese board everyone seems to go for it.

Ingredients
Makes about 1¼ lb (550g)

12 oz (350g) mature Cheddar cheese
4 oz (100g) butter
6 tbs stout, beer or lager

mustard and Worcester sauce (optional)
pepper
4 oz (100g) walnut halves

Grate the cheese. Cream the butter until soft, beat in the grated cheese and gradually work in stout or beer until creamy (very quick with the food processor). Season with pepper and add mustard and Worcester sauce if the cheese is poor in flavour.

Line a round pot with muslin, line the base with walnut halves, pack in half the cheese, put another layer of walnuts in the middle, then the remaining cheese. Turn out before serving. Or mound the cheese into a good shape and press walnuts all over the surface. Chill. Can be used almost at once, but the walnuts become moist and succulent if it's made 24 hours ahead. Will keep for a week or more.

*   Anchoiade

Stale bread cut thick, toasted on one side and pressed with pounded anchovies. Serve it piping hot with drinks or as a simple first course. Men in particular seem to adore it.

Ingredients
4–6 people

6 thick slices white bread
2 tins anchovies in oil
1 clove garlic

2–3 tbs olive oil
pepper

Pound the garlic and the anchovies with their oil in a mortar or process in a food processor, drip in about 2–3 tbs olive oil and season with pepper.

Toast the bread on one side only, then spread generously on the untoasted side with the anchovy mixture, pressing it well in. Pop into a hot oven for about 8 minutes or heat under the grill for about 4 minutes or until really hot. Cut in half and eat in your fingers at once.

Puddings

*   Pêche or Poire Délice

A quickly whisked-up mixture to spoon over fresh or drained tinned fruit.

Ingredients
4–6 people

4–6 fresh peaches or pears (or tinned in
   emergency)
2 tbs thin honey
2–3 tbs rum
¼ pt (150ml) double cream
a squeeze of lemon juice
a few browned flaked almonds

Place the honey and rum in a bowl and stir until the honey dissolves (thick honey can be warmed with the rum, then cooled). Add the cream, whisk until the mixture is softly whipped, add a squeeze of lemon juice and spoon carefully over the peeled and sliced fruit in individual glasses. Top with a few flaked almonds.

*   Flambé Bananas

An excellent pudding of bananas in a rich toffee-like sauce, flamed in rum.

Ingredients
4–6 people

1½ oz (35g) butter	1 lemon
4–6 bananas	cinnamon
2 oz (50g) soft brown sugar	4 tbs rum

Melt the butter in a large frying pan. Peel the bananas and cut in half lengthways, then cut each piece in half across. Lay in foaming hot butter and sprinkle with some of the sugar, cinnamon and lemon juice. Brown on one side, then turn and sprinkle with the remaining sugar, lemon juice, grated lemon rind and cinnamon. When the bananas are browned and the sauce is getting sticky, pour over the rum and flame. Serve at once with ice cream or whipped cream.

* Instant Raspberry Syllabub

A remarkably lavish-tasting syllabub that can be whipped up in minutes.

Ingredients
4–6 people

14 oz (400g) tin raspberries
½ pt (300ml) double cream
2 oz (50g) castor sugar or to taste

2–3 tbs brandy
½ teasp rosewater (optional but gives an elusive scent)
a good squeeze of lemon juice.

Drain, purée and sieve the raspberries, then make up the purée to 8 fl oz (225ml) with the raspberry syrup. Add the brandy and rosewater. Whip the cream and gradually beat in the sugar and raspberry purée until it is all absorbed and the cream is just holding its shape. Pour into a bowl or individual glasses.

Although this can be eaten immediately, it can also be made 24 hours ahead and served chilled.

F * Chocolate Baked Pears

Pears baked in chocolate syrup, good hot or cold. A useful stand-by from the freezer.

Ingredients
4–6 people

4–6 cooking or firm eating pears
4 oz (100g) vanilla sugar
¼ pt (150ml) water

½ vanilla pod
2 oz (50g) plain eating chocolate
½ oz (12g) butter

Dissolve the vanilla sugar in water with the vanilla pod, then bring to the boil and boil for 5 minutes. Remove the vanilla pod. Slip in the peeled, cored and quartered pears and simmer until nearly done. Place the broken-up chocolate in a small bowl over hot water and when soft gradually stir in some cooled pear liquid and the butter. Pour back over the pears and continue cooking very slowly until the pears are done. Serve with ice cream or whipped cream.

*   Rice Pudding Brûlé

The cheating instant pudding that can always be yours with the aid of a tin of rice pudding, brown sugar and a grill!

Ingredients
4–6 people

2 x 14-oz (400g) tins creamed rice pudding
soft dark brown sugar

Heat the grill. Turn the rice pudding into a shallow dish which it almost fills. Cover with a good ¼" (½cm) layer of sugar and put under the grill at once (or the sugar may dissolve) until bubbling and caramelised in parts. Serve at once, hot on top and cold underneath, or leave to cool.

*   Spiced Peach Crumble

A sugar and spicy crumble scattered over drained peaches and cooked for almost instant success.

Ingredients
4–6 people

2 lb (900g) tin sliced peaches
5 oz (125g) flour
4 oz (100g) brown sugar
4 oz (100g) butter

2 oz (50g) Jordan's Original Crunchy or toasted oatflakes
grated rind of 1 lemon
¼ teasp ground cinnamon or mixed spice

Place the drained peaches in a buttered pie dish and sprinkle with a little cinnamon or mixed spice.

Rub the butter into the flour, sugar, grated lemon rind and cinnamon or spice until it resembles large breadcrumbs. Or mix in the food processor with plastic blade. Stir in the Crunchy and scatter on top of the peaches. Bake in a moderate oven (350°F/180°C/Gas 4) for 20–30 minutes until brown and bubbling.

F ✷✷   Pancakes with Barbados Butter Sauce

This can be made with ingredients which you probably have around. Or keep a stock of pancakes in the freezer. The sauce, which is very quick to make, is invaluable with ice cream too.

Ingredients
4–6 people

Pancakes (about 12–14)
2 eggs
5 oz (125g) flour
½ pt (300ml) milk and water mixed
pinch of salt
4 tbs oil
a little lard or oil

Barbados Butter Sauce
4–6 oz (100–175g) butter
4–6 oz (100–175g) golden syrup
2 tbs Barbados rum

Pancakes. Break the eggs into the food processor or liquidiser and add half the milk and water mixture, the flour and salt. Process until smooth, adding the remaining liquid and finally the oil. Rest the mixture for 15–20 minutes, or about 1–2 hours if you have made it by hand.

Heat and lightly grease a heavy flat based 8″ (20cm) frying pan with lard or oil. Pour in about half a coffee cup (2–3 tbs) of the mixture and swirl around the pan. Cook until lightly brown, turn, and cook the second side. Turn out and pile up ready to use, remembering to cool the base of the pan in cold water before making the next pancake. You should not need to grease the pan after the first time as there is enough oil in the mixture to keep it greased. Should your first pancake stick, scrape it out, clean the pan with salt and kitchen paper but do *not* wash it. Heat it, grease it and try again; after 2–3 tries the most stubborn pan should comply!

Fold the pancakes into quarters and lay overlapping in a well-buttered oven-proof dish, pour over the sauce and heat through in a slow oven (300°F/150°C/Gas 2). Flame with rum for great effect.

Barbados Butter Sauce. Place first the chopped up butter and then the syrup and rum in a heavy pan. When the butter melts whisk continuously and boil the mixture for 2–3 minutes only (or you have toffee).

F ** **Crêpes Suzanne**

Pancakes filled with butter-cream flavoured with Grand Marnier and brandy which turns to hot alcoholic sauce when heated; not quite a Crêpe Suzette but just as good. Store in the freezer and remove the number required for a seven to eight minute flash in the hot oven.

Ingredients
4–6 people

Crêpes (10–12 pancakes)
4 oz (100g) flour
pinch of salt
1 egg
2 egg yolks
½ pt (300ml) milk
1½ oz (35g) unsalted butter

Orange Cream
4 oz (100g) butter
3 oz (75g) castor sugar
**1 orange and ½ lemon squeezed to make
  ¼ pt (150ml) juice**
1 tbs Grand Marnier or Orange Curaçao
1 tbs brandy

To Finish
sugar
1 tbs Grand Marnier
1 tbs brandy

Crêpes. Place the eggs and half the milk in a liquidiser or food processor and add the flour and salt. Process until well mixed, then add the remaining milk, and the butter which has been melted over gentle heat so that it does not separate. Rest for 20 minutes, then make very thin pancakes (*see facing page*). Thin the mixture with water if necessary.

Orange Cream. Cream the softened butter until very light and fluffy or use a food processor with plastic blade. Beat in the very finely grated rind from the orange and lemon and the sugar, then gradually the Grand Marnier or Curaçao and brandy. Now beat in the orange and lemon juice, stopping if the butter won't hold it all.

To Finish. Spread the orange cream evenly on half of each crêpe, fold in half, then in quarters. Lay overlapping in a well-buttered ovenproof dish, sprinkle heavily with sugar and heat in a hot oven (425°F/220°C/Gas 7) for 5–6 minutes. Sprinkle with the brandy and Grand Marnier and bring sizzling to the table.

F **   Crêpes de Noël

Pancakes stuffed with mincemeat and heated to the sizzle. They freeze immaculately and can be taken from the freezer individually.

Ingredients
4–6 people

Pancakes (about 12–14)
2 eggs
5 oz (125g) flour
½ pt (300ml) milk and water mixed
pinch of salt
4 tbs oil
a little lard or oil

Filling
¾ lb (350g) good mincemeat
1 Cox's Orange Pippin apple
2 oz (50g) chopped flaked almonds
2–3 tbs Grand Marnier or brandy

To Finish
1 teasp cinnamon
3 tbs castor sugar

Pancakes. Break the eggs into the food processor or liquidiser and add half the milk and water mixture, the flour and salt. Process until smooth, adding the remaining liquid and finally the oil. Rest the mixture for 15–20 minutes, or about 1–2 hours if you have made it by hand. Make very thin pancakes (*see page 234*).

Filling. Add the peeled and diced apple, the almonds and the Grand Marnier to the mincemeat.

To Finish. Spread the filling over half of each pancake, fold in half and then in quarters. Lay overlapping in a well-buttered ovenproof dish and sprinkle heavily with sugar and cinnamon mixed. Place in a hot oven (425°F/220°C/Gas 7) for 6–8 minutes. Serve with dollops of cream or ice cream.

*   Ice Cream Ecossais

Scoops of bought ice cream with a little something added for style.

Ingredients
4–6 people

1 block of best dairy ice cream or 1 pt
   (600ml) home-made vanilla ice cream
4 tbs honey
4–6 fl oz (100–175ml) whisky

Very gently warm the honey and mix with the whisky. When it is well mixed cool. Scoop the ice cream into chilled glasses and pour the honey whisky sauce round it. Serve with wafers, biscuits or Tuiles d'Amandes (*see page 243*).

F **   Chocolate Icebox Gâteau

An elegant 'cake' made of sponge fingers and rich butter-cream. It freezes well, and slices can be cut from the frozen cake to thaw on the plate in minutes.

Ingredients
4–6 people

2 boxes sponge fingers (16 to a box)
¼ pt (150ml) milk
2 tbs brandy or rum

To Serve
¼ pt (150ml) cream
vanilla sugar
plain eating chocolate

Chocolate Cream
4 oz (100g) plain eating chocolate
2–3 tbs milk
1 teasp instant coffee powder
6 oz (175g) unsalted or lightly salted butter
6 oz (175g) icing sugar
2 egg yolks

Oil a large square of tinfoil. Combine the milk and brandy in a flat dish. Dip one side of the sponge fingers briefly in this mixture and lay eight in a row on the tinfoil, dipped side down. Cover with a layer of the chocolate cream. Continue until you have four layers of sponge fingers and chocolate and finally spread chocolate all round the cake as well. Draw up the tinfoil sides and make a parcel. Chill in the refrigerator for 3–4 hours.

Chocolate Cream. Place the broken-up chocolate, milk and coffee powder in a bowl over hot water to melt. Cool. Cream the butter (food processor with plastic blade) really well and add the sifted icing sugar, the cooled chocolate and the egg yolks. Beat well.

To Serve. Whisk the cream sweetened with vanilla sugar until of piping consistency and turn into a piping bag with a large rose nozzle. Unwrap the cake and decorate with cream and a few curls of chocolate. Serve well chilled.

F *   Iced Mango Cream

A quickly made but most delicious pudding that just needs chilling well, or it can be frozen and thawed before serving.

Ingredients
4–6 people

14-oz (400g) tin mangoes
½ pt (300ml) double cream

1 lemon

Strain the mangoes, purée, and sieve to remove the fibres. Whip the cream and gradually beat in the mango purée and lemon juice to taste. Turn into individual pots or glasses or a bowl and freeze for several hours before serving lightly frozen, accompanied by little biscuits or Tuiles d'Amandes (*see page 243*).

SECTION 7

Bread, Biscuits and Other Ideas

T ✸✸ **Wholemeal Bread**

This is our basic loaf at home and we make it every week. I find it too solid when just made with wholemeal flour but sometimes vary the proportions of white to wholemeal.

Ingredients
4 loaves

1½ lb (675g) 'strong' white flour
1½ lb (675g) wholemeal or Granary flour
1½ oz (35g) sea salt
1 oz (25g) fresh yeast
1 teasp sugar
1½ pts (900ml) water (approx)
a few drops oil

Fresh yeast is to my mind very much better than dried, and it will keep for 1–2 weeks in the fridge in a little polythene bag if bought from a good source (a health food shop or a baker with a quick turnover). I find freezing fresh yeast a bit chancy; sometimes it's fine but at other times it won't work. If you have to use dried yeast, use only 2 teaspoonfuls in place of 1 oz (25g) of fresh as it is the over-yeasting which makes bread go stale so quickly. Treat your dough like a baby, not too hot, not too cold, no draughts and it will love you!

Place the flour and salt in a bowl in a warm place (try putting the bags of flour on the radiator over-night and your flour will make a delicious warm bed for the yeast to develop in). Cream the yeast and sugar together until runny, add ½ pt (300ml) tepid water and pour into a well in the flour. Flick flour over the liquid and leave in a warm place for 10 minutes or until cracks appear in the flour and the yeast is beginning to froth. Stir into the flour, adding about another 1 pint (600ml) tepid water until you have a medium soft dough. Knead for 10–15 minutes (or process in four batches in food processor ¾–1 minute each) until pliable and elastic, then form into a ball. Put a few drops of oil in the bottom of your clean bowl, turn the ball of dough in the oil and flip over so that the oily side is uppermost. Cover the bowl, which should have room for the dough to double in size, with a plastic bag or damp cloth and leave in a draught-free place to rise. A slow rise is best to develop the flavour of your flour, but you can gear the process to suit yourself from about ¾–1 hour in a warm airing cupboard or above the stove to 12 hours in a cool larder; or you can even turn your dough into prepared greased bread tins and give it only one rise, but the bread will be more crumbly.

When the dough has doubled in size, knock it down and knead for a few moments only, then divide equally into four, press out flat and roll up carefully to form free standing loaves. Slash the tops 2–3 times. Place on a greased and floured baking tin (or, even better, a tin sprinkled with fine maize meal, cover again with a plastic bag, and leave until well risen and again double the size. Remove the bag and bake in a hot oven (425°F/220°C/Gas 7) for 20 minutes, then turn down to moderately hot (375°F/190°C/Gas 5) for a further 20 minutes or so. The loaves are done when they sound hollow when knocked on the bottom. Cool on a rack.

F ** Brioche Loaf

Easy to make, delicious, impressive, and good with rich pâtés.

Ingredients
1 loaf

8 oz (225g) 'strong' white flour	4 oz (100g) butter
½ oz (12g) fresh yeast	2 eggs
4 fl oz (100ml) tepid milk	½ teasp salt
1 tbs white sugar	

Cream the sugar and yeast until runny and stir in the milk. Sieve the flour and salt into a bowl or food processor. Rub in the butter until it is of breadcrumb consistency, then add the yeast mixture and the eggs to make a very soft dough. Beat with your hand or a wooden spoon for 10 minutes (or 1 minute in the food processor).

Scrape the mixture from the sides of the bowl, cover with a plastic bag or damp cloth and leave to rise for about 1 hour until double in size. Knead for a few moments or process for 10 seconds and turn into an oiled 1 lb (450g) loaf tin or brioche mould. Cover with the plastic bag and leave to double in bulk and fill the mould, again for about 1 hour. Transfer carefully to a moderately hot oven (375°F/190°C/Gas 5) and bake for 35–40 minutes. Cover the top if it starts getting too brown. Turn out on to a wire rack and cool. If time is short turn the dough into the tin after kneading, allow to rise only once, and cook.

F ✳✳ Rich Sesame or Poppy-seed Rolls

Light rich rolls topped with sesame or poppy-seed, or indeed caraway and gros sel if you prefer. They freeze superbly and can be used for breakfast, lunch, tea or supper.

Ingredients
24 rolls

1 lb (450g) 'strong' white flour
1 teasp salt
1 oz (25g) fresh yeast
1 teasp sugar

4 oz (100g) butter
12 fl oz (350ml) mixed tepid milk and
　water (approx)
a few drops oil
a little egg wash or white of egg
sesame or poppy-seeds

Sift the flour and salt into a large bowl and warm a little. Cream the sugar and yeast until runny, then add half the tepid liquid. Pour into a well in the flour and flick flour over to cover the liquid. Leave for 10 minutes or so until the flour cracks and the yeast bubbles. Melt the butter and, when tepid, combine it and the remaining liquid and add to the flour to make a soft dough. Knead for 10 minutes or process in a food processor in two batches for ¾–1 minute, until the dough is smooth, elastic and no longer sticking to everything. Put a few drops of oil in the bowl and turn the ball of dough in it. Turn over, leaving the greased side upwards, and cover with a plastic bag or damp cloth. Leave to rise in a warm draught-free room for 1–1½ hours or until doubled in bulk.

Turn out on to a floured surface, knead briefly and cut into 24 equal pieces. Form each into a flattish round bun or roll and space out on a greased and floured roasting tin or baking sheet. Brush with egg and scatter with sesame or poppy seed. Cover with a plastic bag and leave to rise for about ¾–1 hour until well risen and double in bulk. Do let them rise well or they will be solid inside, but don't let them rise too much or they will collapse. Bake in a hot oven (425°F/220°C/Gas 7) for 10–15 minutes until brown and cooked. Cool on a rack and cover with a cloth if you want a soft crust.

Best kept in a freezer so that they stay fresh. They only take a few minutes to thaw and warm in the oven or under a low grill.

*** Croissants

Croissants aren't easy and can be time-consuming to make, but we find this version relatively quick. The whole secret is keeping everything at the right temperature; too warm and the butter starts to ooze; cool it and the yeast goes on strike; but if you keep it at 65°–70°F all should be well. And let's face it, the flavour of real butter croissants is something very special these days. You very seldom find them even in France.

Ingredients

16 croissants

1 lb (450g) 'strong' white flour	1 teasp sugar
1 oz (25g) lard	8 fl oz (225ml) warm water
1 oz (25g) fresh yeast	1 egg
a few drops oil	6 oz (175g) lightly salted or unsalted butter
	1 teasp salt
	1 beaten egg

Sift the flour and salt into a bowl and rub in the lard; set the bowl in a warm place. Cream the yeast and sugar together until runny, then add the tepid water and whisk in the egg. Pour into a nest in the flour, flick flour over the top and leave in a warm place for about 10 minutes until the yeast starts to work. Work up to a dough and knead for 10 minutes or so until elastic and smooth. Place a few drops of oil in the bowl, turn the dough round in the oil and leave it oily side up. Cover with a plastic bag or damp cloth and leave to rise in a warm place for about 40 minutes until double in size.

Knead briefly and roll out on a floured surface to a 10″ × 16″ (25cm × 40cm) rectangle. Cover the top two-thirds of dough with a quarter of the firm but spreadable butter in flakes and sprinkle lightly with flour; turn the bottom third of dough up and the top third down (as for flaky pastry). Press the edges together and give the dough a turn to your right. Roll and turn four times in all, adding a quarter of the butter each time, but work briskly so that the butter does not get too soft and start to come through (if it does, and you have to chill it, the yeast often gets very sullen and takes ages to start working).

Cut the dough in half and roll each half to a 10″ (25cm) circle. Cut each circle into 8 segments. Brush all over each segment with beaten egg and roll up loosely from base to point, attaching the point carefully. Lay well apart on a greased baking sheet, point side up and ends curved round away from the point to form a crescent. Cover with a large plastic bag or damp cloth. Leave to rise in a warm place (but not above 65–70°F/18–20°C) until well doubled in size, which usually takes about ¾–2 hours. Brush with beaten egg and bake in a hot oven (425°F/220°C/Gas 7) for 10–15 minutes until a good brown. Cool on a rack.

*   **Sesame Fingers**

Crisp bread fingers crowded with sesame seeds make a nice crunchy accompaniment for any smooth first course where contrast is needed. It is surprising how often these little extras seem to make the dishes.

Ingredients
16 fingers

4 slices white or brown bread   sesame seeds
2–3 oz (50–75g) butter   salt

Take the crusts off the bread and cut into fingers. Dip both sides briefly in the melted butter, place on a rack, sprinkle heavily with sesame seeds and season. Cook in a slow oven (300°F/150°C/Gas 2) until crisp right through. Serve hot or cold to accompany soups, mousses or anything where a little crunch is needed to complete the effect. Sesame fingers keep well in a carefully sealed tin.

𝓕 *   **Heart-Shaped Croûtes**

You need stale bread for these and it must go stale naturally, which takes about a week with bought bread. With fresh bread or instantly staled bread (shoved in the oven to dry out!) they are chewy but not crunchy. So when you have a stale loaf make lots of croûtes and freeze them for instant re-warming. Shallow fry them in butter and olive oil for flavour or deep fry them for speed in a deep fat fryer.

Ingredients
20 croûtes

10–20 thick ½" (1cm) slices of stale white   4 oz (100g) butter
       bread   4 tbs olive oil

Stamp out 20 heart-shaped croûtes. To fry a large number of these impeccably, clarify your butter so that it will not burn after cooking several batches. (Melt the butter in a small pan, skim off the froth and pour the butter carefully, without sediment, into the frying pan.) Heat the butter and oil in a frying pan until pretty hot but not smoking; too cool and the bread sucks up all the precious butter and oil and is greasy; too hot and it or the fat burns! Add some croûtes to the pan, brown one side, turn and brown the second side, and remove to absorbent paper to drain. Continue until all are done. Keep the croûtes warm or rewarm in a slow oven (300°F/150°C/Gas 2).

**   Tuiles d'Amandes

These crisp, lacy little biscuits, studded with almonds and cooled on a rolling pin or broom handle for a curvy shape, go well with syllabubs and creamy puddings. They are fiddly because only a few can go in to the oven at once, but everyone enjoys them.

Ingredients
2–3 dozen

4 oz (100g) castor sugar
2 oz (50g) soft butter
1¼ oz (30g) flour

3 oz (75g) flaked almonds
½ lemon

Cream the butter and sugar together, sift in the flour and add the grated rind and juice of the lemon and the almonds; mix well together. Place ½-teaspoon blobs of the mixture well apart on a buttered baking sheet. Bake in hot oven (400°F/200°C/Gas 6) for a few minutes, until they are light brown, but be careful for they burn very easily. They spread a lot and should be thin and lacy. If they are too lacy add a sprinkle more flour to the mixture. If they won't spread of their own accord add a squeeze more lemon. Remove from the oven, leave 1–2 minutes to cool, then with the aid of a spatula remove the biscuits and lay them over a rolling pin to get a curvy shape as they cool (use a broom handle for smaller ones). Work speedily because the biscuits cool quickly and then they won't bend, though they can be re-warmed in the oven. Continue to cook in batches. When cold seal in an air-tight tin, because they go soft very soon if the atmosphere is humid, and can't easily be re-crisped. If I want to keep them for a few days I put a bag of dried silica gel in the tin with them and seal the tin with sellotape.

*   Shortbread Fingers

So simple and quick, we call this 4-8-12 because of the proportions. Serve it for tea, to accompany puddings, fools and sorbets, or with the coffee.

Ingredients
20–30 pieces

4 oz (100g) castor sugar
8 oz (225g) butter (margarine is quite
   good, too)
12 oz (350g) plain flour

Sift the flour into a food processor or bowl and add the castor sugar and the butter cut into hazelnut-sized pieces. Rub in or process to fine breadcrumbs. Press out thinly into an 8″ × 10″ (20cm × 25cm) greased tin and bake in a moderate oven (350°F/180°C/Gas 4) for 20–30 minutes until pale golden brown and cooked right through. Remove from the oven and leave for 5 minutes or so before cutting into fingers and cooling on a wire rack.

CONVERSION TABLES

Weights		Liquid Measures	
Imperial	*Recommended Metric Conversion*	*Imperial*	*Recommended Metric Conversion*
¼ oz	6g	1 fl oz	25ml
½ oz	12g	2 fl oz	50ml
¾ oz	20g	3 fl oz	75ml
1 oz	25g	4 fl oz	100ml
1½ oz	35g	5 fl oz (¼ pt/1 gill)	150ml
2 oz	50g		
3 oz	75g	6 fl oz	175ml
4 oz (¼ lb)	100g	7 fl oz (⅓ pt)	200ml
		8 fl oz	225ml
5 oz	125g	9 fl oz	250ml
6 oz	175g	10 fl oz (½ pt)	300ml
7 oz	200g		
8 oz (½ lb)	225g	11 fl oz	325ml
		12 fl oz	350ml
9 oz	250g	13 fl oz	400ml
10 oz	275g	14 fl oz	425ml
11 oz	300g	15 fl oz (¾ pt)	450ml
12 oz (¾ lb)	350g		
13 oz	375g	16 fl oz	475ml
14 oz	400g	17 fl oz	500ml
15 oz	425g	18 fl oz	550ml
16 oz (1 lb)	450g	19 fl oz	575ml
		20 fl oz (1 pt)	600ml
1½ lb	675g		
2 lb	900g	1½ pts	900ml
2½ lb	1.15kg	1¾ pts	1l
3 lb	1.35kg	2 pts	1.2l
3½ lb	1.6kg	2½ pts	1.5l
4 lb	1.8kg	3 pts	1.7l
5 lb	2.25kg	4 pts	2.25l
6 lb	2.7kg	5 pts	2.8l
7 lb	3.2kg		
8 lb	3.6kg		
9 lb	4.0kg		
10 lb	4.5kg		

Oven Temperature Chart			
Very Slow	225°F	110°C	Gas ½
Very Slow	250°F	130°C	Gas 1
Slow	300°F	150°C	Gas 2
Very Moderate	325°F	170°C	Gas 3
Moderate	350°F	180°C	Gas 4
Moderately Hot	375°F	190°C	Gas 5
Hot	400°F	200°C	Gas 6
Hot	425°F	220°C	Gas 7
Very Hot	450°F	230°C	Gas 8
Very Hot	475°F	240°C	Gas 9

Approximate Meat Roasting Thermometer Readings		
140°F	60°C	Very Rare
150°F	65°C	Beef
160°F	70°C	Lamb
170°F	75°C	Duck and Pâté
180°F	80°C	Pork and Chicken
190°F	85°C	Well done
200°F	90°C	Very well done

The reading will usually rise by 5°F after removing the meat from the oven.

INDEX

References to recipes are indicated by bold type